T0305268

The Mathematics of Banking and Finance

About the authors

DENNIS COX is CEO of Risk Reward Limited, a Strategy and Risk Consultancy for the financial services industry, as well as being a director of a number of other companies. He was formerly Director, Risk Management at HSBC Operational Risk Consultancy and Global Risk Director at Prudential Portfolio Managers Limited, having spent 12 years in practice with Arthur Young and BDO Binder Hamlyn. Among a range of external interests he is a senior Council member of the ICAEW, a member of the Professional Standards Board, Chairman of the Financial Planning Committee of the London Society and a member of the Money Laundering Committee; together with being the Chairman of the Risk Forum for the Securities and Investments Institute. He also represents the public interest in the regulation of the Institute of Actuaries for financial service matters.

MICHAEL COX has spent 25 years teaching quantitative methods to a wide variety of undergraduate students in departments ranging from agriculture, engineering, history, economics, business and medicine. For over 20 years he has taught both statistics and management science to MBA students.

During his career he has published some 50 referred papers in such diverse areas as statistical process control, total quality management, multidimensional scaling and the analytical hierarchy process. In addition Michael has co-authored two text books and developed a major piece of software.

Michael works in applicable mathematics, the solution of real world problems employing statistical and management science techniques. Most of this research has included computer applications.

The Mathematics of banking and finance

"To survive in banking you need to be numerate. Gone are the days when human relationships were all – now you must also see the relationships among numbers. This is an excellent text to make numbers relevant to the non-numerate or to move the numerate from the classroom to banking applications."

—Professor Michael Mainelli, Executive Chairman, Z/Yen Limited

The Mathematics of Banking and Finance

Dennis Cox and Michael Cox

John Wiley & Sons, Ltd

Other Wiley Editorial Offices

John Wiley & Sons Inc., 111 River Street, Hoboken, NJ 07030, USA

Jossey-Bass, 989 Market Street, San Francisco, CA 94103-1741, USA

Wiley-VCH Verlag GmbH, Boschstr. 12, D-69469 Weinheim, Germany

John Wiley & Sons Australia Ltd, 42 McDougall Street, Milton, Queensland 4064, Australia

John Wiley & Sons (Asia) Pte Ltd, 2 Clementi Loop #02-01, Jin Xing Distripark, Singapore 129809

John Wiley & Sons Canada Ltd, 22 Worcester Road, Etobicoke, Ontario, Canada M9W 1L1

Wiley also publishes its books in a variety of electronic formats. Some content that appears
in print may not be available in electronic books.

Library of Congress Cataloging-in-Publication Data

Cox, Dennis W.
  The mathematics of banking and finance / Dennis Cox and Michael Cox.
    p. cm.
  ISBN-13: 978-0-470-01489-9
  ISBN-10: 0-470-01489-X
  1. Business mathematics. 2. Banks and banking—Mathematics. I. Cox, Michael. II. Title.
  HF5691.M335   2006
  332.101′513—dc22

                                                       2006001400

British Library Cataloguing in Publication Data

A catalogue record for this book is available from the British Library

ISBN 13 978-0-470-01489-9 (HB)
ISBN 10 0-470-01489-X (HB)

Typeset in 10/12pt Times by TechBooks, New Delhi, India

Contents

Introduction

Within business in general and specifically within the banking industry, there are wide ranges of mathematical techniques that are in regular use. These are often embedded into computer systems, which means that the user of the system may be totally unaware of the mathematical calculations and assumptions that are being made. In other cases it would also appear that the banking industry uses mathematical techniques as a form of jargon to create its own mystique, effectively creating a barrier to entry to anyone seeking to join the industry. It also serves to effectively baffle clients with science.

But in practice things can be much worse than this. Business systems, including specifically those used by bankers or in treasury functions, make regular use of a variety of mathematical techniques without the users having a real appreciation of the objective of the technique, or of its limitations. The consequence of this is that a range of things can go wrong:

1. The user will not understand the output from the system and so will be unable to interpret the information that comes out.
2. The user will not appreciate the limitations in the modelling approach adopted, and will assume that the model works when it would not be valid in the circumstances under consideration.
3. The user may misinterpret the information arising and provide inaccurate information to management.
4. The user may not understand the uncertainties inherent in the model and may pass it to management without highlighting these uncertainties.
5. The user may use an invalid model to try to model something and come up with results that are not meaningful.
6. Management may not understand the information being provided to them by the analysts and may either ignore or misinterpret the information.

The consequence of this is that models and the mathematics that underpins them are one of the greatest risks that a business can encounter.

Within the banking industry the development of the rules for operational risk by the Bank for International Settlements have exacerbated the problem. In the past, operational areas would not be closely involved with mathematics, instead this would have been left to analysts, risk management and planning professionals. However, these new rules put a range of requirements on all levels of staff and have increased the incidence of the use of modelling in operational risk areas.

It is the challenge of this text to try to provide the reader with some understanding of the nature of the tools that they are using on a day-to-day basis. At present much of the mathematics are hidden – all the user sees is a menu of choices from which to select a particular approach. The system then produces a range of data, but without understanding, gives no information. Therefore we have attempted to provide these users with sufficient information to enable them to understand the basic nature of the concept and, in particular, any weaknesses or inherent problems.

In this work we attempt to remove the mystique of mathematical techniques and notation so that someone who has not done mathematics for many years will be able to gain some understanding of the issues involved. While we do use mathematical notation, this is either described in the chapter itself or in the Appendix on page 279. If you do not follow what we are trying to say with the mathematical notation, explanatory details are embedded within the chapters and the range of worked examples will provide the understanding you require.

Our objective is to try to reduce the number of times that we see the wrong model being used in the wrong place. Even at conferences and in presentations we often see invalid conclusions being drawn from incorrectly analysed material. This is an entry book to the subject. If you wish to know about any of the specific techniques included herein in detail, we suggest that you refer to more specialist works.

1
Introduction to How to Display Data and the Scatter Plot

1.1 INTRODUCTION

The initial chapters of the book are related to data and how it should be portrayed. Often useful data is poorly served by poor data displays, which, while they might look attractive, are actually very difficult to interpret and mask trends in the data.

It has been said many times that 'a picture is worth a thousand words' and this 'original' thought has been attributed to at least two historical heavyweights (Mark Twain and Benjamin Disraeli). While tables of figures can be hard or difficult to interpret, some form of pictorial presentation of the data enables management to gain an immediate indication of the key issues highlighted within the data set. It enables senior management to identify some of the major trends within a complex data set without the requirement to undertake detailed mathematical work. It is important that the author of a pictorial presentation of data follows certain basic rules when plotting data to avoid introducing bias, either accidentally or deliberately, or producing inappropriate or misleading representations of the original data.

When asked to prepare a report for management which is either to analyse or present some data that has been accumulated, the first step is often to present it in a tabular format and then produce a simple presentation of the information, frequently referred to as a plot. It is claimed that a plot is interpreted with more ease than the actual data set out in some form of a table. Many businesses have standardised reporting packages, which enable data to be quickly transformed into a pictorial presentation, offering a variety of potential styles. While many of these software packages produce plots, they should be used with care. Just because a computer produces a graph does not mean it is an honest representation of the data. The key issue for the author of such a plot is to see if the key trends inherent in the data are better highlighted by the pictorial representation. If this is not the case then an alternative approach should be adopted.

Whenever you are seeking to portray data there are always a series of choices to be made:

1. What is the best way to show the data?
2. Can I amend the presentation so that key trends in the data are more easily seen?
3. Will the reader understand what the presentation means?

Often people just look at the options available on their systems and choose the version that looks the prettiest, without taking into consideration the best way in which the material should be portrayed.

Many people are put off by mathematics and statistics – perhaps rightly in many cases since the language and terminology are difficult to penetrate. The objective of good data presentation is not to master all the mathematical techniques, but rather to use those that are appropriate, given the nature of what you are trying to achieve.

In this chapter we consider some of the most commonly used graphical presentational approaches and try to assist you in establishing which is most appropriate for the particular data set that is to be presented. We start with some of the simplest forms of data presentation, the scatter plot, the matrix plot and the histogram.

1.2   SCATTER PLOTS

Scatter plots are best used for data sets in which there is likely to be some form of relationship or association between two different elements included within the data. These different elements are generally referred to as *variables*. Scatter plots use horizontal and vertical axes to enable the author to input the information into the scatter plot, or, in mathematical jargon, to plot the various *data points*. This style of presentation effectively shows how one variable affects another. Such a relationship will reveal itself by highlighting any trend that will be apparent to the reader from a review of the chart.

1.3   DATA IDENTIFICATION

A scatter plot is a plot of the values of Y on the vertical axis, or *ordinate*, taken against the corresponding values of X on the horizontal axis, or *abscissa*. Here the letters X and Y are taken to replace the actual variables, which might be something like losses arising in a month (Y) against time (X).

- X is usually the independent variable.
- Y is usually the response or dependent variable that may be related to the independent variable.

We shall explain these terms further through consideration of a simple example.

1.3.1   An example of salary against age

Figure 1.1 presents the relationship between salary and age for 474 employees of a company. This type of data would be expected to show some form of trend since, as the staff gains experience, you would expect their value to the company to increase and therefore their salary to also increase.

The raw data were obtained from personnel records. The first individual sampled was 28.50 years old and had a salary of £16,080. To put this data onto a *scatter plot* we insert age onto the horizontal axis and salary onto the vertical axis. The different entries onto the plot are the 474 combinations of age and salary resulting from a selection of 474 employees, with each individual observation being a single point on the chart.

This figure shows that in fact for this company there is no obvious relation between salary and age. From the plot it can be seen that the age range of employees is from 23 to 65. It can also be seen that a lone individual earns a considerably higher salary than all the others and that starters and those nearing retirement are actually on similar salaries.

You will see that the length of the axis has been chosen to match the range of the available data. For instance, no employees were younger than 20 and none older than 70. It is not essential that the axis should terminate at the origin. The objective is to find the clearest way to show the data, so making best use of the full space available clearly makes sense. The process of starting from 20 for age and 6,000 for salaries is called *truncation* and enables the actual data to cover the whole of the area of the plot, rather than being stuck in one quarter.

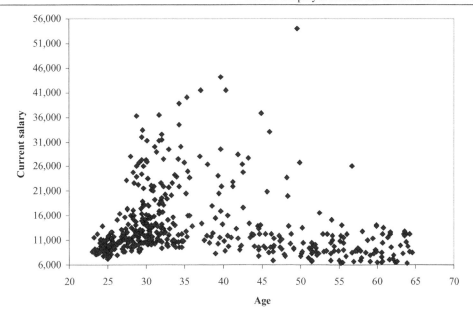

Figure 1.1   Scatter plot of current salary against age.

1.4   WHY DRAW A SCATTER PLOT?

Having drawn the plot it is necessary to interpret it. The author should do this before it is passed to any user. The most obvious relationship between the variables X and Y would be a straight line or a linear one. If such a relationship can be clearly demonstrated then it will be of assistance to the reader if this is shown explicitly on the scatter plot. This procedure is known as *linear regression* and is discussed in Chapter 13.

An example of data where a straight line would be appropriate would be as follows. Consider a company that always charges out staff at £1,000 per day, regardless of the size of the contract and never allows discounts. That would mean that a one-day contract would cost £1,000 whereas a 7-day contract would cost £7,000 (seven times the amount per day). If you were to plot 500 contracts of differing lengths by taking the value of the contract against the number of days, then this would represent a straight line scatter plot.

In looking at data sets, various questions may be posed. Scatter plots can provide answers to the following questions:

- Do two variables X and Y appear to be related? Given what the scatter plot portrays, could this be used to give some form of prediction of the potential value for Y that would correspond to a potential value of X?
- Are the two variables X and Y actually related in a straight line or linear relationship? Would a straight line fit through the data?
- Are the two variables X and Y instead related in some non-linear way? If the relationship is non-linear, will any other form of line be appropriate that might enable predictions of Y to be made? Might this be some form of distribution? If we are able to use a distribution this will enable us to use the underlying mathematics to make predictions about the variables. This is discussed in Chapter 7.

- Does the amount by which Y changes depend on the amount by which X changes? Does the coverage or spread in the Y values depend on the choice of X? This type of analysis always helps to gain an additional insight into the data being portrayed.
- Are there data points that sit away from the majority of the items on the chart, referred to as *outliers*? Some of these may highlight errors in the data set itself that may need to be rechecked.

1.5   MATRIX PLOTS

Scatter plots can also be combined into multiple plots on a single page if you have more than two variables to consider. This type of analysis is often seen in investment analysis, for example, where there could be a number of different things all impacting upon the same data set. Multiple plots enable the reader to gain a better understanding of more complex trends hidden within data sets that include more than two variables. If you wish to show more than two variables on a scatter plot grid, or matrix, then you still need to generate a series of pairs of data to input into the plots. Figure 1.2 shows a typical example.

In this example four variables (a, b, c, d) have been examined by producing all possible scatter plots. Clearly while you could technically include even more variables, this would make the plot almost impossible to interpret as the individual scatter plots become increasingly small.

Returning to the analysis we set out earlier of salary and age (Figure 1.1), let us now differentiate between male salaries and female salaries, by age. This plot is shown as Figure 1.3.

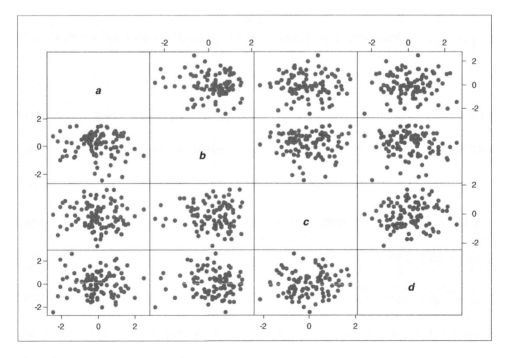

Figure 1.2   Example of a matrix plot.

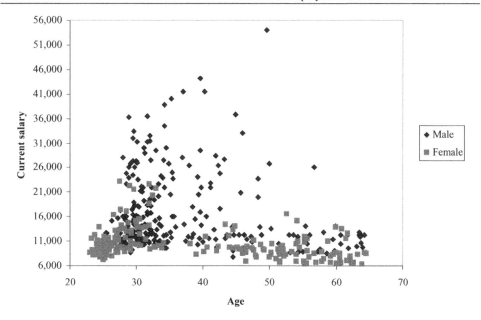

Figure 1.3   Scatter plot of current salary against age, including the comparison of male and female workers.

1.5.1   An example of salary against age: Revisited

It now becomes very clear that women have the majority of the lower paid jobs and that their salaries appear to be even less age dependent than those of men. This type of analysis would be of interest to the Human Resources function of the company to enable it to monitor compliance with legislation on sexual discrimination, for example. Of course there may be a range of other factors that need to be considered, including differentiating between full- and part-time employment by using either another colour or plotting symbol.

It is the role of the data presentation to facilitate the highlighting of trends that might be there. It is then up to the user to properly interpret the story that is being presented.

In summary the scatter plot attempts to uncover any relationship in the data. 'Relationship' means that there may be some structural association between two variables X and Y. Scatter plots are a useful diagnostic tool for highlighting whether there is any form of potential association, but they cannot in themselves suggest an underlying cause-and-effect mechanism. A scatter plot can never prove cause and effect; this needs to be achieved through further detailed investigation, which should use the scatter plot to set out the areas where the investigation into the underlying data should commence.

2
Bar Charts

2.1 INTRODUCTION

While a scatter plot is a useful way to show a lot of data on one chart, it does tend to need a reasonable amount of data and also quite a bit of analysis. By moving the data into discrete bands you are able to formulate the information into a *bar chart* or *histogram*. Bar charts (with vertical bars) or pie charts (where data is shown as segments of a pie) are probably the most commonly used of all data presentation formats in practice. Bar charts are suitable where there is discrete data, whereas histograms are more suitable when you have continuous data. Histograms are considered in Chapter 3.

2.2 DISCRETE DATA

Discrete data refers to a series of events, results, measurements or readings that may occur over a period of time. It may then be classified into categories or groups. Each individual event is normally referred to as an *observation*. In this context observations may be grouped into multiples of a single unit, for example:

- The number of transactions in a queue
- The number of orders received
- The number of calls taken in a call centre.

Since discrete data can only take integer values, this is the simplest type of data that a firm may want to present pictorially. Consider the following example:

A company has obtained the following data on the number of repairs required annually on the 550 personal computers (PCs) registered on their fixed asset ledger. In each case, when there is to be a repair to a PC, the registered holder of the PC is required to complete a repair record and submit this to the IT department for approval and action. There have been 341 individual repair records received by the IT department in a year and these have been summarised by the IT department in Table 2.1, where the data has been presented in columns rather than rows. This recognises that people are more accustomed to this form of presentation and therefore find it easier to discern trends in the data if it is presented in this way. Such a simple data set could also be represented by a bar chart. This type of presentation will assist the reader in undertaking an initial investigation of the data at a glance as the presentation will effectively highlight any salient features of the data. This first examination of the data may again reveal any extreme values (outliers), simple mistakes or missing values.

Using mathematical notation, this data is replaced by $(x_i, f_i: i = 1, \ldots, n)$. The notation adopted denotes the occurrence of variable x_i (the number of repairs) with frequency f_i (how often this happens). In the example, when $i = 1$, x_1 is 0 and f_1 is 295, because 0 is the first observation, which is that there have been no repairs to these PCs. Similarly when $i = 2$, x_2 is 1 and f_2 is 190 and so on until the end of the series, which is normally shown as the letter

Table 2.1 Frequency of repairs to PCs

Number of repairs	Frequency
0	295
1	190
2	53
3	5
4	5
5	2
Total	**550**

n. In this data set $n = 6$, x_6 has the value 5 and f_6 is 2. If the variable x is plotted on the horizontal axis and the frequency on the vertical axis, the vertical column of height f_i occurs at the position where there are x_i repairs. As explained below, a scaled form of the data is adopted since there needs to be some way to standardise the data to enable comparisons to be made between a number of plots.

Certain basic rules should be followed when plotting the data to ensure that the bar chart is an effective representation of the underlying data. These include the following:

- Every plot must be correctly labelled. This means a label on each axis and a heading for the graph as a whole.
- Every bar in the plot must be of an equal width. This is particularly important, since the eye is naturally drawn to wider bars and gives them greater significance than would actually be appropriate.
- There should be a space between adjacent bars, stressing the discrete nature of the categories.
- It is sensible to plot relative frequency vertically. While this is not essential it does facilitate the comparison of two plots.

2.3 RELATIVE FREQUENCIES

The IT department then calculates relative frequencies and intends to present them as another table. The relative frequency is basically the proportion of occurrences. This is a case where the superscript is used to denote successive frequencies. The relative frequency of f_i is shown as f_i'. To obtain the relative frequencies (f_i': $i = 1, \ldots, 6$), the observed frequency is divided by the total of all the observations, which in this case is 550.

This relationship may be expressed mathematically as follows: $f_i' = f_i/F$, where $F = f_1 + \ldots + f_6$, in other words, the total of the number of possible observations. It is usual to write the expression $f_1 + \ldots + f_6$ as $\sum_{i=1}^{6} f_i$ or, in words, 'the sum from 1 to 6 of f_i'. This gives the property that the relative frequencies sum to 1. This data is best converted into a bar chart or histogram to enable senior management to quickly review the data set. This new representation of the data is shown in Table 2.2.

The total number of events is 550; therefore this is used to scale the total data set such that the total population occurs with a total relative frequency of 1. This table represents a subsidiary step in the generation of a bar chart. It is not something that would normally be presented to management since it is providing a greater level of information than they are likely to require and analysis is difficult without some form of pictorial presentation. The bar chart will represent a better representation of the data and will make it easier for the reader to analyse the data quickly. The resulting bar chart is shown in Figure 2.1.

Table 2.2   Relative frequency of repairs to PCs

Number of repairs	Frequency	Relative frequency
0	295	0.5364
1	190	0.3455
2	53	0.0964
3	5	0.0091
4	5	0.0091
5	2	0.0036
Total	**550**	**1**

Here the zero has been shifted on the horizontal axis away from the vertical axis to enable the first bar to be clearly reviewed in a form consistent with all of the other columns. While inclusion of an origin for the vertical axis is essential, an origin for a horizontal axis is only required if the observation 'O' was included in the original data. In general, we do not recommend the use of three-dimensional representations since the eye may be misled by the inclusion of perspective into exaggerating the importance of bars of similar height by subconsciously assigning them more weight. They may look attractive, but they do not assist the reader in discovering key trends within the data set itself. Similarly the author should always be careful in using a variety of colours since this could have the unfortunate consequence of reinforcing a specific part of the data set and should therefore be used with care.

From the plot it may be concluded that while the majority of PCs are actually trouble free, a significant proportion, 10%, exhibit two failures. While very few exhibit more than three or more failures, it is these that need investigating and any common causes of these faults identified and action taken by management. Obviously this is a simple data set and the

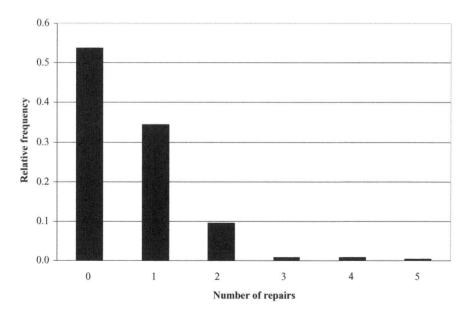

Figure 2.1   Bar chart of repairs to PCs.

information should have been clear from Table 2.2, but management will be able to save time by quickly reviewing the data as shown in the chart.

It is always best to include a narrative explanation to guide the reader to identify the key trends in the data set presented. It is also important for the author to ensure that anything that is to be compared is presented on equal scales, otherwise the relationships between the variables could be distorted. For extensive data sets the plot provides a concise summary of the raw data.

Here is an example of the use of comparative data.

An insurance company introduces a new homeowner's policy. It covers the same range of risks as the traditional policy with the added benefit of an additional 'new for old' replacement clause. The analyst has been asked to assess whether the frequency of claim type varies between the two options.

Both policies cover

1. Hail damage – to roofs, air-conditioning units, windows and fences
2. Wind damage – to roofs, fences and windows
3. Water damage – any damage caused by leaking pipes, toilets, bathtubs, shower units, sinks, fridge freezers, dishwashers and washing machines
4. Fire damage
5. Vandalism
6. Smoke damage.

The analyst was able to obtain the information shown in Table 2.3 from the records of the insurance company.

Table 2.3   Frequency of claim type

	Frequency	
Claim type	Traditional policy	New for old policy
Hail damage	1,029	98
Wind damage	449	47
Water damage	2,730	254
Fire damage	4,355	453
Vandalism	70	7
Smoke damage	1,458	159
Total	**10,091**	**1,018**

The difference in the number of claims for each policy makes any comparisons difficult and trends within the data are unclear. It is easy to see that most claims are for fire damage and the least for vandalism, but relative performance is hard to identify. The analyst then converted the data into a series of relative frequencies, which are set out in Table 2.4, and then used them to produce the bar chart shown as Figure 2.2.

The similarity between the two policies is now clear. However, some key questions need to be addressed.

How might the chart be improved?

• It might be useful to prioritise the type of claim, showing those that occur least frequently to the right of the plot.

Table 2.4   Relative frequency of claim type

	Frequency		Relative frequency	
Claim type	Traditional policy	New for old policy	Traditional policy	New for old policy
Hail damage	1,029	98	0.1020	0.0963
Wind damage	449	47	0.0445	0.0462
Water damage	2,730	254	0.2705	0.2495
Fire damage	4,355	453	0.4316	0.4450
Vandalism	70	7	0.0069	0.0069
Smoke damage	1,458	159	0.1445	0.1562
Total	**10,091**	**1,018**	**1**	**1**

What information has been lost?

• There is no information about the number of claims for each policy, only the relative frequency.
• There is no information about the cost, since all claims have been treated equally.
• There is no calendar information. The new policy would be expected to exhibit a growing number of claims as more customers adopt it. Older policies will have been in force for longer and therefore are more likely to exhibit claims.

This is a simple but useful form of data presentation, since it enables us to see simple trends in the data. There are more complex methods of showing data, which we consider in later chapters.

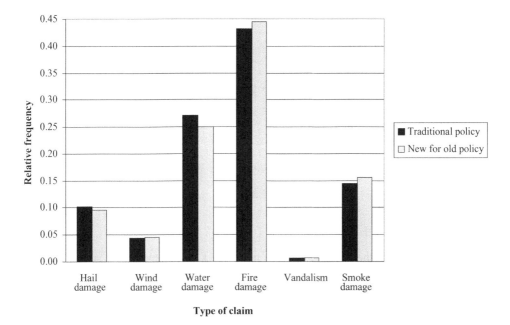

Figure 2.2   Bar chart of claim type against frequency.

2.4   PIE CHARTS

Pie charts are often used in business to show data where there is a contribution to the total population from a series of events. Contribution to profit by the divisions of a company can be shown as a pie chart, which operates by transforming the lines in a table into segments of a circle.

Taking the information from Table 2.2, this can easily be changed into percentages as shown in Table 2.5. This can also be produced as a pie chart, as shown in Figure 2.3.

Table 2.5   Repair to PCs prepared for a pie chart

Number of repairs	Frequency	%
0	295	53.64
1	190	34.55
2	53	9.64
3	5	9.10
4	5	9.10
5	2	3.60
Total	**550**	**100**

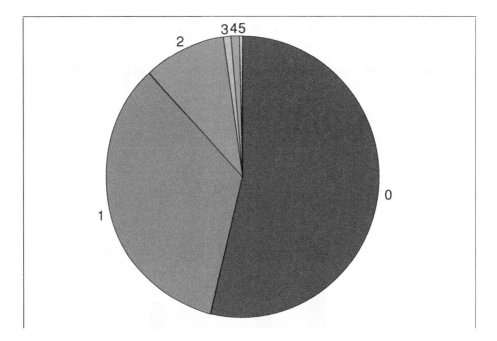

Figure 2.3   Example of a pie chart.

The one advantage of the pie chart is that you can quickly see which is the largest segment. On the other hand, that is also obvious from a quick look at the underlying table. The problem with pie charts is that very little information is actually shown – again all you have is the relative frequency. Further, it is difficult to compare different pie charts with each other. As a presentation to make it easy for the reader to understand the trends in data, it is generally rather poor. However, in practice it is a well-used and popular form of data presentation.

Histograms

3.1 CONTINUOUS VARIABLES

The next issue is how to present observations of continuous variables successfully, for example:

- Height or weight of a company's employees
- The time taken by a series of teams to process an invoice.

While we use a bar chart where there is discrete data, a histogram is employed where there is continuous data. Many of the basic rules employed for bar charts are also used in histograms. However, there is one additional requirement: there is a need to standardise class intervals. This has an echo from bar charts, where it was insisted that all bars were to be of equal width.

The actual form of presentation will be based on the specific data set selected. Displayed in Table 3.1 is some data collected on overtime payments made to the processing and IT functions within a financial institution. All such payments are made weekly and it is expected that staff will work some overtime to supplement their salaries.

The range is referred to as the class interval and the following notation is adopted:

L_i = the left point of the ith class interval,
R_i = the right point, and
f_i = the observed frequency in the interval.

In the example, L_1 is £210, R_1 is £217 with a frequency f_1 of 1. So one employee earns a salary in the range, £210 ≤ salary < £217. The final interval has L_{25} at £355 with R_{25} at £380 and a frequency f_{25} of 4.

There are two issues with plotting this type of data.

Firstly (which is not a problem here), there is the possibility that a right end point may not be identical to the following left end point, so that a gap exists. For example, if $R_1 = 216.5$ and $L_2 = 217$, then an intermediate value of 216.75 would be used to summarise the data, and this would be adopted for both end points.

Secondly, a problem is raised by unequal class intervals which occurs when the difference between the left end point and the right end point is not a constant throughout the data set. Using the notation where [335, 355) means 335 ≤ x < 355, there may for instance in another data set be 12 items in the range [335, 355) and six in the range [237, 241), and to compare these values it is best to think of the 12 items as being 12/5 of an item in each interval [335, 336), ..., [354, 355). Using mathematical notation you should replace f_i by $f_i'' = f_i/[(R_i - L_i)F]$, where $F = f_1 + \ldots + f_{25}$. This has two important properties: (1) it correctly represents the proportional height for each range, and (2) it forces the total area under the graph to become 1. The data from Table 3.1 needs to be prepared for plotting, as shown in Table 3.2, with the resulting histogram shown in Figure 3.1.

An alternative way to show the same information is the cumulative frequency polygon or *ogive*.

Table 3.1 Overtime earnings for processing staff

Overtime earnings (£ per week)		Number of staff
210	217	1
217	221	1
221	225	2
225	229	1
229	233	1
233	237	2
237	241	6
241	245	19
245	249	57
249	253	128
253	257	151
257	261	163
261	265	155
265	269	161
269	273	167
273	277	163
277	281	96
281	285	108
285	295	76
295	305	121
305	315	62
315	325	24
325	335	25
335	355	12
355	380	4
Total		**1,706**

3.2 CUMULATIVE FREQUENCY POLYGON

A cumulative frequency polygon is constructed to indicate what proportions of the observations have been achieved prior to a particular point on the horizontal axis. Employing the relative frequencies, using the calculations in section 2.3, there have been 0 observations before L_1 and f_1' prior to reaching R_1. So the points $(0, L_1)$ and (f_1', R_1) are joined. Similarly the proportion $f_1' + f_2'$ is observed by R_2 and the second line segment can then be drawn. In general, the cumulative distribution is defined by $F_i = f_1' + \ldots + f_i'$. The final right end point must correspond to the cumulative frequency of 1.

The calculations are summarised in Table 3.3 with the results presented in Figure 3.2.

The same employer has data on the weekly overtime earnings of contractors analysed by the sex of the contractor (Table 3.4). Here a histogram can be employed to represent the data and enable the reader to make comparisons.

The figures in Table 3.5 are then required to enable the histograms in Figures 3.3 and 3.4 to be prepared.

To enable these two charts to be compared, the data should be presented on axes that have identical scales. To further facilitate comparison it would be worth while to overlay the figures, as shown in Figure 3.5.

Table 3.2 Overtime payments prepared for plotting a histogram

Overtime (£ per week)		Number of staff	Length of class interval	Relative frequency / Length of class interval
210	217	1	7	0.0001
217	221	1	4	0.0001
221	225	2	4	0.0003
225	229	1	4	0.0001
229	233	1	4	0.0001
233	237	2	4	0.0003
237	241	6	4	0.0009
241	245	19	4	0.0028
245	249	57	4	0.0084
249	253	128	4	0.0188
253	257	151	4	0.0221
257	261	163	4	0.0239
261	265	155	4	0.0227
265	269	161	4	0.0236
269	273	167	4	0.0245
273	277	163	4	0.0239
277	281	96	4	0.0141
281	285	108	4	0.0158
285	295	76	10	0.0045
295	305	121	10	0.0071
305	315	62	10	0.0036
315	325	24	10	0.0014
325	335	25	10	0.0015
335	355	12	20	0.0004
355	380	4	25	0.0001

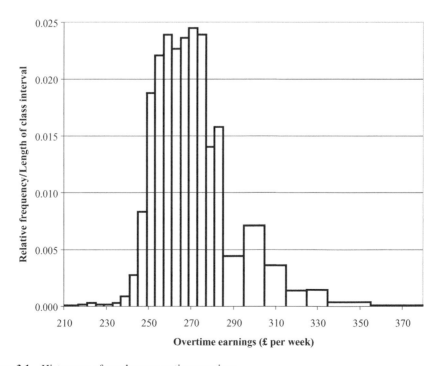

Figure 3.1 Histogram of employee overtime earnings.

Table 3.3 Overtime payments to employees prepared for plotting a cumulative frequency polygon

Overtime payments (£ per week)		Number of staff	Cumulative relative frequency
210	217	1	0.0006
217	221	1	0.0012
221	225	2	0.0023
225	229	1	0.0029
229	233	1	0.0035
233	237	2	0.0047
237	241	6	0.0082
241	245	19	0.0193
245	249	57	0.0528
249	253	128	0.1278
253	257	151	0.2163
257	261	163	0.3118
261	265	155	0.4027
265	269	161	0.4971
269	273	167	0.5950
273	277	163	0.6905
277	281	96	0.7468
281	285	108	0.8101
285	295	76	0.8546
295	305	121	0.9256
305	315	62	0.9619
315	325	24	0.9760
325	335	25	0.9906
335	355	12	0.9977
355	380	4	1.0000

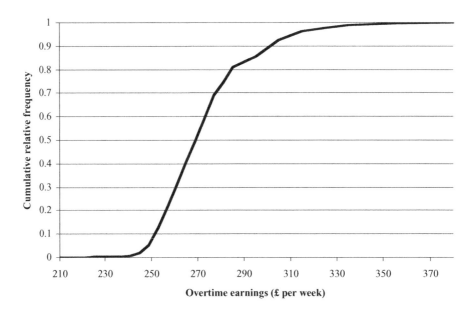

Figure 3.2 Histogram of overtime payments to employees.

Table 3.4   Overtime payments to contractors

Overtime payments (£ per week)		Number of men	Number of women
221	225	0	2
225	229	0	1
229	233	0	19
233	237	0	26
237	241	3	35
241	245	1	57
245	249	4	33
249	253	4	27
253	257	11	24
257	261	16	25
261	265	23	14
265	269	20	17
269	273	31	6
273	277	20	5
277	281	18	5
281	285	20	2
285	295	10	1
295	305	26	1
305	315	11	0
315	325	5	0
325	335	7	0
335	355	8	0
355	375	2	0
Total		**240**	**300**

It is important to be aware of the reliability and accuracy of the original data. This will need to be explained to any user of the information so that they do not draw invalid or unreliable conclusions. In addition, care must be taken with the sampling technique employed, to ensure that no form of bias has been unintentionally introduced into the data presentation. This needs to address both the size of the population selected and how the individual items are selected.

Bearing these points in mind, it is still clear from the above histogram that male contractors are in general earning more overtime than female contractors. However, before drawing incorrect conclusions, other factors need to be assessed. On comparing the two groups, were they equivalent? Factors that might lead to overtime payment differentials are:

- Age
- Experience
- Education
- Training
- Nature of role
- Hours worked
- Seniority
- Responsibility.

Table 3.5 Overtime payments to contractors prepared for plotting a histogram

Overtime payments (£ per week)		Number of men	Length of class interval	Relative frequency Length of class interval	Number of women	Relative frequency Length of class interval
221	225	0	4	0.0000	2	0.0017
225	229	0	4	0.0000	1	0.0008
229	233	0	4	0.0000	19	0.0158
233	237	0	4	0.0000	26	0.0217
237	241	3	4	0.0031	35	0.0292
241	245	1	4	0.0010	57	0.0475
245	249	4	4	0.0042	33	0.0275
249	253	4	4	0.0042	27	0.0225
253	257	11	4	0.0115	24	0.0200
257	261	16	4	0.0167	25	0.0208
261	265	23	4	0.0240	14	0.0117
265	269	20	4	0.0208	17	0.0142
269	273	31	4	0.0323	6	0.0050
273	277	20	4	0.0208	5	0.0042
277	281	18	4	0.0188	5	0.0042
281	285	20	4	0.0208	2	0.0017
285	295	10	10	0.0042	1	0.0003
295	305	26	10	0.0108	1	0.0003
305	315	11	10	0.0046	0	0.0000
315	325	5	10	0.0021	0	0.0000
325	335	7	10	0.0029	0	0.0000
335	355	8	20	0.0017	0	0.0000
355	375	2	20	0.0004	0	0.0000

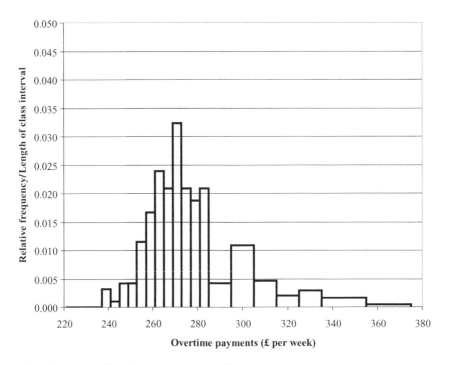

Figure 3.3 Histogram of overtime payments to male contractors.

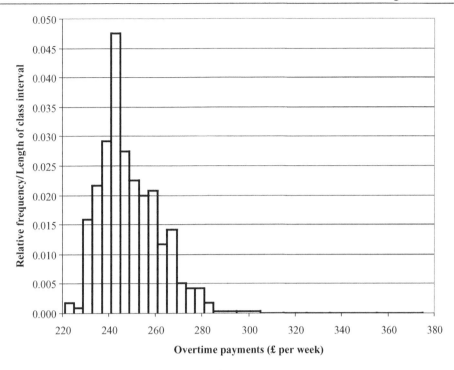

Figure 3.4   Histogram of overtime payments to female contractors.

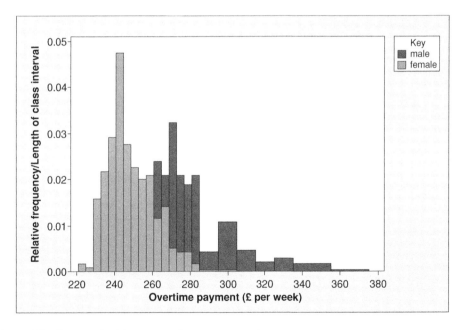

Figure 3.5   Comparative histograms of contractor overtime payments.

3.3 STURGES' FORMULA

It is often difficult to decide, for a given quantity of data, on the number and width of the class intervals. As a rough guide, equal width intervals may be adopted with the number given by what is known as Sturges' formula, which is:

$$k = 1 + 3.3 \log_{10}(n)$$

where k classes are required to accommodate n measurements. Quite often wider intervals are used to investigate the tails of the distributions.

The logarithm, or log, is the power to which a base, such as 10, must be raised to produce a given number. If $n^x = a$, the logarithm of a, with n as the base, is x; symbolically, $\log_n(a) = x$. For example, $10^3 = 1{,}000$, therefore, $\log_{10}(1{,}000) = 3$. The kinds of logarithm most often used are the common logarithm (base 10), the natural logarithm (base e) and the binary logarithm (base 2).

Log is normally found as a button on the calculator or as a function within spreadsheet software.

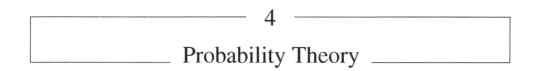

4

Probability Theory

4.1 INTRODUCTION

Most people have some knowledge, if only intuitively, of probability. They may have played simple games of chance, placed a bet or simply made a decision. Within business, probability is encountered throughout the company in all areas where there is a level of uncertainty. Examples would include the likelihood of success of a particular sales strategy and the expected error rate in a particular process.

In this context, a decision is the adoption of any specific course of action where there are a number of options available. This definition could apply equally to the day-to-day operations of a business, as it would to its long-term success and strategic decision-making. Before making such a decision, the basic facts need to be systematically obtained. Typical steps in this process are:

- Identify the specific problem you are trying to solve.
- Gain a total overview of the issues involved.
- Make a value judgement on the totality of the information obtained.
- Formally define your problem.
- List the various alternative actions that could be adopted.
- Contrast the impact of the alternative actions in terms of time, cost and labour.
- Obtain the necessary approval for the preferred course of action.
- Obtain the necessary resources in terms of time, money and labour.
- Follow the agreed course of action.
- Establish that the approved course of action actually solves the problem originally identified.

A number of tools will be described in this chapter that can assist in this process.

4.2 BASIC PROBABILITY CONCEPTS

It may be many years since some people in business, who are now users or authors of decisions, actually learned probability. As a consequence, a few of the key ideas may now have become hazy. Accordingly we need to refresh knowledge regarding some of the concepts that are used generally throughout business. Starting with basic simple probability, we could say, for example, that if a coin were tossed there would be a probability of 1:2 that it landed showing a head. This implies that in 50% of the occasions that a coin is tossed it will land head uppermost. This is the probability that one of two equally likely events actually occur.

The probability that a particular event A occurs is denoted in mathematical notation by Prob(A). This is the ratio of the number of outcomes relating to event A to the total number of possible outcomes from the total population of all outcomes.

Looking at another common probability example, consider a dice being rolled. When a fair dice is rolled the appearance of each of the six faces would be expected to be equally likely.

That means that the probability of a 2 is 1/6, or in one-sixth of the rolls a 2 would be expected to appear. Further, a 2 is equally likely to appear on any subsequent roll of the dice.

4.3   ESTIMATION OF PROBABILITIES

There are a number of ways in which you can arrive at an estimate of Prob(A) for the event A. Three possible approaches are:

- A *subjective* approach, or 'guess work', which is used when an experiment cannot be easily repeated, even conceptually. Typical examples of this include horse racing and Brownian motion. Brownian motion represents the random motion of small particles suspended in a gas or liquid and is seen, for example, in the random walk pattern of a drunken man.
- The *classical* approach, which is usually adopted if all sample points are equally likely (as is the case in the rolling of a dice as discussed above). The probability may be measured with certainty by analysing the event. Using the same mathematical notation, a mathematical definition of this is:

$$\text{Prob}(A) = \frac{\text{Number of events classifiable as } A}{\text{Total number of possible events}}$$

  A typical example of such a probability is a lottery.
- The *frequentist* approach, which may be adopted when a number of trials have been conducted. The number of successes within the population of trials is counted (that is the occurrence of event A) and is immediately referred to the mathematical definition of probability to calculate the actual probability of the occurrence of A, Prob(A). This leads to the following simple definition:

$$\text{Prob}(A) = \frac{\text{Number of times } A \text{ has occurred}}{\text{Total number of occurrences}}$$

This is probability estimated by experiment. As the total number of occurrences is increased, you would expect the number of times A has occurred to increase and the accuracy of the estimation of Prob(A) to improve.

The laws that govern probability are now briefly described. Firstly, some further definitions are required.

4.4   EXCLUSIVE EVENTS

Two events, A and B, are considered to be *mutually exclusive* if they cannot occur simultaneously. For example, when rolling a dice the events of rolling a 2 and a 3 are mutually exclusive. If a 2 has been rolled, this then prevents a 3 being rolled at the same time on the same dice. However, the next time that the dice is rolled the result is that any side of the dice could be selected with an equal probability.

4.5   INDEPENDENT EVENTS

Two events, A and B, are considered to be *independent* if the occurrence of A has no effect on the occurrence of B. For example, if you choose to toss a coin twice and the first toss shows a head uppermost, then this tells you nothing about the outcome of the second toss, which would still be that the head or the tail would occur with identical probability.

Two events are not independent if the occurrence of the first changes the likelihood of the occurrence of the second. Taking again the example of a dice, if we say that each face of the dice may only be selected once, this changes the probabilities. The first roll of the dice comes up with a 3, which had a one in six probability of being selected. Since there are only five faces now available for the second roll, the probability of any particular face being selected now is one in five. Therefore the first roll has changed the probability of rolling a 6 on the second roll from one in six to one in five.

4.6   COMPARISON OF EXCLUSIVITY AND INDEPENDENCE

It is not uncommon for people to confuse the concepts of mutually exclusive events and independent events.

- *Exclusive events* – If event *A* happens, then event *B* cannot, or vice versa. For example, if a head appears on the toss of a coin, it is definitely not a tail.
- *Independent events* – The outcome of event *A* has no effect on the outcome of event *B*. That is, taking the idea that after a coin has been tossed and a head results, this does not change the probability of either a head or tail on the next toss of the coin.

So, if *A* and *B* are mutually exclusive, they cannot be independent. If *A* and *B* are independent, they cannot be mutually exclusive.

4.7   VENN DIAGRAMS

A Venn diagram provides a simple pictorial representation of probabilities. The set of all possible outcomes for the event being considered is referred to as the *sample space*. An area on the page is then taken to represent this, with a rectangle usually being used. Any particular event, *A*, is a subset of the sample space and is drawn as a shape (conventionally a circle) within the sample space, as shown in Figure 4.1. The figure is purely schematic; no information is provided within the Venn diagram concerning the relative size of the areas.

Now we shall introduce a second event, *B*. The event that *A* or *B* both occur is the area covered by the two events. The event that *A* and *B* both occur is the area common to the two events, as shown in Figure 4.2.

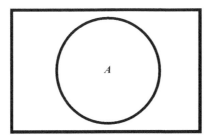

Figure 4.1   Venn diagram of a single event.

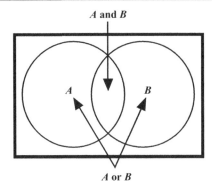

Figure 4.2   Venn diagram of two events.

There are a number of issues that follow from this:

1. The probability of A or B occurring is greater than, or equal to, the probability of A occurring and the probability of B occurring at the same time. In mathematical notation this is shown as Prob(A or B) ≥ Prob(A and B).
2. If A and B are mutually exclusive then the probability of A and B occurring at the same event is equal to zero. Basically the event (A and B) cannot occur (Prob(A and B) = 0). This would be shown as two separate circles, within the sample space, that do not overlap.
3. It might be easier to calculate the probability that event A does not occur (written $\bar{A}$), rather than the probability that it does. In the Venn diagram this is the area outside of the circle representing A.

4.8   THE ADDITION RULE FOR PROBABILITIES

The addition rule for probabilities is simply that they can be added together. However, you must always make sure that any overlapping probabilities are not double counted. Looking at the Venn diagram in Figure 4.2, this means excluding the common area 'A and B'. In mathematical notation this equation would appear as:

$$\text{Prob}(A \text{ or } B) = \text{Prob}(A) + \text{Prob}(B) - \text{Prob}(A \text{ and } B)$$

This applies where allowance has to be made for the fact that the event (A and B) occurs within both event A and event B.

If the two events are A and $\bar{A}$ (i.e. the probability that A occurs and the probability that A does not occur), then Prob(A and $\bar{A}$) = 0 since these must be mutually exclusive events. On the other hand, the probability that either A or $\bar{A}$ occurs must cover all eventualities since A either must occur, or must not. Accordingly the probability is written as Prob(A or $\bar{A}$) = 1. This applies since the two events cover every possibility and therefore one must occur with certainty. From the addition law the result follows that:

$$\text{Prob}(A) + \text{Prob}(\bar{A}) = 1.$$

4.8.1   A simple probability example using a Venn diagram

Orders have been placed for an identical product with two suppliers X and Y. From previous experience the following table of probabilities have been obtained:

$$\text{Prob}(X \text{ replies within one week}) = 0.19$$
$$\text{Prob}(Y \text{ replies within one week}) = 0.25$$
$$\text{Prob}(\text{both } X \text{ and } Y \text{ reply within one week}) = 0.06$$

The problem then is to calculate the probability that no replies are received within the first week and also to calculate the probability that exactly one reply is received.

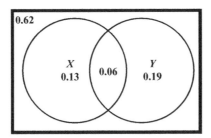

Figure 4.3   Venn diagram for the orders example.

The probabilities are illustrated in Figure 4.3. Note that the areas are evaluated sequentially, starting with the probability that both reply, then working out the probabilities that only one replies, and finally calculating the probability that there is no reply.

Therefore the probability of no replies is 0.62, or, more formally,

$$\text{Prob}(\text{no reply}) = 1 - \text{Prob}(X \text{ or } Y \text{ reply})$$
$$= 1 - [\text{Prob}(X \text{ replies}) + \text{Prob}(Y \text{ replies}) - \text{Prob}(X \text{ and } Y \text{ reply})]$$
$$= 1 - 0.19 - 0.25 + 0.06 = 0.62.$$

The Venn diagram also shows that the probability of obtaining exactly one reply is 0.32, because:

$$\text{Prob}(\text{exactly one reply}) = \text{Prob}(X \text{ or } Y \text{ replies}) - \text{Prob}(X \text{ and } Y \text{ reply})$$
$$= \text{Prob}(X \text{ replies}) + \text{Prob}(Y \text{ replies})$$
$$- \text{Prob}(X \text{ and } Y \text{ reply}) - \text{Prob}(X \text{ and } Y \text{ reply})$$
$$= 0.19 + 0.25 - 0.06 - 0.06 = 0.32.$$

Therefore, in summary, probabilities are additive, as long as overlapping probabilities are properly considered. Such techniques underpin much of the work that is discussed in the remainder of this book.

4.9   CONDITIONAL PROBABILITY

The probability of event A occurring, given that B has already occurred, is written $\text{Prob}(A|B)$. An example of such a probability would be the probability of accepting a new account having received a request from a new customer. This can be written using the frequentist approach (see section 4.3) as:

$$\text{Prob}(A \mid B) = \frac{f_{A \text{ and } B}}{f_B}$$

where an event x occurs with frequency f_x. Dividing top and bottom by N, the number of events in the sample space, gives,

$$\text{Prob}(A \mid B) = \frac{\frac{f_{A \text{ and } B}}{N}}{\frac{f_B}{N}} = \frac{\text{Prob}(A \text{ and } B)}{\text{Prob}(B)}$$

4.9.1   An example of conditional probability

A bank offers two types of deposit account, fixed rate and floating rate. Of the total range of 20 products available, 15 have fixed interest rates, 7 have variable interest rates and 3 have both fixed and floating interest rate options. We are told that an account, selected at random, has a fixed interest rate. What is the probability that it also has a variable interest rate option?

If an account is selected at random the following probabilities will then apply:

$$
\begin{aligned}
\text{Prob(fixed rate)} &= 15/20 \\
\text{Prob(variable rate)} &= 7/20 \\
\text{Prob(both fixed and variable rate)} &= 3/20
\end{aligned}
$$

Therefore,

$$
\begin{aligned}
\text{Prob(variable rate} \mid \text{fixed rate)} &= \frac{\text{Prob(both fixed and variable rate)}}{\text{Prob(fixed rate)}} \\
&= \frac{3/20}{15/20} = 0.2
\end{aligned}
$$

4.10   THE MULTIPLICATION RULE FOR PROBABILITIES

There may be times when you need to multiply two or more probabilities. This will typically occur when there are at least two events with different probabilities that need to be combined. For example, what is the probability of a customer taking a fixed rate deposit given that he or she has previously opened another deposit account? The previous deposit account could be either fixed rate or floating rate. If we represent fixed rate by A and floating rate by B, then the probability that the next account is also fixed rate could be written as follows:

$$\text{Prob}(A \text{ and } B) = \text{Prob}(A)\,\text{Prob}(B \mid A) + \text{Prob}(B)\,\text{Prob}(A \mid B)$$

This means that there are two ways in which A and B can occur. Either the choice is B after the first choice of A, or the choice is A after a first choice of B. This general result holds for any two events, A and B. However if the events A and B are independent, then,

$$\text{Prob}(B \mid A) = \text{Prob}(B) \quad \text{and} \quad \text{Prob}(A \text{ and } B) = \text{Prob}(A)\,\text{Prob}(B)$$

4.10.1 A classical example of conditional probability

A population of transactions contains nine items, four of which are errors and five of which are correct. Two transactions are chosen at random from this population without replacement, then:

1. The probability that the first transaction selected is correct = 5/9.
2. The probability that the second transaction selected is correct given that the first selection was correct = 4/8, since after one correct item has been selected there remain eight transactions, four of which are errors and four of which are correct.
3. However, the probability that at the outset you select two transactions that are both correct is 5/9 (for the first transaction) times (4/8) for the second transaction, i.e. $(5 \times 4)/(9 \times 8) =$ 20/72 using the multiplication rule.
4. The probability that one selection is correct and one is an error has two available options. If the first selection is correct, the second selection must be an error and if the first selection is an error, the second must be correct. This then uses both the multiplication rule and the addition rule, as follows:

$$\left(\frac{5 \times 4}{9 \times 8}\right) + \left(\frac{4 \times 5}{9 \times 8}\right) = \frac{40}{72}$$

So, in this case there are two factors since the transactions may be selected in either order.

Any two event selection, for example the first being correct and the second being correct, cannot be wholly independent, since

$$\text{Prob(second correct)} = \text{Prob(first correct and second correct)}$$
$$+ \text{Prob(first error and second correct)}$$
$$= (20/72) + (20/72) = 40/72$$
$$\neq 4/8 \text{ (from item 2 above)}$$

That means that

$$\text{Prob}(A \mid B) \neq \text{Prob}(B)$$

This type of analysis is best used when there are only a few variables to deal with. However, in reality there is often the need to deal with extremely complicated problems involving a number of different possible outcomes, and in such cases more complex mathematical approaches need to be adopted.

4.11 BAYES' THEOREM

So far we have considered only two events with differing probabilities. To deal with multiple probabilities mathematically we need to refer to Bayes' theorem. This type of modelling has become increasingly popular in areas such as modelling for operational risk where there is a large number of variables to consider.

Bayes' theorem says that if there are n disjoint events (events that have no elements in common) that cover the sample space, then:

$$\text{Prob}(E_i \mid A) = \frac{\text{Prob}(E_i)\,\text{Prob}(A \mid E_i)}{\sum\limits_{j=1}^{n} \text{Prob}(E_j)\,\text{Prob}(A \mid E_j)}$$

where the symbol in the denominator represents the action of taking the sum (or total) of all of the various clauses as set out when added together.

The terms E_i are referred to as *priors*, which are assigned before the samples are chosen, and are associated with a variable A. To aid in interpreting the theorem, a Venn diagram is presented in Figure 4.4.

To make sense of the above, let us consider a practical example.

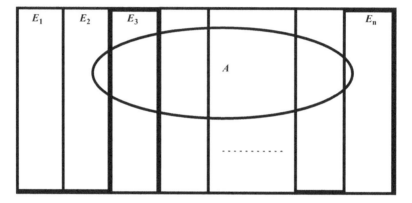

Figure 4.4   Venn diagram for Bayes' theorem.

4.11.1   An example of Bayes' theorem

Two branches of a retail bank, C and D, have each reported eight transactions to risk manage-ment for review. Of these, four of the transactions reported by branch C have actually been found to represent errors, whereas six of the transactions reported by branch D were errors. The question, which we shall answer, is: Given that an error has been identified by senior management as requiring special attention, what is the probability that this originated from branch C?

It is known that:

$$\text{Prob(error} \mid C) = 4/8 = 0.5$$
$$\text{Prob(error} \mid D) = 6/8 = 0.75$$
$$\text{Prob}(C) = \text{Prob}(D) = 1/2 \text{ (since each branch is equally likely, having}$$
$$\text{each reported eight transactions)}$$

Then, using the same mathematical notation as above,

$$\text{Prob}(C \mid \text{error}) = \frac{\text{Prob}(C)\text{Prob}(\text{error} \mid C)}{\text{Prob}(C)\text{Prob}(\text{error} \mid C) + \text{Prob}(D)\text{Prob}(\text{error} \mid D)}$$

$$= \frac{0.5 \times 0.5}{0.5 \times 0.5 + 0.5 \times 0.75} = 0.4$$

This provides the required result. However, we have only so far considered how to combine the results of two branches; the same approach could have been taken for any number of branches, say 70, just by using a greater number of clauses.

4.11.2   Bayes' theorem in action for more groups

Transactions are reported to risk management from three departments (M_1, M_2, M_3) according to Table 4.1.

Table 4.1   Reports to risk management

	M_1	M_2	M_3
Percentage supplied	60	30	10
Probability transaction not resulting in a loss	0.95	0.8	0.65

If a transaction is found to actually result in a loss, what is the probability that department M_1 supplied it? From the table the probabilities of actual losses are 0.05, 0.20 and 0.35 respectively. Now using Bayes' theorem,

$$\text{Prob}(M_1 \mid s) = \frac{\text{Prob}(s \mid M_1)\,\text{Prob}(M_1)}{\text{Prob}(s \mid M_1)\text{Prob}(M_1) + \text{Prob}(s \mid M_2)\text{Prob}(M_2) + \text{Prob}(s \mid M_3)\text{Prob}(M_3)}$$

$$= \frac{0.60 \times 0.05}{0.05 \times 0.60 + 0.20 \times 0.30 + 0.35 \times 0.10} = 0.24$$

It is therefore unlikely that branch M_1 will have caused the loss, even though they represent 60% of the population of transactions, since there is a 0.76 probability that the loss was caused by another branch.

4.11.3   Bayes' theorem applied to insurance

Let us consider in a further example the type of analysis that is often undertaken in industries such as the insurance industry.

In Newcastle 60% of the registered car drivers are at least 30 years old. Of these drivers 4% are annually convicted of a motoring offence. This figure rises to 10% for younger drivers. An employee of your company has recently been charged for speeding. What is the probability that the employee is over 30 years old?

The required probability is Prob(Age $\geq$ 30 | a motoring offence). To change this into the notation used above we shall let A represent a motoring offence. There are two choices in respect of the variable 'the age of the employees'. These are:

$$E_1 = \text{Age} \geq 30 \quad \text{and} \quad E_2 = \text{Age} < 30$$

These are the priors in this case. It is known that the probability of a motoring offence occurring if the employee is at least 30 is:

$$\text{Prob}(A \mid E_1) = 0.04,$$

whereas the probability of a motoring offence occurring if the employee is younger than 30 is:

$$\text{Prob}(A \mid E_2) = 0.1.$$

We also know that the probability that the employee is at least 30, and the probability that the employee is younger than 30, are represented by:

$$\text{Prob}(E_1) = 0.6, \qquad \text{Prob}(E_2) = 0.4$$

Using Bayes' theorem this gives the following answer:

$$\text{Prob}(E_1 \mid A) = \frac{\text{Prob}(E_1)\text{Prob}(A \mid E_1)}{\text{Prob}(E_1)\text{Prob}(A \mid E_1) + \text{Prob}(E_2)\text{Prob}(A \mid E_2)}$$
$$= \frac{0.6 \times 0.04}{0.6 \times 0.04 + 0.4 \times 0.1} = 0.375$$

It is therefore unlikely that the employee is over 30 years old, which is also why insurance premiums are higher for younger drivers. There is a 37.5% likelihood that they will be at least 30 and a 62.5% likelihood that they are younger than 30.

A diagrammatic approach may be used to provide a solution to this type of problem.

4.12   TREE DIAGRAM

If a problem involves a sequence of events it is useful to employ a tree diagram to explore the full range of possibilities. This is best demonstrated by Figure 4.5, which presents the outcomes for practical example from section 4.11. The information we need to analyse is given in Table 4.1.

The circles in Figure 4.5 represent *events*, with the individual points being referred to as *nodes*. The probabilities associated with the events resulting from any node must always add to 1 since each event must actually occur. The individual events are then arranged sequentially, as shown in Figure 4.5.

The branches marked as irrelevant represent the probabilities that a transaction has been reported to risk management but there has not actually been a loss. They are of limited interest to senior management in this context.

Looking at the probability of following path M_1, the probability that there is no loss will be $0.6 \times 0.95 = 0.57$. The six possible probabilities $(0.57 + 0.03 + 0.24 + 0.06 + 0.065 + 0.035)$ must add to 1. However, three of these possible outcomes are irrelevant since the transactions do not result in losses. The remaining terminal probabilities are scaled to achieve a total of 1. Therefore the probability that a loss emanates from branch M_1 is:

$$\text{Prob}(M_1 \mid s) = \frac{0.03}{0.03 + 0.06 + 0.035} = 0.24.$$

4.12.1   An example of prediction of success

The Strategy Director has estimated that the probability that your company's latest product will be a success is 0.75. An independent research organisation has been hired to study expected

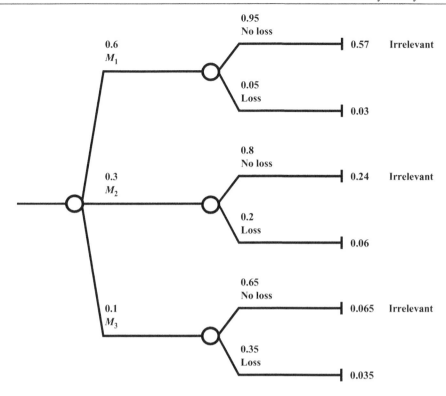

Figure 4.5   Tree diagram for the three division error reporting problem.

customer reaction to the new product and they also expect the product to succeed. With hindsight, the research organisation has previously been proved wrong in 1 survey out of 20. Does this new information change the probability of success originally estimated by the Strategy Director?

This example provides the following information to combine:

$$\text{Prob(success predicted)} = 0.75$$
$$\text{Prob(research correct | success predicted)} = 0.95$$

What you are trying to calculate is the probability that success is predicted, given that the research is correct, or:

$$\text{Prob(success predicted | research correct)}$$

This is an exercise again employing Bayes' theorem, with the priors being the predictions of success and failure. The first objective is to calculate the following term:

$$\text{Prob(success predicted)} \times \text{Prob(research correct | success predicted)}$$

Using the calculation for independence on the conditional probability (see section 4.9)

$$\text{Prob(success predicted)} \times \text{Prob(research correct in success)} = 0.75 \times 0.95$$

for the opposite result the equation becomes:

$$\text{Prob(failure predicted)} \times \text{Prob(research correct | failure predicted)}$$

Again using the calculation for independence in the conditional probability

$$\text{Prob(failure predicted)} \times \text{Prob(research correct in failure)} = 0.25 \times 0.05.$$

So that:

$$\text{Prob(success predicted | research correct)} = \frac{0.75 \times 0.95}{0.75 \times 0.95 + 0.25 \times 0.05} = 0.983$$

In this particular use of the theorem, where there is independence, a diagram (Figure 4.6) could also be used to derive a solution. The areas of interest are the two events on the diagonal giving the result obtained above. Alternatively, tree diagrams (Figures 4.7 and 4.8) could be employed to obtain the required probabilities.

	Research is correct	Research is wrong	
E_1	Agree	Disagree	0.75
E_2	Disagree	Agree	0.25
	0.95	0.05	

Figure 4.6   Venn diagram for the prediction of success example.

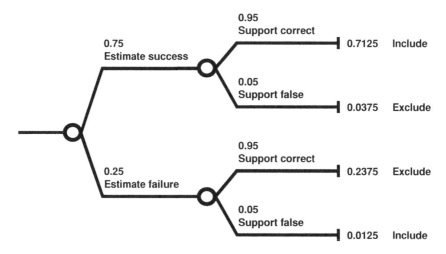

Figure 4.7   First tree diagram for prediction of success.

The original estimation of the Strategy Director is shown first with that of the research agency representing the second branch. It can be applied to each option separately. They could both

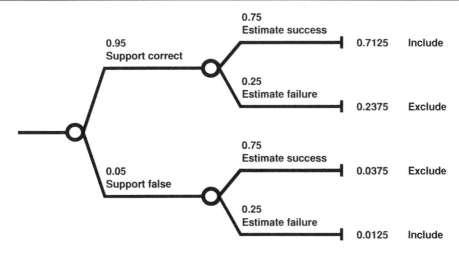

Figure 4.8   Second tree diagram for prediction of success.

be correct, both wrong, or one correct and one wrong. Both of these events are independent, so a tree may be drawn with the events in a different sequence. This is particularly useful in deciding which overall events to discard and which to retain.

Here we have reversed the two estimates, putting that of the research agency first and then adding the supporting information from the Strategy Director. The problem is to assess which probabilities to retain from Figures 4.7 and 4.8. Clearly 'support correct' and 'estimate success' should be retained. From Figure 4.7 we eliminate 'estimate success' and 'support false' while from Figure 4.8 we eliminate 'support correct' and 'estimate failure'. Hence the event retained is 'support false' and 'estimate failure', a double negative. On rescaling the retained probabilities the same result as in Figure 4.7 is obtained.

This sort of approach is useful when you are conducting any form of 'what/if' analysis. These ask the question: Given that A has happened, how likely is B to happen? Such questions turn up where there is quality control – for example, when the problem is to trace back defects to the original fault.

On adopting a more formal approach to the general problem, there is always the issue of posing the correct question. This is often a question of semantics; loose verbal definitions can make the problem posed intractable. For the problem in Figure 4.8, some notation might be introduced:

$$\text{Prob(success)} = x$$
$$\text{Prob(research predicts success} \mid \text{success)} = y$$

then,

$$\text{Prob(success} \mid \text{research predicts success)} = \frac{xy}{xy + (1 - x)(1 - y)}$$

The break-even point, with conditional probability of a half, corresponds to the line $x + y = 1$.

4.12.2   An example from an American game show: The Monty Hall problem

The set of Monty Hall's game show *Let's Make a Deal* has three closed doors (*A*, *B* and *C*). Behind one of these doors is a car; behind the other two are goats. The contestant does not know where the car is, but Monty Hall does.

The contestant picks a door and Monty opens one of the remaining doors, one he knows does not hide the car. If the contestant has already chosen the correct door, Monty is equally likely to open either of the two remaining doors, since each would have a goat behind it.

After Monty has shown a goat behind the door that he opens, the contestant is always given the option to switch doors. What is the probability of winning the car if the contestant stays with his first choice? What if he decides to switch?

The simplest approach is to construct a tree diagram (Figure 4.9). From the tree diagram the probabilities in Table 4.2 may be summarised.

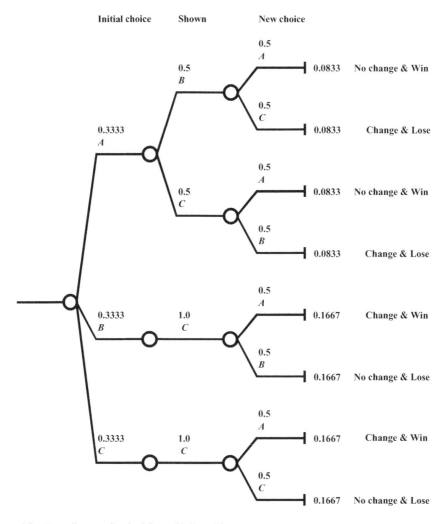

Figure 4.9   Tree diagram for the Monty Hall problem.

Table 4.2 Summary probabilities for Monty Hall problem

	Win	Lose
Change	0.3333	0.1667
No change	0.1667	0.3333

Therefore in order to maximise the chance of winning, the optimal strategy is for the contestant to change his choice, since he is twice as likely to win than if he fails to switch. Monty has shown the contestant additional information by opening one of the doors, which has provided the contestant with a better chance of winning.

Taking the information from the diagram:

$$\text{Prob(change)} = \text{Prob(no change)} = \frac{1}{2}$$

$$\text{Prob(win | change)} = \frac{\text{Prob (win \& change)}}{\text{Prob (change)}} = \frac{2}{3}$$

$$\text{Prob(win | no change)} = \frac{\text{Prob(win \& no change)}}{\text{Prob(no change)}} = \frac{1}{3}$$

Looking at this in more detail . . .

Prob(initial choice is a winner) $= 1/3$

Prob(initial choice is not a winner) $= 2/3$

Prob(change choice | any initial choice) $= 1/2$ since these are independent for the player

Prob(win & change) $=$ Prob(initial choice is not a winner)

$\times$ Prob(change | initial choice is not a winner)

$= 2/3 \times 1/2 = 1/3$

Prob(win & do not change) $=$ Prob(initial choice is a winner)

$\times$ Prob(do not change choice | initial choice is a winner)

$= 1/3 \times 1/2 = 1/6$

These are the same results as those obtained above.

4.13   CONCLUSION

In conclusion, it is particularly important to understand the impact of independence and conditional probabilities when trying to consider the probability of a particular outcome given specific circumstances. It is ignoring these properties that leads to serious errors of judgement due to the provision of incorrect or inaccurate information.

5
Standard Terms in Statistics

5.1 INTRODUCTION

Within statistics there are a variety of terms that are generally applied. For anyone becoming involved with statistics for the first time, it is essential (1) that the standard vocabulary is used to describe data and (2) that this vocabulary is fully understood.

The following terms are explained in this chapter:

- Maximum and minimum
- Mean
- Mode
- Median
- Upper and lower quartile
- MQMQM or Box plot
- Skewness
- Variance and standard deviation.

The chapter concludes with consideration of the measures available for continuous data.

5.2 MAXIMUM AND MINIMUM

At its simplest, the maximum is the largest item in any data set and the minimum is the smallest. Where there are a large number of observed values, the maximum and minimum can be used to represent the extreme values of some attribute within the data set. Consider a typical set of observations $(x_i: i = 1, \ldots, n)$ then we can define maximum and minimum using mathematical equations as follows:

$$\text{the maximum is } x_j, \quad \text{where } x_j \geq x_i \quad \text{for} \quad i = 1, \ldots, n$$
$$\text{the minimum is } x_j, \quad \text{where } x_j \leq x_i \quad \text{for} \quad i = 1, \ldots, n$$

What this is saying is that item j has a value x_j that is the greatest (maximum) or the least (minimum) in the population. Therefore the maximum and minimum can be said to be providing bounds to the data set.

There are three forms of average, which are in common usage – the mean, the median and the mode.

5.2.1 Mean

The mean (also called the arithmetic mean) is the average in a set of data obtained by adding all the items together and dividing by the number of items in the data set. Using mathematical notation it can be defined to be:

$$\text{mean}(x) = \frac{x_1 + x_2 + \ldots + x_n}{n} = \frac{1}{n}\sum_{i=1}^{n} x_i$$

This is often written as $\bar{x}$ and is the most frequently used type of average.

For example, consider the data set $\{1, 2, 2, 3, 3, 4, 4, 4, 4, 4, 5, 5, 5, 5, 6, 6, 6, 7, 7, 8, 10\}$ then the mean is

$$\frac{1 + 2 + 2 + 3 + 3 + 4 + 4 + 4 + 4 + 4 + 5 + 5 + 5 + 5 + 6 + 6 + 6 + 7 + 7 + 8 + 10}{21}$$

which is

$$\frac{101}{21} = 4.81$$

This style of averaging is often used in practice where a range of outcomes is possible. It effectively deals with weighting by giving each outcome an identical weight. No single outcome is more important than another. In the example a number of the observations appear more than once. This is referred to as grouped data and is summarised in Table 5.1, which shows, for example, that observation x_i occurs with a frequency f_i.

Table 5.1 Grouped specimen data

Observation (x_i)	1	2	3	4	5	6	7	8	9	10
Frequency (f_i)	1	2	2	5	4	3	2	1	0	1

For grouped data the mean is then

$$\text{mean}(x) = \frac{\sum_{i=1}^{10} f_i x_i}{\sum_{i=1}^{10} f_i}$$

Therefore forming the column $f_i x_i$ (the product of the observations and the frequencies) and adding is identical to simply performing the summation on x. This effectively means that the mean of x is the total of all the observations multiplied by their frequency, divided by the total number of observations. This saves the labour of, for instance, adding in the value 4 five times. Then we can employ the calculations presented in Table 5.2, to recalculate the mean.

The data has the following values for its descriptors, mean $101/21 = 4.81$, a minimum of 1 and a maximum of 10.

Of course this average needs to be used with care. There is no observation 4.81 since all the observations actually have integer values. So if the population is, for example, the number of errors in reconciliations discovered by month, then the '4.81' suggests that you should plan for either 4 or 5 errors normally occurring.

5.2.2 Median

The median is the central value of the observations when they are placed in numerical order. If there is an odd number of observations, it is $x_{(n+1)/2}$ while for an even number it is:

$$(x_{n/2} + x_{(n/2)+1})/2.$$

Table 5.2   Specimen data to calculate the mean

Observation x_i	Frequency f_i	$f_i x_i$	Cumulative frequency
1	1	1	1
2	2	4	3
3	2	6	5
4	5	20	10
5	4	20	14
6	3	18	17
7	2	14	19
8	1	8	20
9	0	0	20
10	1	10	21
Total	**21**	**101**	

This means that if there is an odd number of observations, the median is the central observation. However, if there is an even number of observations, the median is the average of the amounts before and after the middle of the distribution. The consequence of this is that when there is an even number of observations, the median does not need to actually have one of the x values. The median is often used when one or two extreme x values distort the mean.

The alternative approach, where there are some extreme values, is to exclude these outliers from the data set in the first place as being unrepresentative.

5.2.3   Mode

The mode is the most commonly occurring value and would be of importance to a manufacturer when assessing the style of product to market.

In the example above the observation 4 appears to have occurred five times, it is therefore the most frequently appearing and consequently can also be referred to as the *mode*. Another way of looking at this is to assume that the same table refers to a single day's sale of 10 products. In this case there have been more sales of product 4 than sales of the other nine products on offer.

5.3   UPPER AND LOWER QUARTILE

The purpose of the upper and lower quartiles is to provide some further initial analysis of the shape or distribution of possible outcomes. If there are n observations in the data then the upper quartile and lower quartile values may be defined as having values that correspond to $3(n + 1)/4$ and $(n + 1)/4$ positioned entries of the ordered data. They also give the range within which 50% of the observations lie. Again if these calculations do not produce integers, then the correct proportions of the values neighbouring these points are taken. This covers the case where the quartile sits between two observations.

Returning to the data in Table 5.2, the measures are:

- The population (n) is 21.
- The median is at position 11, which is observation 5 (between 10 and 14 cumulative frequency).

- The lower quartile (Q_1) is at $(n + 1)/4 = 5.5$, since the fifth entry is the last observation of observation 3 and the sixth entry is the first entry of observation 4, so $Q_1 = 3 + 0.5 \times (4-3) = 3.5$.
- The upper quartile (Q_3) is at $3(n + 1)/4 = 16.5$ since the 16th and 17th entries are both 6, so $Q_3 = 6$.

In most real life scenarios there are a wide range of outcomes, and the upper and lower quartiles will just be calculated in the way shown above without any rounding being employed. The rounding would itself introduce a level of inaccuracy that may be misleading.

A useful plot to summarise some of these measures is the MQMQM plot, also known as a box plot. These plots are particularly useful in summarising and rapidly comparing multiple data sets.

5.4 MQMQM PLOT

Some of the values calculated above may be combined in an MQMQM plot (Figure 5.1), where the letters represent

Minimum

Lower Quartile

Median

Upper Quartile

Maximum

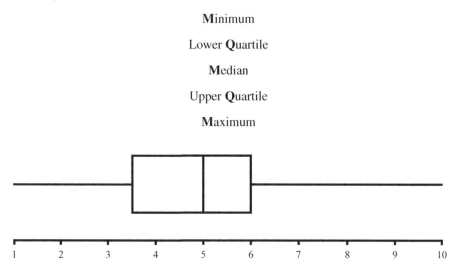

Figure 5.1 MQMQM plot of the specimen data.

The outer solid lines are bounded by the maximum and minimum. The central block is bounded by the upper and lower quartiles with the central line representing the median.

The problem caused by extreme values occurring in a data set was mentioned earlier. Ideally most analysts would like a set of observations to occur in a nice even spread that is effectively symmetric. Unfortunately, this is not normally the case and most data sets will have a few unusual events that have specific characteristics. For example, if you are looking at the daily movements in interest rates, most items will be within the boundary of 0% and 1% since it is unusual for interest rates to move by more than 1% in a day. However, if there has been a major change to the financial environment then there will be a much greater movement. This is a non-standard outcome, which will normally be excluded from your data set for short-term sensitivity analysis considerations, but used separately for scenario analysis (see Chapter 30).

5.5   SKEWNESS

Observations are positively skewed if a histogram (see Chapter 3) of the observations shows a 'hump' towards the low values. In this case the descriptors would be ordered,

mode < median < mean

A typical example of this would be errors in processing transactions where most of the errors are small.

Alternatively, there could be a bias towards the high values, which is known as being negatively skewed, and the order would become:

mean < median < mode

This distribution could occur when you are summarising salaries for senior management, for example.

As a memory aid for the order, the values are alphabetically ordered for negative skew and in the reverse order for positive skew. These two cases, plus a symmetric example without any skew, are illustrated in Figure 5.2.

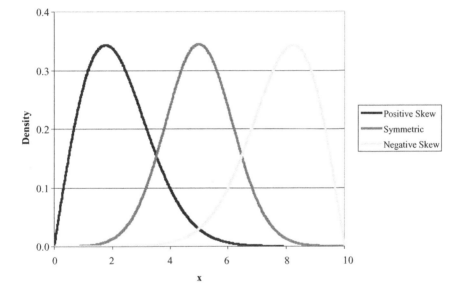

Figure 5.2   Illustration of skewness.

All the measures used so far have related to the actual observed values. There are however a number of terms that provide a summary of the data and are used for additional data analysis. The most important of these are the variance and standard deviation.

5.6   VARIANCE AND STANDARD DEVIATION

The variance and the standard deviation give a measure of the range of the observations. They provide some information regarding the distribution of the data around the centre. Whether the set of data is closely clustered or whether it is more diffuse, for example. The two terms are related to each other as follows:

- The variance calculates the average difference squared between the observations and their mean.
- The standard deviation is defined to be the square root of the variance.

Using mathematical notation, for a sample of n observations from a population, the variance, written as var(x), is defined to be:

$$\text{var}(x) = \frac{\sum_{i=1}^{n} (x_i - \bar{x})^2}{n - 1}$$

and the standard deviation, written as std(x), is defined to be:

$$\text{std}(x) = \sqrt{\text{var}(x)}.$$

An alternative expression for the variance of grouped data is:

$$\text{var}(x) = \frac{\sum_{i=1}^{n} f_i (x_i - \bar{x})^2}{\left(\sum_{i=1}^{n} f_i\right) - 1}$$

The divisor is $n - 1$ in all cases where a sample has been taken from the population. If the complete population has been sampled, a divisor of n should be adopted. If the sample is large enough, the difference in dividing by n or $n - 1$ is not likely to be significant.

The variance and standard deviation are frequently calculated when undertaking statistical analysis. Returning to the previous example the variance can be calculated employing the values in Table 5.3.

Table 5.3   Specimen data to calculate the variance

Observation x_i	Frequency f_i	$f_i x_i$	Deviation $(x_i - \bar{x})$	$(x_i - \bar{x})^2$	$f_i (x_i - \bar{x})^2$
1	1	1	−3.81	14.51	14.51
2	2	4	−2.81	7.89	15.79
3	2	6	−1.81	3.27	6.55
4	5	20	−0.81	0.66	3.28
5	4	20	0.19	0.04	0.15
6	3	18	1.19	1.42	4.25
7	2	14	2.19	4.80	9.60
8	1	8	3.19	10.18	10.18
9	0	0	4.19	17.56	0.00
10	1	10	5.19	26.94	26.94
Total	**21**	**101**			**91.24**

In section 5.3 the mean was calculated as mean $= 101/21 = 4.81$. Using the equations above, this gives the following calculations for the variance and standard deviation:

$$\text{Variance} = \frac{91.24}{21 - 1} = 4.56$$

$$\text{Standard deviation} = \sqrt{4.56} = 2.14$$

While the above presentation is valid, it may prove inefficient for manual calculation. To enable these calculations to be conducted more easily, the equation for the variance, for ungrouped data, may be rewritten as

$$\text{var}(x) = \frac{\sum\limits_{i=1}^{n} x_i^2 - \frac{1}{n}\left(\sum\limits_{i=1}^{n} x_i\right)^2}{n - 1}$$

Which is equivalent to the following equation:

$$\text{var}(x) = \frac{\sum\limits_{i=1}^{m} f_i x_i^2 - \frac{1}{N}\left(\sum\limits_{i=1}^{m} f_i x_i\right)^2}{N - 1}$$

where $N = \sum\limits_{i=1}^{m} f_i$.

This applies to grouped data. Repeating the previous calculation, we can use the figures shown in Table 5.4.

Table 5.4   Specimen data to calculate the variance with greater ease

Observation x_i	Frequency f_i	$f_i x_i$	$f_i x_i^2$
1	1	1	1
2	2	4	8
3	2	6	18
4	5	20	80
5	4	20	100
6	3	18	108
7	2	14	98
8	1	8	64
9	0	0	0
10	1	10	100
Total	**21**	**101**	**577**

Using the equations above, this new formula gives the variance calculation as follows:

$$\text{Variance} = \frac{577 - \frac{1}{21}101^2}{21 - 1} = 4.56$$

As expected the result is identical to that obtained above.

In practical examples the mean and standard deviation can provide useful summaries about the raw data. If the data follows the symmetric form in Figure 5.2, then, typically, 95% of the data lies in the range defined by the mean $-2\times$ standard deviation and mean $+2\times$ standard deviation. If, on a typical day in a bank, the mean amount deposited is £90 with a standard deviation of £15, it is not unreasonable to then say that typically 95% of deposits lie between £60 (£90 $-$ £15 $\times$ 2) and £120 (£90 $+$ £15 $\times$ 2).

5.7   MEASURES FOR CONTINUOUS DATA

All the data considered so far has been discrete data. It may be necessary to calculate the mean and variance of some continuous data that has been gathered into class intervals. To use the equations defined above, simply equate each class interval to its mid-point. That is $x_i = (R_i + L_i)/2$, the centre of the left and right end points. Let us consider Table 5.5, which sets out the weekly overtime earnings of contractors, all of whom are expected to do at least some overtime. The required calculations are displayed in the data. For this data the mean is given by the following calculation:

$$\text{Mean} = \frac{67{,}383}{240} = 280.76$$

then, using the equation where $N = \sum_{i=1}^{m} f_i$

$$\text{var}(x) = \frac{\sum_{i=1}^{m} f_i x_i^2 - \frac{1}{N} \left(\sum_{i=1}^{m} f_i x_i \right)^2}{N - 1}$$

This gives the following calculation for the variance:

$$\text{Variance} = \frac{19{,}054{,}829 - \frac{1}{240} 67{,}383^2}{240 - 1} = 569.91$$

Table 5.5   Weekly overtime payments for contractors

Weekly overtime payments (£ per week)		Number of contractors	Mid-point	$f_i x_i$	$f_i x_i^2$
237	241	3	239	717	171,363
241	245	1	243	243	59,049
245	249	4	247	988	244,036
249	253	4	251	1,004	252,004
253	257	11	255	2,805	715,275
257	261	16	259	4,144	1,073,296
261	265	23	263	6,049	1,590,887
265	269	20	267	5,340	1,425,780
269	273	31	271	8,401	2,276,671
273	277	20	275	5,500	1,512,500
277	281	18	279	5,022	1,401,138
281	285	20	283	5,660	1,601,780
285	295	10	290	2,900	841,000
295	305	26	300	7,800	2,340,000
305	315	11	310	3,410	1,057,100
315	325	5	320	1,600	512,000
325	335	7	330	2,310	762,300
335	355	8	345	2,760	952,200
355	375	2	365	730	266,450
Total		**240**		**67,383**	**19,054,829**

The standard deviation is the square root of the variance, which in this case is 23.87.

In summary, the mean provides a measure of the centrality, while the standard deviation provides an indication of the spread. The variance is really only a stage in the calculation to obtain the more useful standard deviation, but in practice is also often shown in reports.

As discussed above, for normal data 95% of the observations lie within ± two standard deviations of the mean.

6

Sampling

6.1 INTRODUCTION

In previous chapters we have considered how data should be presented, and some of the basic measures and techniques related to data and their analysis. We have not yet considered any of the issues relating to the actual collection of data.

Prior to collecting any information the objective that the company is seeking to achieve must be clear. If you are unsure what you are trying to analyse, you may not collect the data you require and no amount of detailed analysis will then improve the fact that the wrong data has initially been collated.

6.2 PLANNING DATA COLLECTION

Before you start to collect data it is well worth spending some time giving the objectives that you are seeking to address a degree of thought. This stage of the planning will include deciding what is the total set of variables that could be considered and identifying precisely which are of interest. It is a waste of resources, both time and money, to collect redundant data or data that does not illustrate the properties of the variables you are seeking to analyse.

The units of measurement that are to be used should be formally established. If you were collecting a set of trade transactions that are to be shown in one currency, you would not want the observations to be in different currencies since you would only then have to translate them back into a single currency. It would have been better had the transactions initially been recorded in local currency equivalents, for example, to aid comparison.

It is wise, at the outset, to decide on the level of accuracy required from the observations. For example, if you are intending to use data for strategic management purposes, it will be pointless to know the answer to four decimal places. The data could be given to the nearest unit and would still achieve the objectives of your management.

As part of the initial planning process, the population to be sampled should be both identified and defined. Data could be held in a series of different systems and therefore it will be important to identify all the systems that hold the relevant data to ensure that a complete and fair population is sampled. This will avoid introducing unnecessary bias into the sampling process.

The next question is to consider whether it is essential to examine every member of the population or to consider whether a sample would suffice. This will depend on the level of accuracy required, the size of the underlying population and the time and resources available.

Having selected the key criteria, the next decision is to consider how cost effective the sampling and analysis is likely to be. Will the size of the sample that can realistically be collected be sufficient to obtain the desired level of accuracy?

6.3   METHODS FOR SURVEY ANALYSIS

If a company intends to undertake a major survey of their clients' satisfaction, for example, it would be possible for every customer to be contacted by a single analyst. While this would fully cover the population, it could prove costly and time consuming. The one advantage of using a single analyst to undertake the entire task would be that the data should be consistent in both the application of collection techniques and also the subsequent data analysis. To enable the firm to get a better understanding of the specific requirements of the survey, it would be advisable for a pilot survey to be conducted.

An alternative approach would be for the firm to employ either an internal or an external team to carry out the survey. However, if the team approach is adopted it will be essential to ensure that every person employed in the survey knows exactly what information he or she is expected to collect, from which population and also how the information is to be collected and analysed.

If there are insufficient funds, or it is considered impractical to conduct a detailed series of structured interviews, then the use of questionnaires should be considered. These may be used to either replace or supplement the series of structured interviews. Having prepared the questionnaire, the key benefits are:

1. They are cheap to distribute and collect.
2. Each question will be asked in the same way without bias.

However the quality of the response to questionnaires is not normally as good as the results achieved from structured interviews. Many of your customers may not return the forms, while others may misinterpret questions or lose interest and fail to complete all questions.

When preparing the questions many issues need to be considered, including:

- There should not be too many questions.
- The questions must be precisely phrased in plain English and should not be too long.
- The answers should not be suggested by the questions.
- The questions should be sufficient to obtain the required information.
- The questions should be designed to minimise the cost of analysing the responses.
- A sample survey should be conducted to ensure that the order of the questions does not affect the answers given. Ideally companies that have assisted with the pilot survey should be retested with the main survey to ensure that the questions are robust. On balance these customers should provide the same responses on both occasions.

However, the use of a questionnaire-based approach may be preferable to a team of ill-informed or biased interviewers, since it should be completely standard with the same question asked of each customer in the same way.

Finally there is the option of conducting a literature search, in its broadest sense. The data required might already be available – for example, in the company's records. Would it be possible to combine the results of a number of independent but related studies using statistical methods to retrieve, select and combine the data – a process referred to as meta-analysis?

The case may also occur where a range of independent surveys has already been conducted and their results published. While the results on a survey in the USA may not be directly applicable to the business you are looking at in the United Kingdom, the conclusions are likely to be of interest and the questions employed may also be suitable for your purposes.

Having settled on the testing approach to be employed, the sample must then be chosen. The choice of the sample size is highly dependent on the criteria outlined above (accuracy, cost, etc.). The sample chosen must be large enough to counteract the effect of any particular sampled item having an exceptional result, referred to as an outlier. Alternatively such outliers could be excluded from the analysed population, with their exclusion being specifically highlighted.

There are a number of ways in which a sample may be chosen.

6.3.1   Random samples

In a random sample, the chance of any member of the population being selected is equal. To do this, every member of the population – for example, the complete list of depositors – must be listed and assigned a number. Having done this, a 'lottery' approach could be adopted to select numbers from a fully mixed sample until sufficient depositors have been chosen. An alternative would be to make use of random number tables (such as Table 6.1), which contain banks of random numbers.

Table 6.1   A specimen set of random numbers

17623	47441	27821	91845	45054	58410	. . .

The important thing is to use these numbers sequentially, either by rows or columns. If you imagine a sample consisting of 450 people, the numbers from Table 6.1 would be taken in blocks of three. This would give the following sequence of three digit numbers: 176, 234, 744, 127 . . . and so on. Some of the numbers will be beyond the range of the data, which in this case is 450. This is not a problem since the numbers that are outside of the range, for example 744, are simply ignored. This selection process continues until the sample is complete.

In some cases it may be impractical or inappropriate to generate a random sample, in which case a number of other options could be considered, as set out below.

6.3.2   Systematic sampling

In systematic sampling the population is first set out in a list, which is assumed to have no regular bias. This would avoid cases where, for example, the order of the entries always runs as January, February, March, etc.

The next stage is to select two random numbers, m and n . Here the mth data item is first sampled then the $(m + n)$th, $(m + 2n)$th and so on. Therefore, if $m = 7$ and $n = 9$ you will select data item 16, 25, 34 and so on. To produce a greater degree of randomness, a second pair of numbers could be taken periodically; however, if there is no bias in the population this is probably unnecessary.

6.3.3   Stratified sampling

This method can be adopted when the population can be partitioned into distinct layers or strata. For example, consider the following population of customers at a branch of a bank, as displayed in Table 6.2.

To consider 10% of the customers, 10 customers should be selected randomly from the group that do not have any deposit accounts, with 15, 25 and 10 being selected from the three remaining groups.

Table 6.2   Number of deposits held by customers

Number of deposit accounts	Total
0	100
1	150
2	250
3 or more	100

6.3.4 Multistage sampling

It is often inefficient to initially construct a complete list of all of the items in the population. If the population can be partitioned into a number of groups, then these could be randomly selected using random number tables, as Table 6.1. The process can then be repeated with fresh partitions of the selected groups until a pseudo-population is reached that can be randomly sampled.

For example, a random sample of countries might be selected, then a random sample of towns in these countries chosen in which the bank has a branch and, finally, a random sample of customers in the towns selected.

6.3.5 Quota sampling

This approach can be adopted if a number of details about the population are known. It can then be decided exactly how many should be chosen from each class. These will be collected by chance until each category is complete and the correct sample size collected. This is the approach taken by street-based marketing surveyors who typically require interviews with specific numbers of people with given occupations. This method is generally only used when it is impractical to construct a complete list of the population.

6.3.6 Cluster sampling

This is similar to multistage sampling except that every member of the final partition is considered. This would be adopted if only a partial list of the population were available. For instance, if a list of customers in a selected town were unavailable due to legal issues, then additional members of another selected town will be chosen to replace this unavailable part of the sample population. That the sample has to be amended may impact upon the analysis that is subsequently conducted. If it is significant, this should be highlighted to management when the results of the analysis are delivered.

6.4 HOW IT CAN GO WRONG

There were two infamously bad surveys in America that have lessons for today's companies.

The first was a survey of voting preference conducted in the 1920s. Unfortunately, to save time and money, people were telephoned. Consequently, rather than examine all voters in the total population, only those with telephones were contacted. The equivalent in the modern work is to contact people by either text or e-mail. Both of these techniques will only select the portion of the population that use this medium.

The second bad survey related to the American draft during the Vietnam War. It was decided to call people up by their date of birth. Hence every date in the year in question was placed in a cylinder. Having placed the January cylinders into a receptacle, those for February were then added and the other months were then included one at a time. A mixing process was carried out after each month's population was added. After this mixing process was complete sufficient cylinders were then drawn. Unfortunately the bulk of those selected had dates of birth that fell in the latter part of the year, since the population for December had far less chance to mix than that for January, and so remained near the surface.

6.5   WHAT MIGHT BE IN A SURVEY?

What type of questions should be asked and in what form should the questions be delivered? Should use be made of focus groups, individual interviews, or surveys by mail, for example? The following approach will assist in deciding upon the actual approach that is most suitable in specific circumstances:

Stage 1

- Conduct a survey of those organisations that you know in advance will relate to your questions. You may use a sample or, if the target group is relatively small, you may choose to survey them all.
- Make your mail survey short with yes/no or a/b/c type questions. People will not generally take the time to respond to open-ended questions.
- You should only expect a 3–4% response rate on the initial mailing. If your survey instrument is well structured, you should be able to detect a trend after the return of 25 surveys. You can always conduct a second mail survey if needed.
- You may choose to undertake a follow-up phone interview with non-respondents.

Stage 2

- Tabulate the survey and produce some brief initial conclusions.
- Use the above conclusions to formulate a short personal interview questionnaire.
- Conduct 15–20 personal interviews to validate the initial conclusions. Be careful, the interview questions should not be leading by nature and you should ensure that the interviewer is objective. The interviewer should not be told exactly what answers to expect.
- Tabulate the interview survey.
- Consider whether the personal interviews validate, support or contradict the survey.

6.6   CAUTIONARY NOTES

It is important to realise that anyone setting up a survey can manipulate the results and therefore this source of bias needs to be minimised.

- The vocabulary adopted when designing a survey must be clear, unambiguous and comprehensible to the intended audience. For instance, just how many is 'a few'? Avoid the use of a double negative since this will only serve to confuse respondents.

- Interviewers must also be aware that opinion does not necessarily imply knowledge. Having carefully and fairly worded a question, the responses offered may still exert an undue influence. Asking specific questions may assist respondents in recalling information. Rather than asking, 'During the past year how often did you visit the bank?', use 'When did you last visit the bank?' The analysis you will conduct will enable you to achieve the conclusions you are seeking.
- While telephone surveys are quick and easy, they may also be problematic. Does your survey have access to unlisted numbers, since the likelihood is that otherwise this sort of customer will be excluded? If such customers are excluded, you will need to use some other basis to sample them.
- The order in which questions are asked can be significant. A question will create a certain context, which will be applied by the respondee to successive questions.
- Finally, when management receive the results of a survey, it will be important for them to satisfy themselves on a number of points:
  - Was the sample chosen fairly?
  - Were the questions posed consistently?
  - Did the survey report what people said, or what they really meant?
  - Was the information accurately recorded?
  - Was the sample consistent with other samples obtained?

If a sample appears to be different in profile to other samples, you can review it again or check to see if some form of unconscious bias has been introduced.

7

Probability Distribution Functions

7.1 INTRODUCTION

A probability distribution function, which may also be called a *probability density function*, gives the set of probabilities associated with each of the values that a random variable can take. In practice, distribution functions are used when there are a series of potential results, for example interest rates.

Probability distribution functions enable a lot of information to be portrayed in a form that enables management to understand both the spread of the information and the nature of any uncertainty contained within the observations. In this chapter we introduce a number of important distributions, beginning with the simplest of distributions, the discrete uniform distribution.

7.2 DISCRETE UNIFORM DISTRIBUTION

Taking a simple example, when you are tossing a coin, there are only two options available, heads or tails. These options are displayed in Table 7.1.

Table 7.1 Probability distribution for tossing a coin

Event	Head	Tail
Probability	$\frac{1}{2}$	$\frac{1}{2}$

When rolling a dice, there are six options, each of which can arise with equal probability, as summarised in Table 7.2.

Table 7.2 Probability distribution for rolling a dice

Event	1	2	3	4	5	6
Probability	$\frac{1}{6}$	$\frac{1}{6}$	$\frac{1}{6}$	$\frac{1}{6}$	$\frac{1}{6}$	$\frac{1}{6}$

These are two examples of a discrete uniform distribution. In each case the total of the probabilities is 1 and each possible outcome has an equal chance of occurring. If you graph the values set out in Table 7.2, then a bar chart would be obtained, as shown in Figure 7.1.

Prior to discussing more advanced distributions, it is necessary to introduce some additional terms.

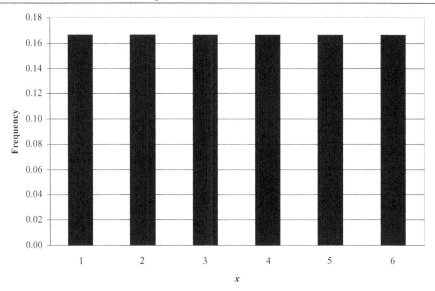

Figure 7.1   Bar chart for the probability distribution for rolling a dice.

7.2.1   Counting techniques

Counting techniques are used to deal with the problem of selecting items from a large sample, with or without having regard to the order in which they appear in the sample. There is a shorthand mathematical notation that is used to represent the total number of ways that a given choice could occur. This is defined as $n!$ (referred to as n factorial) which represents $n(n - 1)(n - 2) \ldots 1$. Therefore if n is positive, then $n! = n(n - 1)!$. Further the initial value, zero factorial, is defined as having the value 1 ($0! = 1$).

7.2.2   Combination

A combination is a group of items selected from a larger set regardless of the order in which they appear. The number of ways to select r items from a set of n unlike items is written

$$_nC_r \quad \text{or} \quad \binom{n}{r} \quad \text{and is equal to} \quad \frac{n!}{r!\,(n - r)!}$$

This works since there are n ways of choosing the first item, $n - 1$ for the second and $n - r$ for the rth. However, since the order is unimportant a factor $r!$ is introduced as a divisor to allow for all the possible orderings of the selected items. Considering the nature of the selection procedure $_nC_r = {}_nC_{n-r}$ since one is the choice for what has been selected while the other is the distribution that applies for what is left.

If, for example, the problem of selecting two debtors from a list of 12 is considered, then there are $_{12}C_2$ ways of making the choice. Using the equation $n!/r!\,(n - r)!$ with $n = 12$ and $r = 2$, this gives $12!/2!\,(12 - 2)!$. Since many of these terms cancel, because $(12 - 2)! = 10!$ and $2! = 2 \times 1 = 2$, the equation simplifies to become $12 \times (12 - 1)/2$ or $12 \times 11/2 = 66$. This means that there are 66 different ways that a sample of two debtors may be selected from a list of 12 debtors.

7.2.3   Permutation

There may of course be the occasion when the order of the items in the sample is important – for example, when ranking performance. In this case the number of permutations is written as $_nP_r$ which takes the value $n!/(n-r)!$ where you are selecting r items from a set of n unlike items. The link between combination (section 7.2.2) and permutation is shown by the equation $_nP_r = r!\,_nC_r$ since $(n!/r!\,(n-r)!)r! = n!/(n-r)!$.

Consider the problem of awarding three team bonuses (first, second and third) to teams within a treasury function, where there are six desks. The remaining three teams do not receive any team bonus at all. There are $_6P_3$ permutations since any one of the desks could win the first prize, but then only five remain for the second prize and four for the third. To calculate the number of ways of giving the bonuses, we use the equation $n!/(n-r)!$. This gives $6!/(6-3)!$ ways, and since $(6-3)! = 3!$, which therefore cancels, the terms become $6 \times 5 \times 4 = 120$. There are therefore a total of 120 ways of giving the awards.

7.3   BINOMIAL DISTRIBUTION

The binomial distribution is used where there are only a limited number of possible outcomes available. It could be as simple as when there can be only one of two events, say, success and failure.

Consider the probability of there being m successes in n trials (m is the number of observations and n the population from which items are to be selected). In this case a probability p is assigned to a success and a probability of $q = 1 - p$ to a failure. Since the successes can occur in any order there are $_nC_m$ ways in which the m observations may occur. Therefore the probability of m successes in n trials, which means there are $n - m$ failures, is written mathematically as $B(m; n, p)$ is $_nC_m p^m q^{n-m}$. This distribution has a mean (see section 5.2.1) of np and a variance (see section 5.6) of $np(1-p)$.

The distribution function for the case where there is a population $n = 10$ and a probability of success $p = 0.4$ is shown in Figure 7.2.

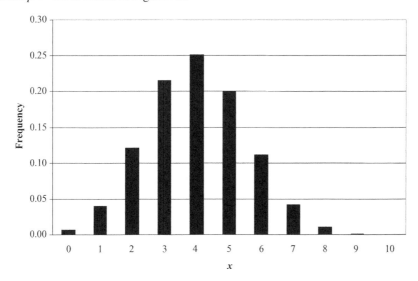

Figure 7.2   Bar chart for the binomial distribution for $n = 10$ and $p = 0.4$.

7.3.1 Example of a binomial distribution

A bank is considering selling a new type of loan product in three areas: rural, residential and inner city. The probability that the product will be successful is viewed as 0.4, which means that there is a probability of failure of 0.6, and it is assumed that all of the areas are independent. The population is the three areas and the bank will want to consider what happens in all cases, corresponding to either a successful product launch, or a failure. The first question is: What would happen if the product were unsuccessful in all three areas? Then using $_nC_m p^m q^{n-m}$, the probability of no successes is:

$$\text{Prob}(0 \text{ success}) = {_3C_0} \times 0.4^0 \times 0.6^3 = 0.216$$

In other words, for there to be no successes the bank needs to select none from three. There are then no successes with a probability of 0.4, whereas there are three failures with a probability of 0.6. There are then three other possible states to consider, which are: one success, two successes and three successes. Using the same equation $_nC_m p^m q^{n-m}$ gives:

$$\text{Prob}(1 \text{ success}) \quad = {_3C_1} \times 0.4^1 \times 0.6^2 = 0.432$$
$$\text{Prob}(2 \text{ successes}) = {_3C_2} \times 0.4^2 \times 0.6^1 = 0.288$$
$$\text{Prob}(3 \text{ successes}) = {_3C_3} \times 0.4^3 \times 0.6^0 = 0.064$$

The four options (no success, one success, two successes and three successes) occur with a total probability of $0.216 + 0.432 + 0.288 + 0.064 = 1$. There are two techniques that can be used to simplify the calculation of the required probabilities.

Firstly, the probabilities can be calculated recursively, since each term is determined by the application of a formula to preceding terms. This means that

$$\text{Prob}(m) = \frac{\text{Prob}(m-1) \times p \times (n-m+1)}{q \times m} \quad \text{with Prob}(0) = q^n.$$

The other technique is to use Pascal's triangle.

7.3.2 Pascal's triangle

Pascal's triangle, named after Blaise Pascal (1623–62), can also be employed to calculate the combinatorial coefficients. Pascal's triangle (see Figure 7.3) works by adding the numbers appearing above but linked to them. So, for example, the fourth line shows 1, then 3 being 1 plus 2, another 3 this time being 2 plus 1 and then the final 1. Pascal's triangle is old, and it was already old when Pascal 'invented' it. See, for example, Chu Shi-Chieh's (1303) *Ssu Yuan Yü Chien*. 'The Old Method Chart of the Seven Multiplying Squares.'

Notice that $_nC_m = {_{n-1}C_m} + {_{n-1}C_{m-1}}$. Illegal combinations such as $_nC_{-1}$ are taken to be zero since you cannot take a negative sample from a population.

In Figure 7.3 we show Pascal's triangle as it is normally shown and then in a form consistent with the notation used in this chapter (Figure 7.4).

In Figure 7.3 each row starts and ends with a 1 and every other entry is the sum of the nearest two entries in the row immediately above it. Using the mathematical notation introduced in this chapter, we would say that the $(m+1)$th entry in the nth row is defined to be $_nC_m$.

To use the figures, you locate the coefficient of interest in Figure 7.4, and the numerical value may then be found occupying the equivalent cell in Figure 7.3.

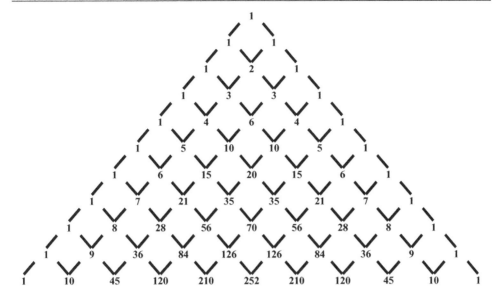

Figure 7.3   The factors for Pascal's triangle.

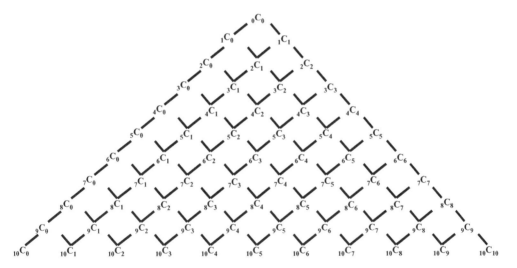

Figure 7.4   The coefficients for Pascal's triangle.

7.3.3   The use of the binomial distribution

The binomial distribution is only appropriate if:

- there is a series of n trials
- there are two possible outcomes for each trial
- the outcomes are mutually exclusive
- the outcomes are independent
- the probability p of the outcomes remains constant across all trials.

An example might be bank failures. This would be appropriate if it could be assumed that each bank has the same probability to fail each year. Such an approach could be used to compare the banking sectors in different countries.

The value of options underlying a risky asset may follow a binomial distribution. In any given time period, the asset may rise by a certain amount with a probability (p) or fail to rise with a probability $(1 - p)$. The performance over a fixed number of time periods (n) may then be found from the binomial distribution.

7.4   THE POISSON DISTRIBUTION

The Poisson distribution is appropriate when you count the number of events across time or over an area. You should consider using a Poisson distribution, as opposed to a binomial distribution, in any situation that involves counting a large series of events. Sometimes, you will see the count represented as a rate per unit continuum, such as the number of transaction errors made by a trading room over a year, or the number of errors made by each dealer.

The Poisson distribution could be considered as a variant of the binomial distribution, which takes into account the need for tail events to appear within the distribution. This equates to the case where the parameter n in the binomial distribution becomes large, and the calculation of the coefficients becomes extremely difficult. Effectively the binomial distribution would give you a very large triangle to calculate. In such cases the distribution becomes:

$$\text{Prob}(x; \lambda) = \frac{\lambda^x \, e^{-\lambda}}{x!}$$

where $\lambda = np$, the product of the population and the probability of success, and x is the number of successes required. The value 'e' is a constant, approximately equal to 2.718, and can be found on most calculators. This distribution has mean λ (see section 5.2.1) and variance λ(see section 5.6). An example is shown in Figure 7.5.

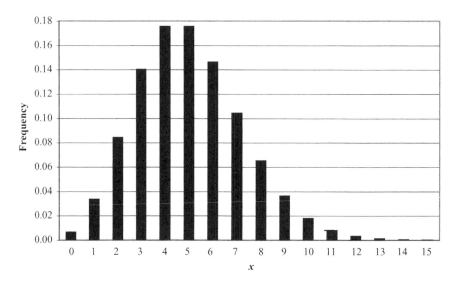

Figure 7.5   Bar chart for the Poisson distribution for $\lambda = 5$.

It is not unreasonable to replace a binomial distribution with a Poisson distribution if the population $n > 20$ and p, the probability of success, is <0.05 or if the population $n > 100$ and the product of the population and the probability of success is less than 10 ($np < 10$).

7.4.1 An example of the Poisson distribution

A case study has been carried out on the number of repairs required on the portable computers owned by a bank within a given year. There are 690 computers, which becomes the population (size N). The data observed is presented in Table 7.3.

Table 7.3   Frequency of computer repair

Number of repairs	Frequency
0	371
1	239
2	66
3	6
4	6
5	2
Total	**690**

The Poisson distribution provides a suitable model for this data. If the model appears to fit the data, then it may be used predictively to answer 'what if' questions. For instance, if we increase the number of computers held, how many repairs may then be anticipated? This then impinges on the number of hardware engineers required and the quantities of spare computers to be held in stock.

The Poisson distribution has a single parameter, λ, which in this case is the mean. Firstly, the mean (see section 5.2.1) number of repairs required, must be calculated:

$$\text{Mean} = \frac{1 \times 239 + 2 \times 66 + 3 \times 6 + 4 \times 6 + 5 \times 2}{690} = \frac{423}{690} = 0.613 = \lambda$$

This number is then used to calculate the probability of x repairs ($x = 0, \ldots, 5$) and therefore the expected number of computers requiring x repairs since $690 \times \text{Prob}(x)$. To ensure that we have the correct total, the final category is replaced by five or more repairs, to bring in the idea of the potential for a long tail. It is possible for a computer to fail 10 times in a year, although you would probably have thrown it out of a window by then. Again these probabilities can be calculated recursively, since,

$$\text{Prob}(x) = \frac{\text{Prob}(x-1) \times \lambda}{x}.$$

In Table 7.4 we look at the fit of the data to the Poisson distribution and compare that to the original results.

Clearly the two frequency columns (frequency and fitted frequency) in Table 7.4 are remarkably similar. To construct the fitted frequencies the only information employed was the mean and the sample size. Based on this information, the fitted frequencies are within a few percent of the actual observed frequencies. Were the bank to expand its operation to include 1,500 computers, how many computers might be expected to require one repair annually? Now N has changed to 1,500, while λ is unchanged. The estimated frequency is $1{,}500 \times 0.3321 = 498.15$,

Table 7.4   Fitted frequency of computer repair

Number of visits x	Frequency f	Fitted probability $\lambda^x e^{-\lambda}/x!$	Fitted frequency $N(\lambda^x e^{-\lambda}/x!)$
0	371	0.5417	373.77
1	239	0.3321	229.14
2	66	0.1018	70.24
3	6	0.0208	14.35
4	6	0.0032	2.20
5+	2	0.0004	0.30
Totals	**690**	**1.0000**	**690.00**

which would be rounded down to 498. Similarly, you could estimate how many computers may require one repair in a two-year period. Again $N = 1,500$; however, the new rate is double the previous rate, $\lambda = 2 \times 0.613 = 1.226$, and therefore estimated frequency is

$$N\frac{\lambda e^{-\lambda}}{1!} = 1,500 \times 1.226 \times e^{-1.226} = 539.68$$

which would be rounded to 540.

7.4.2   Uses of the Poisson distribution

The Poisson distribution is only appropriate if

- the outcomes are independent
- the rate per unit continuum is constant.

Typical applications would include the number of customers that visit an ATM during a given period of time, the number of spelling mistakes made while typing a single page, the number of phone calls received by a helpline during a day, or the number of times a website is accessed in an hour. In all cases a count of events is required during a fixed time period, and to enable the Poisson distribution to be applied, the rate of occurrence must be fixed.

7.5   USES OF THE BINOMIAL AND POISSON DISTRIBUTIONS

A securities house trades securities that are processed in batches. Out of each batch, 100 trades are tested to ensure that they are priced within an acceptable tolerance of the market price to seek out off-market pricing. If five or more trades are found to be outside the expected tolerance, then the whole batch is retested. What is the probability that a particular batch will be rejected if the total population contains 1% of transactions that are outside of the required level of tolerance?

Two approaches will be adopted. Assuming a binomial distribution, then:

$$\text{Prob(defective)} = 0.01$$

We also know that:

$$\text{Prob(5 or more defective)} = 1 - (\text{Prob(0 defective)} + \text{Prob(1 defective)} + \text{Prob(2 defective)}$$
$$+ \text{ Prob(3 defective)} + \text{Prob(4 defective)})$$

Using the equation from section 7.3, $(_nC_m\,p^m q^{n-m})$ the individual probabilities summarised in Table 7.5 may be obtained.

Table 7.5 Binomial probabilities

Number of failures	Probability
0	0.3660
1	0.3697
2	0.1849
3	0.0610
4	0.0149
Total	**0.9966**

Therefore the probability of having to retest the population is 0.0034 or 0.34%. Alternatively, since there is a large sample and a relatively small probability of a defect, the Poisson distribution could be employed, with $\lambda = 1$ $(\lambda = np)$. The individual probabilities will be calculated using the equation in section 7.4

$$\text{Prob}(x;\lambda) = \frac{\lambda^x e^{-\lambda}}{x!}$$

which would give the probabilities summarised in Table 7.6, in which the probability of having to retest has risen to 0.0037 or 3.7%, which is 10% more than the estimate calculated by the binomial distribution.

Table 7.6 Poisson probabilities

Number of defectives	Probability
0	0.3679
1	0.3679
2	0.1839
3	0.0613
4	0.0153
Total	**0.9963**

In the context employed here, the Poisson distribution is used as an approximation to the binomial distribution. As a standard rule, and definitely in this case, four-figure accuracy is required. To avoid excessive calculation, it is best to employ recursion in both cases rather than work from the basic equations. In addition, it is always best to employ the 'e' button on the calculator rather than use a numerical approximation.

Recognise that an assumption has been made that the observations of off-market pricing are independent and also that only a sample of transactions has been considered. If either of these assumptions is not valid then the distribution will suggest an inaccurate answer. The key question is whether the data is reliable as an indicator of the process.

Applications might involve considerable cost in either accepting or rejecting batches erroneously. A typical Poisson distribution application would be to consider queue length or the occurrence of industrial injuries. Another popular area is in quality where the binomial distribution would record the number of faults, while the Poisson distribution counts flaws per unit.

7.5.1 Is suicide a Poisson process?

A large trading house is worried that the pressure resulting from annual performance reviews may be an instigator of suicide attempts. Obviously attempted suicide is a matter for concern by the caring employer and they are also concerned about the possible impact of negative publicity. The aim here is to investigate if the Poisson distribution provides a plausible model for the data provided. If the attempted suicides do in fact follow a Poisson process, then no suicide has an effect on any other, since they are all independent. Also, the time until the next attempted suicide must be independent of the elapsed time since the last one.

The data is presented in Table 7.7, which also contains subsidiary calculations.

Table 7.7   Dates of the events: attempted staff suicides

Date	Inter-arrival time	Sorted times
7 May 1978		
14 June 1978	38	1
13 May 1979	333	1
12 October 1979	152	2
30 December 1980	445	5
18 May 1983	869	15
10 February 1984	268	20
16 October 1986	979	26
11 November 1986	26	28
9 December 1986	28	38
11 December 1986	2	55
20 February 1988	436	64
19 February 1989	365	120
7 July 1989	138	138
31 August 1989	55	142
13 May 1991	620	152
28 October 1991	168	168
3 September 1996	1,772	168
26 June 1997	296	206
18 January 1998	206	243
12 December 1999	693	268
2 May 2000	142	296
17 May 2000	15	333
29 April 2001	347	347
30 April 2001	1	365
20 May 2001	20	436
4 November 2001	168	445
9 November 2001	5	620
12 January 2002	64	693
12 January 2004	730	730
11 May 2004	120	869
9 January 2005	243	979
10 January 2005	1	1,772

To model the data, the key term is the time between events. This is conventionally referred to as the inter-arrival time and gives the number of days between successive events. To complete the analysis, these periods need to be sorted prior to including them into a distribution.

This sorted data is accumulated into bins to enable a comparison to be made with a Poisson process. Some suitable cut points $\{0, 90, 180, 270, 360, 450, 540, 630, 2{,}000\}$ are selected and displayed with associated frequencies in Table 7.8.

Table 7.8 Accumulated attempted suicide data

Class interval		Observed frequency
0	90	11
90	180	6
180	270	3
270	360	3
360	450	3
450	540	0
540	630	1
630	2,000	5
Total		**32**

To employ a Poisson distribution, it is necessary to calculate the rate per unit continuum. The average number of days between events is 304.56, so the rate is $\lambda = 1/304.53 = 0.0033$. This is directly calculated from the raw data.

The next stage is to calculate the probabilities, assuming a Poisson distribution. We know that the probability of no events by time t in a Poisson process is $e^{-\lambda t}$, since the appropriate rate is λt.

$$
\begin{aligned}
\text{Prob(no suicide by day } b) &= e^{-\lambda b} \\
\text{Prob(no suicide by day } a) &= e^{-\lambda a} \\
\text{Prob(at least one suicide by day } b) &= 1 - e^{-\lambda b} \\
\text{Prob(at least one suicide by day } a) &= 1 - e^{-\lambda a} \\
\text{Prob(at least one suicide between days } a \text{ and } b) &= e^{-\lambda a} - e^{-\lambda b}
\end{aligned}
$$

It is assumed that b exceeds a.

The final formula is employed to complete Table 7.9. For the second row of the table, $b = 180$, $a = 90$ and $\lambda = 0.0033$ and the probability is therefore $e^{-\lambda a} - e^{-\lambda b} = 0.1904$. A

Table 7.9 Expected frequencies of suicide assuming a Poisson distribution

Class interval		Probability	Expected frequency
0	90	0.2558	8.19
90	180	0.1904	6.09
180	270	0.1417	4.53
270	360	0.1054	3.37
360	450	0.0785	2.51
450	540	0.0584	1.87
540	630	0.0434	1.39
630	2000	0.1264	4.04
Total		**1**	**32**

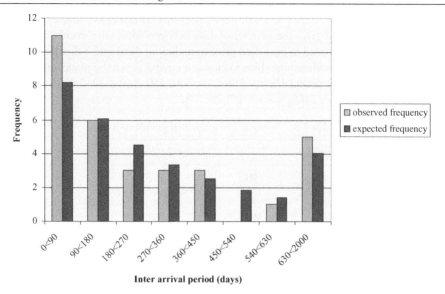

Figure 7.6 Comparison of the observed and expected attempted suicide frequencies.

graph could then be used (Figure 7.6) to compare the actual results to the frequencies that would be expected from the use of the Poisson distribution.

The frequencies are remarkably similar. While a formal statistical test could now be used to show the accuracy of the data fit to the distribution, the relatively low frequencies make such an approach of doubtful value. On adopting fewer class intervals, further evidence becomes available to support the Poisson distribution. While the attempted suicides may be a cause for concern, they do appear to follow a Poisson distribution and therefore occur randomly throughout the period. They are not linked to cyclical events.

A few continuous distributions are now considered. Their probabilities are represented by a function, $f(x)$ for $a < x < b$. Then the probability that x lies in the range $[c, d]$ is the area enclosed between the curve and verticals drawn at c and d. We shall show how this works in practice by considering some of the possible continuous distributions.

7.6 CONTINUOUS UNIFORM DISTRIBUTION

This distribution is used when all outcomes of an experiment are equally likely, and is defined to be

$$f(x) = \frac{1}{b-a} \quad \text{for } a < x < b$$

being zero elsewhere. This distribution has a mean of $(a + b)/2$ and a variance of $(b - a)^2/12$.

These values are found by integrating the distribution, which we refer to as a density function, and considering its moments over the range being evaluated. Integration is a mathematical technique that evaluates the area enclosed between a curve and the horizontal axis. A moment is the expected value of a power of the random variable. It is the integral of the density function times the random variable raised to the desired power. The first moment is the mean of the distribution. The second moment is related to the variance. A discrete form of the distribution was described in section 7.1. An example with range [1, 6] is shown in Figure 7.7.

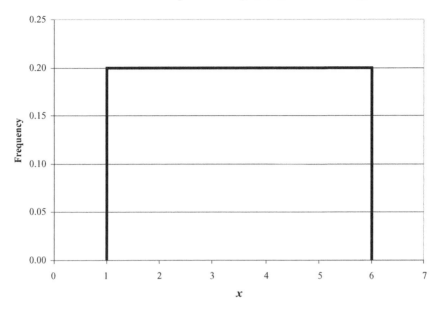

Figure 7.7   The density function of a uniform distribution in the range [1, 6].

The density is featureless and there is not much to be gained from using it. Of much wider applicability is the exponential distribution.

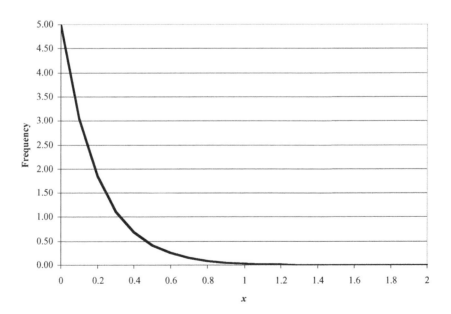

Figure 7.8   The density function of an exponential distribution with mean 0.2.

7.7 EXPONENTIAL DISTRIBUTION

The exponential distribution is also sometimes called the *negative* exponential distribution to stress the minus sign in the exponent of the function, and has a density defined by,

$$f(x) = \lambda\, e^{-\lambda x} \quad \text{for } x > 0$$

The exponential distribution is zero elsewhere. An example with a mean (see section 5.2.1) of 0.2 is shown in Figure 7.8.

This distribution has mean (see section 5.2.1) λ^{-1} and variance (see section 5.6) λ^{-2}. It provides the waiting time to the first success in a Poisson process. In fact this property could be used to define the density. By considering the independence of the individual observations, the exponential distribution can also be used to fit the time between successes in a Poisson process.

Normal Distribution

8.1   INTRODUCTION

The normal distribution is probably the most important probability distribution that will be encountered in practice. This distribution function is symmetric and is often described as being bell shaped. The function has two parameters, the mean μ (see section 5.2.1) and the standard deviation σ (see section 5.6) and has a density function (see section 7.6) described by:

$$\phi\left(x;\mu,\sigma^2\right) = \frac{1}{\sqrt{2\pi}\,\sigma}e^{-\frac{1}{2}((x-\mu)/\sigma)^2}$$

The mean occurs at the central point of the distribution and the width is adjusted by varying the standard deviation. What this distribution expresses is a visual representation of data where the probability that a observation is below, or above, the mean is the same, but where the probability of a specific value decreases as it moves away from the mean. Some examples of normal distributions are shown in Figure 8.1.

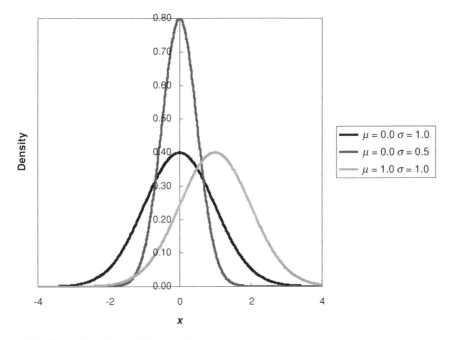

Figure 8.1   Examples of normal density functions.

Each of the curves has the property that the average (mean, median and mode) is at the centre of the distribution. As with any distribution, the area under each curve is 1, since a value must occur.

This distribution has certain specific characteristics that need to be considered. There have also been tables of its cumulative probabilities constructed as shown in Table 8.4 at the end of this chapter. These refer to the standard normal curve with zero mean and unitary variance and can be used to simplify calculations.

8.2   NORMAL DISTRIBUTION

It is conventional to describe a normal distribution, denoted by ϕ, in terms of its key parameters, which are its mean (μ) and variance (σ^2), so ϕ (*mean, variance*). It is shown below how to transform from the standard normal variable z, which has a mean of zero and a variance of 1, or ϕ (0, 1). This is tabulated to x, which is $\phi\left(\mu, \sigma^2\right)$, where x is any real physical variable. In reality normal (0, 1) never occurs but normal (μ, σ^2) does. Tables, for brevity, are always normal (0, 1). The mean being zero in the standard case centres the distribution on the vertical axis, with an equal chance of a value being below or above zero. In practice this will usually be seen as items having an equal chance of being positive or negative.

By using Table 8.4, the value of 0.159 (15.9%) corresponds to a value of -1. That means that the probability of z in the range $[-\infty, -1]$ is 0.159. Since the curve is symmetric and has an area equal to 1, $[100 - (15.9 \times 2)]\% = 68.2\%$ of the curve lies in the region $[-1, 1]$. Infinity (∞) appears because the distribution has a long tail that goes out to infinity.

Again using Table 8.4, a value of -1.96 corresponds to a probability of 0.025, giving 95% (2×47.5) for the range $[-1.96, 1.96]$, similarly $[-2.58, 2.58]$ gives 99%. This is how companies produce statistics that something has a likelihood of 95%, for example. This effectively means that once in 20 times the result is likely to be outside the expected parameters.

You can use Excel to obtain the estimates, as shown in Figure 8.2.

	A	B		A	B
1	Mean	0	1	Mean	0
2	Standard deviation	1.00	2	Standard deviation	1
3	z	1.96	3	z	1.96
4			4		
5	Probability	0.9750	5	Probability	=NORMDIST(B3,B1,B2,TRUE)

Figure 8.2   Excel function to evaluate normal probabilities.

The normal distribution is often set out in the form of a table using the key criteria already discussed. When referring to a normal table it is essential to ensure that you are correctly interpreting it, since a number of conventions are commonly used. The most common form of convention is Prob($-\infty < z < Z$) for various values of Z, alternatives are Prob($0 < z < Z$) and Prob($Z < z < \infty$), where z is $\phi(0, 1)$ and Z is its limit. Using the basic rules of probability these values may be related:

$$\text{Prob}(-\infty < z < Z) = \text{Prob}(0 < z < Z) + \text{Prob}(-\infty < z < 0)$$
$$= \text{Prob}(0 < z < Z) + 0.5 = 1 - \text{Prob}(Z < z < \infty)$$

The equation or transform that links from x, which is $\phi\left(\mu, \sigma^2\right)$, to z, which is $\phi(0, 1)$, is:

$$z = \frac{x - \mu}{\sigma}$$

8.2.1 A simple example of normal probabilities

A company believes that its daily data entry error rate fits the distribution $\phi(8, 4)$. If this were correct, what would be the probability that a sample of the daily transactions would contain between 6 and 12 errors? If we take x to be the actual number of errors found in the sample, then using the above transform to $\phi(0, 1)$, the required probability is:

$$\text{Prob}(6 < x < 12) = \text{Prob}\left(\frac{6 - 8}{2} < z < \frac{12 - 8}{2}\right)$$

This then becomes:

$$\text{Prob}(-1 < z < 2) = \text{Prob}(-\infty < z < 2) - \text{Prob}(-\infty < z < -1)$$

(since we need to refer to the tabulated values, Table 8.4)

$$= (1 - \text{Prob}(2 < z < \infty)) - 0.159$$

(since the total area under the curve is 1)

$$= (1 - \text{Prob}(-\infty < z < -2)) - 0.159$$

(by symmetry, since the positive and negative curves are the same)

$$= 1 - 0.023 - 0.159$$

$$= 0.818$$

The figures are again taken from Table 8.4. What this means is that in at least 81.8% of the samples there would be between six and 12 errors, on the assumption that the distribution is normal (8, 4) so has a mean of eight and a variance of four.

8.2.2 A second example of normal probabilities

A company assumes that the quality criteria for a call centre is normally distributed with a failure mean of 10 and a standard deviation of 0.03. In this context failure represents not achieving the required quality standard.

(a) *What is the proportion of samples that will have a failure rate exceeding 10.075?*
Using $z = \dfrac{x - \mu}{\sigma}$, the required probability is:

$$\text{Prob}(x > 10.075) = \text{Prob}\left(z > \frac{10.075 - 10}{0.03}\right)$$

$$= \text{Prob}(z > 2.5)$$

$$= \text{Prob}(z < -2.5) \quad \text{(by symmetry)}$$

$$= 0.006$$

This therefore gives 0.6% as the proportion. So, using the distribution, the company would conclude that only 0.6% of the samples will have a failure rate as high as this. If, in testing, a higher rate was generally found to be occurring, then this will start to raise questions about the initial parameters selected for the normal distribution, and perhaps the initial choice of using a normal distribution. It may also suggest that there may be some personnel issues that need to be addressed.

(b) *What is the probability that a sample will have an error rate between 9.98 and 10.02?*
   The required probability is:

$$\text{Prob}(9.98 < x < 10.02) = \text{Prob}(-0.667 < z < 0.667) \quad \text{(using the transformation)}$$
$$= 1 - \text{Prob}(z < -0.667) - \text{Prob}(z > 0.667)$$
$$= 1 - 2 \times \text{Prob}(z < -0.667) \quad \text{(by symmetry)}$$
$$= 1 - 2 \times 0.252$$
$$= 0.496$$

The precise value is not tabulated in Table 8.4. The values 0.255 and 0.251 correspond to -0.66 and -0.67 respectively, so we need to use a technique from classical geometry, referred to as *interpolation*. Since 0.255 equates to -0.66 and 0.254 equates to -0.6625, 0.253 to -0.665, 0.252 to -0.6675 and 0.251 to -0.67, we therefore arrive at a value of 0.252.

8.3   ADDITION OF NORMAL VARIABLES

Let x and y be normally distributed with parameters μ_1 and σ_1 (variance $\text{var}_1 = \sigma_1^2$) and μ_2 and σ_2 (variance $\text{var}_2 = \sigma_2^2$), respectively. Then $s = x + y$ is normally distributed with mean $\mu_1 + \mu_2$ and variance $\text{var}_1 + \text{var}_2$. $t = x - y$ is also normally distributed with mean $\mu_1 - \mu_2$ and variance $\text{var}_1 + \text{var}_2$. In both cases the combined variance is always the addition of the individual variances.

Therefore, if x is $\phi(10, 4)$ and y is $\phi(15, 36)$, then $x + y$ is $\phi(25, 40)$ and $x - y$ is $\phi(-5, 40)$.
An important general result, also called the Law of Averages, is the Central Limit Theorem.

8.4   CENTRAL LIMIT THEOREM

If $x_1, x_2, \ldots, x_n$ are independent random variables having the same distribution with mean μ and standard deviation σ, then for a large enough sample (typically $n > 30$) the random variable $z = (\bar{x} - \mu)/(\sigma/\sqrt{n})$ approximates to a standard normal distribution. This result follows regardless of whatever the underlying distribution of the $\{x_i\}$ is.

8.4.1   An example of the Central Limit Theorem

If a sample of 100 transactions is taken from a population that is known to have a mean of 75 and a variance of 225, what is the probability that the sample mean lies in the range [72, 77]?
   In the notation used above, $\mu = 75$, $n = 100$ and $\sigma = 15$, so the average would be expected to have mean of 75 and standard deviation of 1.5 $\left(s = \dfrac{\sigma}{\sqrt{n}} = \dfrac{15}{10} \right)$, so

$$\text{Prob}(72 < \bar{x} < 77) = \text{Prob}\left(\frac{-3}{1.5} < z < \frac{2}{1.5} \right)$$
$$= \text{Prob}(-2 < z < 1.333)$$
$$= (1 - \text{Prob}(-\infty < z < -1.333)) - \text{Prob}(-\infty < z < -2)$$
$$= 1 - 0.091 - 0.023$$
$$= 0.886$$

It may be a requirement to estimate the population mean from an estimate of the sample mean. Again the Central Limit Theorem would be used and the reliability of this estimate can be gauged from the confidence interval. This gives a range of plausible values for the population mean.

8.5   CONFIDENCE INTERVALS FOR THE POPULATION MEAN

For normally distributed data, where the population standard deviation is known, you should use the confidence interval equation $\bar{x} \pm z_\alpha(\sigma/\sqrt{n})$, taking the notation as summarised in Table 8.1 and the appropriate values from the normal distribution tables summarised in Table 8.2.

Table 8.1   Notation required for confidence intervals for the population mean

$\bar{x}$	Sample mean
n	Sample size
σ	Population standard deviation (known)
z_α	Tabulated value of the z-score that achieves a significance level of α in a two-tail test

Table 8.2   Normal values required for confidence intervals for the population mean

α	z_α
90%	1.645
95%	1.960
99%	2.576

8.5.1   An example of confidence intervals for the population mean

Let us assume that it is known that, in a population, measurements are approximately normally distributed with a standard deviation of 16. Tests are carried out on a particular subgroup of the population and the mean value of a sample of 25 transactions is actually found to be 110. Calculate a 95% confidence interval for the population mean.

In summary

$$\bar{x} = 110 \quad n = 25 \quad \sigma = 16 \quad z_\alpha = 1.96$$

Using the earlier equation $\bar{x} \pm z_\alpha(\sigma/\sqrt{n})$, the interval is then:

$$110 \pm 1.96\frac{16}{\sqrt{25}} = [103.728, 116.272]$$

We can now be 95% confident that the population mean lies in this interval.

The normal distribution can also be used to approximate certain discrete distributions (see Chapter 7). The reason that the normal distribution is so useful is due to the ease with which calculations can be carried out, and that is why it is so regularly used. However, recognise that a normal distribution can only be used where observations have an equal chance of being above or below the mean. Where this is not the case the normal distribution should be used with caution.

8.6 NORMAL APPROXIMATION TO THE BINOMIAL DISTRIBUTION

The binomial distribution was discussed in section 7.3. Using the equations from that section, if x is $B(n, p)$ then $z = \dfrac{x - np}{\sqrt{np(1-p)}}$ could be approximated by a standard normal distribution, for a population where n is large enough. This means that the probability that x lies in the range (a, b) can be approximated by a normal probability in the range

$$\left(\frac{a - 0.5 - np}{\sqrt{np(1-p)}}, \quad \frac{b + 0.5 - np}{\sqrt{np(1-p)}} \right)$$

The factor of 0.5 is referred to as the continuity correction and makes allowance for converting from a discrete to a continuous distribution. As a general rule the approximation is employed if the variance $np(1 - p)$ exceeds 10.

8.6.1 An example of the normal approximation to the binomial distribution

A population consists of a series of deposit and lending transactions. Of 7,000 transactions, 3,682 (52.6%) were deposits. In a 20 year period there were two million transactions of which 51.2% related to deposits. The question then is whether the higher proportion in the sample is significantly different from the general experience.

Taking $p = 0.512$ and $n = 7,000$, how likely is that the sample will contain 3,682 or more deposit transactions? The mean for the general population over time is $7,000 \times 0.512 = 3,584$ and the variance is $7,000 \times 0.512 \times 0.488$ giving a standard deviation of 41.82. Using the expression above $\left(\dfrac{a - 0.5 - np}{\sqrt{np(1-p)}}, \dfrac{b + 0.5 - np}{\sqrt{np(1-p)}} \right)$, the required probability is calculated as:

$$\text{Prob}\left(\frac{3,682 - 0.5 - 3,584}{41.82} < z < \frac{7,000 + 0.5 - 3,584}{41.82} \right) = \text{Prob}(2.331 < z < 81.692)$$

$$\approx \text{Prob}(z < -2.331)$$

$$= 0.01$$

This probability is small enough to suggest that the sample of 7,000 does not in fact differ from the general trend. It is then possible to identify a sample as being an outlier, but this in itself carries risks. In such cases, the only real alternative is to consider the total population and assess whether there has been a paradigm shift that needs to be considered.

8.7 NORMAL APPROXIMATION TO THE POISSON DISTRIBUTION

The normal distribution can also be used to approximate the Poisson distribution, which is discussed in section 7.4. Using the equations from that section, for a Poisson distribution with mean (λ) exceeding 10, the probability that the variable lies below a is approximated by a normally distributed variable below $(a + 0.5 - \lambda)/\sqrt{\lambda}$.

8.7.1   An example of fitting a normal curve to the Poisson distribution

This example shows staff that have sued their employer for monetary damages based on their injury. The question is whether the raw data, summarised in Table 8.3, may be modelled by a normal curve.

Table 8.3   Accumulated data on damages awarded

Class interval damages		Frequency
−5,000	0	2
0	5,000	22
5,000	10,000	37
10,000	15,000	65
15,000	20,000	38
20,000	25,000	31
25,000	30,000	4
30,000	35,000	1

The first step in developing an appropriate normal distribution is to estimate the sample mean, which is 13,425.51 and the standard deviation of 6,692.17 of the full data set. Figure 8.3 presents the comparative plots.

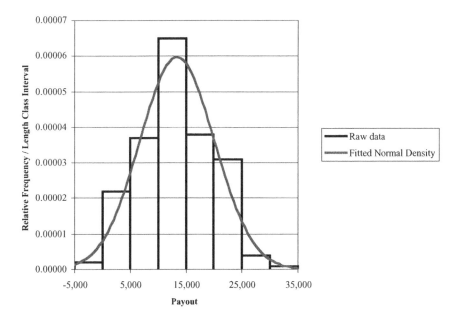

Figure 8.3   Histogram of the damages awarded compared to a normal density.

The normal curve looks plausible, although not perfect (Table 8.4). At any time when you try to fit data to a curve you are giving up some of the data quality for the properties of the curve. The point of doing this is that the curve has properties that can be modelled; therefore giving up some level of data quality can still have benefits. However, if the curve does not fit the data well, then you may be giving up too much data quality and the mathematical modelling that will then be carried out could prove to be unreliable.

Table 8.4   Areas of the standardised normal distribution

The function tabulated is $\dfrac{1}{\sqrt{2\pi}} \displaystyle\int_{-\infty}^{Z} e^{-z^2/2} dz$ the probability that $z < Z$, where $z \sim \phi(0, 1)$.

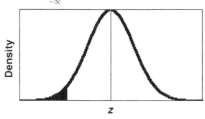

Z	0.00	−0.01	−0.02	−0.03	−0.04	−0.05	−0.06	−0.07	−0.08	−0.09
0.0	0.500	0.496	0.492	0.488	0.484	0.480	0.476	0.472	0.468	0.464
−0.1	0.460	0.456	0.452	0.448	0.444	0.440	0.436	0.433	0.429	0.425
−0.2	0.421	0.417	0.413	0.409	0.405	0.401	0.397	0.394	0.390	0.386
−0.3	0.382	0.378	0.374	0.371	0.367	0.363	0.359	0.356	0.352	0.348
−0.4	0.345	0.341	0.337	0.334	0.330	0.326	0.323	0.319	0.316	0.312
−0.5	0.309	0.305	0.302	0.298	0.295	0.291	0.288	0.284	0.281	0.278
−0.6	0.274	0.271	0.268	0.264	0.261	0.258	0.255	0.251	0.248	0.245
−0.7	0.242	0.239	0.236	0.233	0.230	0.227	0.224	0.221	0.218	0.215
−0.8	0.212	0.209	0.206	0.203	0.200	0.198	0.195	0.192	0.189	0.187
−0.9	0.184	0.181	0.179	0.176	0.174	0.171	0.169	0.166	0.164	0.161
−1.0	0.159	0.156	0.154	0.152	0.149	0.147	0.145	0.142	0.140	0.138
−1.1	0.136	0.133	0.131	0.129	0.127	0.125	0.123	0.121	0.119	0.117
−1.2	0.115	0.113	0.111	0.109	0.107	0.106	0.104	0.102	0.100	0.099
−1.3	0.097	0.095	0.093	0.092	0.090	0.089	0.087	0.085	0.084	0.082
−1.4	0.081	0.079	0.078	0.076	0.075	0.074	0.072	0.071	0.069	0.068
−1.5	0.067	0.066	0.064	0.063	0.062	0.061	0.059	0.058	0.057	0.056
−1.6	0.055	0.054	0.053	0.052	0.051	0.049	0.048	0.047	0.046	0.046
−1.7	0.045	0.044	0.043	0.042	0.041	0.040	0.039	0.038	0.038	0.037
−1.8	0.036	0.035	0.034	0.034	0.033	0.032	0.031	0.031	0.030	0.029
−1.9	0.029	0.028	0.027	0.027	0.026	0.026	0.025	0.024	0.024	0.023
−2.0	0.023	0.022	0.022	0.021	0.021	0.020	0.020	0.019	0.019	0.018
−2.1	0.018	0.017	0.017	0.017	0.016	0.016	0.015	0.015	0.015	0.014
−2.2	0.014	0.014	0.013	0.013	0.013	0.012	0.012	0.012	0.011	0.011
−2.3	0.011	0.010	0.010	0.010	0.010	0.009	0.009	0.009	0.009	0.008
−2.4	0.008	0.008	0.008	0.008	0.007	0.007	0.007	0.007	0.007	0.006
−2.5	0.006	0.006	0.006	0.006	0.006	0.005	0.005	0.005	0.005	0.005
−2.6	0.005	0.005	0.004	0.004	0.004	0.004	0.004	0.004	0.004	0.004
−2.7	0.003	0.003	0.003	0.003	0.003	0.003	0.003	0.003	0.003	0.003
−2.8	0.003	0.002	0.002	0.002	0.002	0.002	0.002	0.002	0.002	0.002
−2.9	0.002	0.002	0.002	0.002	0.002	0.002	0.002	0.001	0.001	0.001
−3.0	0.001	0.001	0.001	0.001	0.001	0.001	0.001	0.001	0.001	0.001

Comparison of the Means, Sample Sizes and Hypothesis Testing

9.1 INTRODUCTION

By comparing the means, a company can see if the observed results appear to be consistent with the results that have been predicted, typically based upon a distribution. Clearly there will be more questions to follow – for example, whether the observed distribution is consistent with the expected distribution – but a review of the means is a useful starting point.

For any sample in excess of 30 observations, the Central Limit theorem (see section 8.4) can be used. However, for smaller samples a different approach, the so-called t statistic is employed. In a random sample of size n from some population with mean μ (usually the value to be estimated), with a sample mean of $\bar{x}$ and a sample standard deviation of s, then $\dfrac{\bar{x} - \mu}{s / \sqrt{n}}$ has a t distribution with $n - 1$ degrees of freedom, where a degree of freedom is just the number of independent parameters required to specify the position and orientation of an object.

Turning to Table 9.5, the value $t_\nu(P)$ is presented, where P is the probability of falling in the positive tail (rejection region) of the distribution and ν is the degrees of freedom. Only positive values of $t_\nu(P)$ are given, because the distribution is symmetric and therefore $t_\nu(1 - P) = -t_\nu(P)$. When ν exceeds 30, the t distribution may be approximated by the normal distribution (see Chapter 8). In fact the final row of some t tables is just the appropriate values from the table for the normal distribution (see Table 8.4).

Where is this type of analysis important? When you are undertaking any kind of modelling within banking you are always looking at the population you are selecting as acting in some way like the distribution you are expecting. This type of modelling appears throughout the investment world, but also in the operational and credit risk worlds. By comparing the mean of your chosen sample to that of the population, you are able to assess whether the sample appears to be representative of the total population or may in fact be an outlier.

If you are in the 'tail' of the distribution then all the assumptions that you normally make in terms of modelling are likely to be invalid and any trading or management decisions that you make are likely to be unreliable.

We will now look at this in more detail by considering some further refinement of the issues and seeing the application to true business examples.

9.2 ESTIMATION OF THE MEAN

For any small data set (particularly any that have less than 30 observations), the mean and variance can be calculated by hand. However, the challenge is to consider whether you can accurately estimate the true (population) mean. In the notation used above the sample mean $\bar{x}$, the sample standard deviation of s and the sample size of n are known. An estimate of the population mean (μ) is required with a probability of α ($100\alpha\%$). The concern is always that the chance of being wrong has a probability of $\beta = (1 - \alpha)/2$, since there are two tails (effectively one above and another below the mean). The population mean then lies in the interval

$$\bar{x} \pm \frac{t_{n-1}(\beta) \times s}{\sqrt{n}}$$

This only tells us that we are able to estimate the mean for the total population from knowing the variance, sample size and also the mean of the sample population. However, there does remain a risk that we could be wrong. At any time when you know there is a tail to the population you are looking at, 1 in every 100 items in the tail will be outside a confidence level of 99%. This means that in one time in every hundred a result outside the expected parameters is likely to occur. If this is sufficiently significant to the company then they will still need to consider such events.

9.2.1 An example of estimating a confidence interval for an experimental mean

A company seeks to estimate how long it takes for the overnight processing batch to run, within 95% certainty. Of the 16 days in the sample, the mean time taken is 300 minutes with a standard deviation of 60 minutes. The values are summarised in Table 9.1.

Table 9.1 Summary of parameters for the example

$\bar{x}$	300
s	60
n	16
ν	15
α	0.05
β	0.025
$t_{15}(0.025)$	2.131

Since this is a small population, using the t statistic:

$$\bar{x} \pm \frac{t_{n-1}(\beta) \times s}{\sqrt{n}}$$

the bounds are given by

$$300 \pm \frac{t_{15}(0.025) \times 60}{\sqrt{16}} = 300 \pm \frac{2.131 \times 60}{4} = [268.03, 331.97]$$

This means that the 95% confidence level would cover processing run times of between 268 and 331 minutes. If the processing time actually took 400 minutes, then this would be outside of the 95% confidence level.

If identical estimates of the mean and variance were obtained from a sample of 25 days, then again, using the t statistic, the range would have been:

$$300 \pm \frac{t_{24}(0.025) \times 60}{\sqrt{25}} = 300 \pm \frac{2.064 \times 60}{5} = [275.23, 324.77]$$

As might be expected, the larger sample gives tighter bounds (268 against 275 at the most efficient processing end and 324 against 331 at the less efficient processing end). Since increasing the population n raises the denominator in the above equation, it decreases the selected value of the t distribution by increasing the degrees of freedom. Effectively, by sampling more items, you are rewarded by having increased accuracy to your estimate. In this example the span of the original estimate was 63.94 and this decreased to 49.54 (a 22.5% reduction) by increasing the sample from 16 to 25 (a 56.3% increase).

A question that commonly arises in practice is: How large should a sample be to obtain a desired level of precision?

9.3   CHOICE OF THE SAMPLE SIZE

If an estimate of the variance (see section 5.6) of a sample is available, you are then able to calculate the number of observations that you need to select to obtain an estimate of the mean to a prescribed level of confidence. The level of confidence required will give you the range that will be available around the mean. If a high level of confidence is required, then a larger sample size will also be needed, whereas if a low level of confidence is acceptable, then a smaller sample size can be used. Mathematically, if the sample mean is required to differ by at most a distance d ($\pm d$) from the population mean, then:

$$d \geq \frac{t_{n-1}(\alpha) \times s}{\sqrt{n}}$$

9.3.1   An example of selecting sample size

If, in the example from section 9.2.1, the sample mean is required to lie within 30 minutes of the population mean with 95% certainty, then the following formula would have to be solved:

$$nd^2 \geq \left(t_{n-1}(\alpha) \times s\right)^2$$

where n is the size of the random sample, the sample standard deviation is s and d is a measure of distance. Clearly both n and $t_{n-1}(\alpha)$ depend on choosing the same variable, the population n. So we are able to divide both sides by d^2 and also by $t_{n-1}(\alpha)^2$. The standard deviation remains at 60. The equation then becomes:

$$\frac{n}{t_{n-1}^2(\alpha)} \geq \frac{s^2}{d^2} = \frac{60^2}{30^2} = 4$$

which can be solved by trial and error, using the results in Table 9.2. A sample of size 18 should suffice since this gives the answer of 4.04, which is the first figure to exceed the required figure of 4.

9.4   HYPOTHESIS TESTING

It is often found necessary to pose a test in more formal language. A hypothesis is just a proposal – it is something that is taken to be true for the purpose of an argument or investigation. Initially a null hypothesis is posed, which is that the observed mean of the sample actually equals the expected mean of the entire population. There are then a series of alternative hypotheses that can then be posed. These could include:

1. Observed mean < Expected mean
2. Observed mean > Expected mean
3. Observed mean $\neq$ Expected mean

Table 9.2

n	$t_{n-1}(0.025)$	$\dfrac{n}{t_{n-1}^2(0.025)}$
5	2.776	0.65
6	2.571	0.91
7	2.447	1.17
8	2.365	1.43
9	2.306	1.69
10	2.262	1.95
11	2.228	2.22
12	2.201	2.48
13	2.179	2.74
14	2.160	3.00
15	2.145	3.26
16	2.131	3.52
17	2.120	3.78
18	2.110	4.04
19	2.101	4.30
20	2.093	4.57

Finally a significance level must be chosen, say α. If hypothesis 1 or 2 is being examined, a one-tail test is adopted and the t statistic $t_{n-1}(1 - \alpha)$ is used. For the third case, a two-tail test is employed, which needs $t_{n-1}\big((1 - \alpha)/2\big)$ since the observed mean could be either above or below the expected mean. The rejection region is then $t_{n-1}s/\sqrt{n}$; that is, if the observed mean falls in this region around the expected mean, the null hypothesis is rejected and the alternative hypothesis is accepted. This implies that the observed mean is not equal to the expected mean. If the mean does not fall in this region, the null hypothesis is accepted and the expected mean and the observed mean are apparently consistent.

The boundary of the rejection region is precisely defined mathematically. However, this is just a mathematical equation and must always be used with care, particularly if the estimate falls near the boundary, since the conclusions that may be drawn may be of variable quality.

It is always worth making sure that anyone using a modelling approach understands the nature of the mathematical assumptions that are inherent in it. The mathematical assumption may be valid but could introduce such a level of uncertainty that the result itself may be undermined in terms of the accuracy it provides.

9.4.1   An example of hypothesis testing

The reconciliations department claims that, on average, they take 28.5 minutes to clear the outstanding items on a reconciliation. The time taken to clear the items outstanding on nine reconciliations provides a mean of 27.7 and a variance 3.24. The question then is to assess whether the assumption made regarding the mean (that it is 28.5) is actually supported by the sample whose results are known.

The null hypothesis is that the mean is 28.5. This would have required the mean of the sample and of the expected result to be the same. The alternative hypothesis is that the mean is not 28.5, so a two-tail test is employed. The t statistic, using the equation $t_{n-1}(\frac{1-\alpha}{2})$ from section 9.4, is:

$$t_{calc} = \frac{28.5 - 27.7}{\sqrt{\dfrac{3.24}{9}}} = \frac{0.8}{0.6} = 1.33$$

This is examined at eight degrees of freedom ($\nu = n - 1 = 9 - 1 = 8$). Since this value lies below $t_8 (0.025)$ (from Table 9.5), the null hypothesis cannot be rejected at the 95% level of certainty. In fact the acceptable bounds at this level are [27.1, 29.9] for μ and [26.3, 29.1] for $\bar{x}$, using equation $\bar{x} \pm (t_{n-1}(\beta) \times s)/\sqrt{n}$ from section 9.2.

9.5 COMPARISON OF TWO SAMPLE MEANS

Two samples are to be compared. The key measurements are, mean $\bar{x}_i$, standard deviation s_i, containing n_i observations for $i = 1, 2$. The techniques described in section 9.1 can still be used. The problem now is which estimate of the variance should be adopted since there will be two – one for each of the samples. In fact the correct procedure is to pool the variances if

$$\frac{\max\left(s_1^2, s_2^2\right)}{\min\left(s_1^2, s_2^2\right)} < 4$$

then we can pool the variances. If the condition given by the above equation is not met, then the variances should not be pooled. The pooled variance is then:

$$s^2 = \frac{(n_1 - 1) \times s_1^2 + (n_2 - 1) \times s_2^2}{n_1 + n_2 - 2}$$

where the choice of divisor is the degrees of freedom. This gives a pooled standard deviation s on taking the square root of the above equation.

The null hypothesis is that $\bar{x}_1 - \bar{x}_2 = 0$; in other words, that the two samples have identical means. The alternative is that $\bar{x}_1 - \bar{x}_2 \neq 0$. The t statistic is $(\bar{x}_1 - \bar{x}_2)/s\sqrt{1/n_1 + 1/n_2}$, which is compared with $t_{n_1+n_2-2}\left((1 - \alpha)/2\right)$.

9.5.1 An example of a two-sample t test

Two samples with values shown in Table 9.3 are to be compared. The pooled standard deviation is 2.70, giving a t statistic of:

$$\frac{\bar{x}_1 - \bar{x}_2}{s\sqrt{\dfrac{1}{n_1} + \dfrac{1}{n_2}}} = \frac{77.4 - 72.2}{2.70\sqrt{\dfrac{1}{5} + \dfrac{1}{6}}} = 3.18$$

This value is significant ($t_9 (0.025) = 2.26$) because $3.18 > 2.26$ and the null hypothesis is rejected since the difference between the two means is 5.2. Therefore the conclusion is that the two sample means are probably not the same.

Table 9.3 Parameters for a two-sample t test

Sample size	Mean	Standard deviation
5	77.4	3.3
6	72.2	2.1

9.6   TYPE I AND TYPE II ERRORS

In a particular experiment the null hypothesis is that the parameter of a given population is x against the alternative that it is y. Either the null hypothesis is accepted, action a, or the alternative is accepted, action b. Thus there are four possible situations (A, B, C, D) as shown in Figure 9.1.

		Statistician	
		a	b
Nature	x	A	B
	y	C	D

Figure 9.1   Type I and Type II errors.

A type I error is said to occur if the event B takes place. The null hypothesis is true and yet the alternative hypothesis is accepted. A type II error corresponds to the event C. In this case the alternative hypothesis is true and yet the null hypothesis is accepted. The events A and D are, of course, correct. This is demonstrated in the following example.

9.6.1   An example of type I and type II errors

Two trading teams have undertaken a series of transactions. Table 9.4 shows the number of trades sampled, the mean profit made and the standard deviation in the sample. Our objective is to test the claim that the mean for the first population exceeds the mean for second population by at least 15.

Table 9.4   Series of transactions

No.	Sample size		Mean £k		Standard deviation £k	
1	n_1	8	$\bar{x}_1$	98	s_1	18
2	n_2	10	$\bar{x}_2$	76	s_2	15

The null hypothesis is $H_0 : \bar{x}_1 > \bar{x}_2 + 15 \equiv \bar{x}_1 - \bar{x}_2 - 15 > 0$, and the alternative is $H_0 : \bar{x}_1 \leq \bar{x}_2 + 15 \equiv \bar{x}_1 - \bar{x}_2 - 15 \leq 0$. Using the equation from section 9.5 $\dfrac{(n_1 - 1) \times s_1^2 + (n_2 - 1) \times s_2^2}{n_1 + n_2 - 2}$, the pooled variance is:

$$\frac{(8 - 1) \times 18^2 + (10 - 1) \times 15^2}{8 + 10 - 2} = 16.38^2$$

The t statistic is obtained by using equation $(\bar{x}_1 - \bar{x}_2)/s\sqrt{1/n_1 + 1/n_2}$ from section 9.5.1, in this case the second mean is moved by 15, as follows:

$$\frac{98 - (76 + 15)}{16.38\sqrt{\frac{1}{10} + \frac{1}{8}}} = 0.90$$

with 16 degrees of freedom, which, using Table 9.5, gives:

$$t_{16}(0.05) = -1.75$$

Table 9.5 Percentage points of the t distribution

For a one-tail test, $\Pr(T_\nu > t_\nu(P)) = P$ for ν degrees of freedom. For a two-tail test,
$\Pr(T_\nu > t_\nu(P) \, or \, T_\nu < -t_\nu(P)) = 2P$ for ν degrees of freedom.

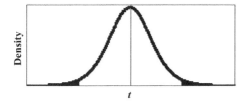 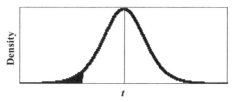

ν	$P = 0.05$	$P = 0.025$	$P = 0.005$	$P = 0.0025$	$P = 0.0010$
1	6.314	12.706	63.657	127.321	318.309
2	2.920	4.303	9.925	14.089	22.327
3	2.353	3.182	5.841	7.453	10.215
4	2.132	2.776	4.604	5.598	7.173
5	2.015	2.571	4.032	4.773	5.893
6	**1.943**	**2.447**	**3.707**	**4.317**	**5.208**
7	**1.895**	**2.365**	**3.499**	**4.029**	**4.785**
8	**1.860**	**2.306**	**3.355**	**3.833**	**4.501**
9	**1.833**	**2.262**	**3.250**	**3.690**	**4.297**
10	**1.812**	**2.228**	**3.169**	**3.581**	**4.144**
11	1.796	2.201	3.106	3.497	4.025
12	1.782	2.179	3.055	3.428	3.930
13	1.771	2.160	3.012	3.372	3.852
14	1.761	2.145	2.977	3.326	3.787
15	1.753	2.131	2.947	3.286	3.733
16	**1.746**	**2.120**	**2.921**	**3.252**	**3.686**
17	**1.740**	**2.110**	**2.898**	**3.222**	**3.646**
18	**1.734**	**2.101**	**2.878**	**3.197**	**3.610**
19	**1.729**	**2.093**	**2.861**	**3.174**	**3.579**
20	**1.725**	**2.086**	**2.845**	**3.153**	**3.552**
21	1.721	2.080	2.831	3.135	3.527
22	1.717	2.074	2.819	3.119	3.505
23	1.714	2.069	2.807	3.104	3.485
24	1.711	2.064	2.797	3.091	3.467
25	1.708	2.060	2.787	3.078	3.450
30	1.697	2.042	2.750	3.030	3.385
40	**1.684**	**2.021**	**2.704**	**2.971**	**3.307**
50	**1.676**	**2.009**	**2.678**	**2.937**	**3.261**
60	**1.671**	**2.000**	**2.660**	**2.915**	**3.232**
80	**1.664**	**1.990**	**2.639**	**2.887**	**3.195**
100	**1.660**	**1.984**	**2.626**	**2.871**	**3.174**

for a one-tail test, which is not significant. This is because $0.90 > -1.75$. Therefore the null hypothesis cannot be rejected and the two sample means are probably consistent with the required difference of 15.

10

Comparison of Variances

10.1 INTRODUCTION

When you are analysing a data set the objective is often to fit the data to a curve whose properties are well understood. The curve characteristics are then used for modelling purposes. Clearly if the properties of the data are not consistent with the properties of the curve then any conclusions developed from the curve analysis are likely to be at best unreliable. We have looked so far at the problems caused by the median not being consistent with the anticipated result arising from the standard approach adopted. In this chapter we consider the impact of changing variances.

10.2 CHI-SQUARED TEST

Given a sample, the question to be answered is whether the observed variance is actually consistent with the expected variance. The distribution that we use to analyse this is called the chi-squared distribution, and the procedure of analysis is called the chi-squared test, or χ^2 test.

The density function for this distribution is shown in Figure 10.1 and explained in Table 10.1.

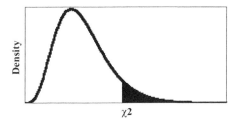

Figure 10.1   Chi-squared density function.

If s is the standard deviation of a random sample of size n from a normal population with standard deviation σ, then $((n-1) \times s^2)/\sigma^2$ has a chi-squared distribution with $n-1$ (ν) degrees of freedom (see section 9.1). The degrees of freedom are a parameter, which in this case is where we have n free observations and the variance is fixed effectively constraining one observation.

Most standard published tables only cover the range to 30 degrees of freedom, as shown in Table 10.1. Beyond this range the chi-squared distribution may be approximated by a normal distribution (see Chapter 8). More advanced statistical tables do exist which give the appropriate relationship beyond this range, but these are not reproduced in this book.

10.2.1   An example of the chi-squared test

A compliance officer would want to know whether a trader was undertaking equity trades within an acceptable tolerance of the market price at the time that a transaction is entered

Table 10.1   Tables for the χ^2 distribution

The values tabulated are $\chi_\nu^2(P)$, where $\Pr\left(\chi_\nu^2 > \chi_\nu^2(P)\right) = P$, for ν degrees of freedom.

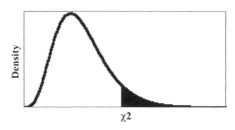

ν	$P = 0.1$	$P = 0.05$	$P = 0.025$	$P = 0.01$	$P = 0.005$	$P = 0.002$
1	2.706	3.841	5.024	6.635	7.879	9.550
2	4.605	5.991	7.378	9.210	10.597	12.429
3	6.251	7.815	9.348	11.345	12.838	14.796
4	7.779	9.488	11.143	13.277	14.860	16.924
5	9.236	11.071	12.833	15.086	16.750	18.907
6	**10.645**	**12.592**	**14.449**	**16.812**	**18.548**	**20.791**
7	**12.017**	**14.067**	**16.013**	**18.475**	**20.278**	**22.601**
8	**13.362**	**15.507**	**17.535**	**20.090**	**21.955**	**24.352**
9	**14.684**	**16.919**	**19.023**	**21.666**	**23.589**	**26.056**
10	**15.987**	**18.307**	**20.483**	**23.209**	**25.188**	**27.722**
11	17.275	19.675	21.920	24.725	26.757	29.354
12	18.549	21.026	23.337	26.217	28.300	30.957
13	19.812	22.362	24.736	27.688	29.819	32.535
14	21.064	23.685	26.119	29.141	31.319	34.091
15	22.307	24.996	27.488	30.578	32.801	35.628
16	**23.542**	**26.296**	**28.845**	**32.000**	**34.267**	**37.146**
17	**24.769**	**27.587**	**30.191**	**33.409**	**35.718**	**38.648**
18	**25.989**	**28.869**	**31.526**	**34.805**	**37.156**	**40.136**
19	**27.204**	**30.144**	**32.852**	**36.191**	**38.582**	**41.610**
20	**28.412**	**31.410**	**34.170**	**37.566**	**39.997**	**43.072**
21	29.615	32.671	35.479	38.932	41.401	44.522
22	30.813	33.924	36.781	40.289	42.796	45.962
23	32.007	35.172	38.076	41.638	44.181	47.392
24	33.196	36.415	39.364	42.980	45.559	48.812
25	34.382	37.652	40.646	44.314	46.928	50.223
30	**40.256**	**43.773**	**46.979**	**50.892**	**53.672**	**57.167**
35	**46.059**	**49.802**	**53.203**	**57.342**	**60.275**	**63.955**
40	**51.805**	**55.758**	**59.342**	**63.691**	**66.766**	**70.618**
50	**63.167**	**67.505**	**71.420**	**76.154**	**79.490**	**83.656**
60	**74.397**	**79.082**	**83.298**	**88.379**	**91.952**	**96.404**
80	96.578	101.879	106.629	112.329	116.321	121.281
100	118.498	124.342	129.561	135.807	140.170	145.577

into. This is stated to be a standard deviation of 0.003, or 3 basis points. To make the check, a sample of 25 transactions is periodically analysed. The compliance officer needs to be informed if at most one of the samples is rejected because the trade price differs from the market price by more than 0.003. Another issue would be: What is the cut-off value on the measured variance?

Since the population $n = 25$, $\chi^2_{24}(0.01) = 42.98$ (from Table 10.1) is required for one trade to fail (i.e. the other 24 must pass), and so, using the equation from section 10.2, the variance must lie below:

$$\frac{\chi^2_{24}(0.01) \times \sigma^2}{n-1} = \frac{42.98 \times 0.003^2}{25-1} = 0.000016$$

or a standard deviation of 0.004. In other words, a variance that exceeds 0.003 may occur by chance, however a variance as extreme as 0.004 indicates a significant deviation.

10.3   F TEST

To compare variances we will use an F distribution. The version of the F distribution used will depend on the number of degrees of freedom needed to work out the mean sum of squares within the sample and between the samples, respectively the denominator and numerator of the test statistic, plus the desired tail area.

In practice, the results of this are read from a table, extensive examples of which are presented in Tables 10.2, 10.3 and 10.4. Using the notation outlined in section 10.2 above; the F statistic is written as:

$$F^{n_1-1}_{n_2-1}(\alpha) = \frac{s^2_1}{s^2_2}$$

Again two hypotheses may be posed. The null hypothesis is that the standard deviations are equal, or $s_1 = s_2$, whereas the alternative hypothesis is that these values are not equal. A significance level is set to define when the numbers are materially different. Therefore, if we set a level of significance at 0.01 or 1%, and the null hypothesis is accepted, then you would only expect the critical or expected value to be exceeded in less than 1% of cases.

The F statistic also has the following characteristic:

$$F^{v_1}_{v_2}(1-\alpha) = \frac{1}{F^{v_2}_{v_1}(\alpha)}$$

This operation is required if a two-tail test is desired. Generally, published tables only give one tail to save space, so you therefore need this equation to obtain the second tail.

10.3.1   An example of the F test

Two samples of size 10 have been obtained; the first has a variance of 12.8 and the second a variance of 3.2. The question then is whether the claim that the two variances are equal is actually supported. Let us assume that 0.05 or 5% is taken as being the critical value in this case.

Using the equation $F^{n_1-1}_{n_2-1}(\alpha) = s^2_1/s^2_2$, the calculated statistic is $F_{calc} = 12.8/3.2 = 4$. This exceeds $F^9_9(0.05)$, which, from Table 10.3, is 3.18. Therefore the null hypothesis cannot be accepted. This means that the two populations do actually have significantly different variances.

10.3.2   An example considering the normal distribution

It is thought by management that a normal population has a standard deviation of 2. It is decided that, on examining a sample of nine transactions, the estimate will be rejected if the sample variance exceeds 8.8. What is the probability that this estimate will be rejected even though the standard deviation is actually 2? In other words, what is the chance that we will discard a good estimate incorrectly?

Using the chi-squared statistic from section 10.2, $((n-1) \times s^2)/\sigma^2$, we now have $n = 9$, $s = 8.8$ and $\sigma = 2$, giving $((9-1) \times 8.8)/4 = 17.6$. This is compared to the chi-squared statistic with 8 degrees of freedom. From Table 10.1, at 8 degrees of freedom, the figure 17.535 appears at 0.025, so since 17.6 exceeds this figure you can conclude that there is a probability of 0.025 (2.5%) of rejecting the valid initial assumption. In most banking scenarios this will be far too high and would be considered to be an unacceptable risk since most business is conducted at 99.9% confidence levels, so larger samples will need to be selected or the variance and standard deviation would need to be reduced.

The values tabulated in Table 10.2 are $F_{v_2}^{v_1}(0.10)$, such that $\Pr(F_{v_2}^{v_1} > F_{v_2}^{v_1}(0.10)) = 0.10$, where v_1 is the degree of freedom of the numerator and v_2 is the degree of freedom of the denominator. The lower percentage points of the distribution are obtained using the relationship $F_{v_2}^{v_1}(0.90) = 1/F_{v_1}^{v_2}(0.10)$.

The values tabulated in Table 10.3 are $F_{v_2}^{v_1}(0.05)$, such that $\Pr(F_{v_2}^{v_1} > F_{v_2}^{v_1}(0.05)) = 0.05$, where v_1 is the degree of freedom of the numerator and v_2 is the degree of freedom of the denominator. The lower percentage points of the distribution are obtained using the relationship $F_{v_2}^{v_1}(0.95) = 1/F_{v_1}^{v_2}(0.05)$.

The values tabulated in Table 10.4 are $F_{v_2}^{v_1}(0.025)$, such that $\Pr(F_{v_2}^{v_1} > F_{v_2}^{v_1}(0.025)) = 0.025$, where v_1 is the degree of freedom of the numerator and v_2 is the degree of freedom of the denominator. The lower percentage points of the distribution are obtained using the relationship $F_{v_2}^{v_1}(0.975) = 1/F_{v_1}^{v_2}(0.025)$.

Table 10.2   Percentage points of the F distribution – upper 10% points

ν_2 \ ν_1	1	2	3	4	5	6	7	8	9	10	11	12	13	14	15	16	17	18	19	20	40	60	100
1	39.86	49.50	53.59	55.83	57.24	58.20	58.91	59.44	59.86	60.20	60.47	60.71	60.90	61.07	61.22	61.35	61.35	61.57	61.66	61.74	62.53	62.79	63.01
2	8.53	9.00	9.16	9.24	9.29	9.33	9.35	9.37	9.38	9.39	9.40	9.41	9.42	9.42	9.43	9.43	9.43	9.44	9.44	9.44	9.47	9.48	9.48
3	5.54	5.46	5.39	5.34	5.31	5.29	5.27	5.25	5.24	5.23	5.22	5.22	5.21	5.21	5.20	5.20	5.20	5.19	5.19	5.18	5.16	5.15	5.14
4	4.55	4.33	4.19	4.11	4.05	4.01	3.98	3.96	3.94	3.92	3.91	3.90	3.89	3.88	3.87	3.86	3.86	3.85	3.85	3.84	3.80	3.79	3.78
5	4.06	3.78	3.62	3.52	3.45	3.41	3.37	3.34	3.32	3.30	3.28	3.27	3.26	3.25	3.24	3.23	3.23	3.22	3.21	3.21	3.16	3.14	3.13
6	3.78	3.46	3.29	3.18	3.11	3.06	3.01	2.98	2.96	2.94	2.92	2.91	2.89	2.88	2.87	2.86	2.86	2.85	2.84	2.84	2.78	2.76	2.75
7	3.59	3.26	3.07	2.96	2.88	2.83	2.79	2.75	2.73	2.70	2.68	2.67	2.65	2.64	2.63	2.62	2.62	2.61	2.60	2.60	2.54	2.51	2.50
8	3.46	3.11	2.92	2.81	2.73	2.67	2.62	2.59	2.56	2.54	2.52	2.50	2.49	2.48	2.46	2.46	2.46	2.44	2.43	2.43	2.36	2.34	2.32
9	3.36	3.01	2.81	2.69	2.61	2.55	2.51	2.47	2.44	2.42	2.40	2.38	2.36	2.35	2.34	2.33	2.33	2.31	2.31	2.30	2.23	2.21	2.19
10	3.29	2.92	2.73	2.61	2.52	2.46	2.41	2.38	2.35	2.32	2.30	2.28	2.27	2.26	2.24	2.23	2.23	2.22	2.21	2.20	2.13	2.11	2.09
11	3.23	2.86	2.66	2.54	2.45	2.39	2.34	2.30	2.27	2.25	2.23	2.21	2.19	2.18	2.17	2.16	2.16	2.14	2.13	2.12	2.05	2.03	2.01
12	3.18	2.81	2.61	2.48	2.39	2.33	2.28	2.25	2.21	2.19	2.17	2.15	2.13	2.12	2.11	2.09	2.09	2.08	2.07	2.06	1.99	1.96	1.94
13	3.14	2.76	2.56	2.43	2.35	2.28	2.23	2.20	2.16	2.14	2.12	2.10	2.08	2.07	2.05	2.04	2.04	2.02	2.01	2.01	1.93	1.90	1.88
14	3.10	2.73	2.52	2.40	2.31	2.24	2.19	2.15	2.12	2.10	2.07	2.05	2.04	2.02	2.01	2.00	2.00	1.98	1.97	1.96	1.89	1.86	1.83
15	3.07	2.70	2.49	2.36	2.27	2.21	2.16	2.12	2.09	2.06	2.04	2.02	2.00	1.99	1.97	1.96	1.96	1.94	1.93	1.92	1.85	1.82	1.79
16	3.05	2.67	2.46	2.33	2.24	2.18	2.13	2.09	2.06	2.03	2.01	1.99	1.97	1.95	1.94	1.93	1.93	1.91	1.90	1.89	1.81	1.78	1.76
17	3.05	2.67	2.46	2.33	2.24	2.18	2.13	2.09	2.06	2.03	2.01	1.99	1.97	1.95	1.94	1.93	1.93	1.91	1.90	1.89	1.81	1.78	1.76
18	3.01	2.62	2.42	2.29	2.20	2.13	2.08	2.04	2.01	1.98	1.95	1.93	1.92	1.90	1.89	1.88	1.88	1.85	1.85	1.84	1.75	1.72	1.70
19	2.99	2.61	2.40	2.27	2.18	2.11	2.06	2.02	1.98	1.96	1.93	1.91	1.89	1.88	1.87	1.85	1.85	1.83	1.82	1.81	1.73	1.70	1.67
20	2.98	2.59	2.38	2.25	2.16	2.09	2.04	2.00	1.97	1.94	1.91	1.89	1.88	1.86	1.85	1.83	1.83	1.81	1.80	1.79	1.71	1.68	1.65
40	2.84	2.44	2.23	2.09	2.00	1.93	1.87	1.83	1.79	1.76	1.74	1.72	1.70	1.68	1.66	1.65	1.65	1.63	1.62	1.61	1.51	1.47	1.43
60	2.79	2.39	2.18	2.04	1.95	1.88	1.82	1.78	1.74	1.71	1.68	1.66	1.64	1.62	1.60	1.59	1.59	1.56	1.55	1.54	1.44	1.40	1.36
100	2.76	2.36	2.14	2.00	1.91	1.83	1.78	1.73	1.70	1.66	1.64	1.61	1.59	1.57	1.56	1.54	1.54	1.52	1.51	1.49	1.38	1.34	1.29

Table 10.3 Percentage points of the F distribution – upper 5% points

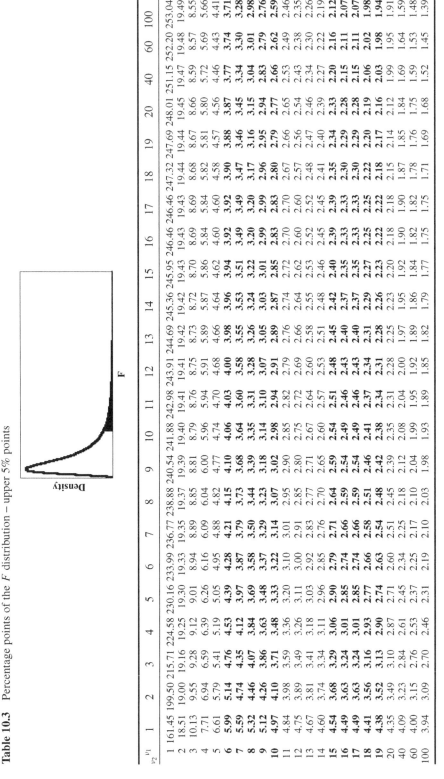

ν_2 \ ν_1	1	2	3	4	5	6	7	8	9	10	11	12	13	14	15	16	17	18	19	20	40	60	100
1	161.45	199.50	215.71	224.58	230.16	233.99	236.77	238.88	240.54	241.88	242.98	243.91	244.69	245.36	245.95	246.46	246.46	247.32	247.69	248.01	251.15	252.20	253.04
2	18.51	19.00	19.16	19.25	19.30	19.33	19.35	19.37	19.39	19.40	19.41	19.41	19.42	19.42	19.43	19.43	19.43	19.44	19.44	19.45	19.47	19.48	19.49
3	10.13	9.55	9.28	9.12	9.01	8.94	8.89	8.85	8.81	8.79	8.76	8.75	8.73	8.72	8.70	8.69	8.69	8.68	8.67	8.66	8.59	8.57	8.55
4	7.71	6.94	6.59	6.39	6.26	6.16	6.09	6.04	6.00	5.96	5.94	5.91	5.89	5.87	5.86	5.84	5.84	5.82	5.81	5.80	5.72	5.69	5.66
5	6.61	5.79	5.41	5.19	5.05	4.95	4.88	4.82	4.77	4.74	4.70	4.68	4.66	4.64	4.62	4.60	4.60	4.58	4.57	4.56	4.46	4.43	4.41
6	**5.99**	**5.14**	**4.76**	**4.53**	**4.39**	**4.28**	**4.21**	**4.15**	**4.10**	**4.06**	**4.03**	**4.00**	**3.98**	**3.96**	**3.94**	**3.92**	**3.92**	**3.90**	**3.88**	**3.87**	**3.77**	**3.74**	**3.71**
7	**5.59**	**4.74**	**4.35**	**4.12**	**3.97**	**3.87**	**3.79**	**3.73**	**3.68**	**3.64**	**3.60**	**3.58**	**3.55**	**3.53**	**3.51**	**3.49**	**3.49**	**3.47**	**3.46**	**3.45**	**3.34**	**3.30**	**3.28**
8	**5.32**	**4.46**	**4.07**	**3.84**	**3.69**	**3.58**	**3.50**	**3.44**	**3.39**	**3.35**	**3.31**	**3.28**	**3.26**	**3.24**	**3.22**	**3.20**	**3.20**	**3.17**	**3.16**	**3.15**	**3.04**	**3.01**	**2.98**
9	**5.12**	**4.26**	**3.86**	**3.63**	**3.48**	**3.37**	**3.29**	**3.23**	**3.18**	**3.14**	**3.10**	**3.07**	**3.05**	**3.03**	**3.01**	**2.99**	**2.99**	**2.96**	**2.95**	**2.94**	**2.83**	**2.79**	**2.76**
10	**4.97**	**4.10**	**3.71**	**3.48**	**3.33**	**3.22**	**3.14**	**3.07**	**3.02**	**2.98**	**2.94**	**2.91**	**2.89**	**2.87**	**2.85**	**2.83**	**2.83**	**2.80**	**2.79**	**2.77**	**2.66**	**2.62**	**2.59**
11	4.84	3.98	3.59	3.36	3.20	3.10	3.01	2.95	2.90	2.85	2.82	2.79	2.76	2.74	2.72	2.70	2.70	2.67	2.66	2.65	2.53	2.49	2.46
12	4.75	3.89	3.49	3.26	3.11	3.00	2.91	2.85	2.80	2.75	2.72	2.69	2.66	2.64	2.62	2.60	2.60	2.57	2.56	2.54	2.43	2.38	2.35
13	4.67	3.81	3.41	3.18	3.03	2.92	2.83	2.77	2.71	2.67	2.64	2.60	2.58	2.55	2.53	2.52	2.52	2.48	2.47	2.46	2.34	2.30	2.26
14	4.60	3.74	3.34	3.11	2.96	2.85	2.76	2.70	2.65	2.60	2.57	2.53	2.51	2.48	2.46	2.45	2.45	2.41	2.40	2.39	2.27	2.22	2.19
15	**4.54**	**3.68**	**3.29**	**3.06**	**2.90**	**2.79**	**2.71**	**2.64**	**2.59**	**2.54**	**2.51**	**2.48**	**2.45**	**2.42**	**2.40**	**2.39**	**2.39**	**2.35**	**2.34**	**2.33**	**2.20**	**2.16**	**2.12**
16	**4.49**	**3.63**	**3.24**	**3.01**	**2.85**	**2.74**	**2.66**	**2.59**	**2.54**	**2.49**	**2.46**	**2.43**	**2.40**	**2.37**	**2.35**	**2.33**	**2.33**	**2.30**	**2.29**	**2.28**	**2.15**	**2.11**	**2.07**
17	**4.49**	**3.63**	**3.24**	**3.01**	**2.85**	**2.74**	**2.66**	**2.59**	**2.54**	**2.49**	**2.46**	**2.43**	**2.40**	**2.37**	**2.35**	**2.33**	**2.33**	**2.30**	**2.29**	**2.28**	**2.15**	**2.11**	**2.07**
18	**4.41**	**3.56**	**3.16**	**2.93**	**2.77**	**2.66**	**2.58**	**2.51**	**2.46**	**2.41**	**2.37**	**2.34**	**2.31**	**2.29**	**2.27**	**2.25**	**2.25**	**2.22**	**2.20**	**2.19**	**2.06**	**2.02**	**1.98**
19	**4.38**	**3.52**	**3.13**	**2.90**	**2.74**	**2.63**	**2.54**	**2.48**	**2.42**	**2.38**	**2.34**	**2.31**	**2.28**	**2.26**	**2.23**	**2.22**	**2.22**	**2.18**	**2.17**	**2.16**	**2.03**	**1.98**	**1.94**
20	4.35	3.49	3.10	2.87	2.71	2.60	2.51	2.45	2.39	2.35	2.31	2.28	2.25	2.23	2.20	2.18	2.18	2.15	2.14	2.12	1.99	1.95	1.91
40	4.09	3.23	2.84	2.61	2.45	2.34	2.25	2.18	2.12	2.08	2.04	2.00	1.97	1.95	1.92	1.90	1.90	1.87	1.85	1.84	1.69	1.64	1.59
60	4.00	3.15	2.76	2.53	2.37	2.25	2.17	2.10	2.04	1.99	1.95	1.92	1.89	1.86	1.84	1.82	1.82	1.78	1.76	1.75	1.59	1.53	1.48
100	3.94	3.09	2.70	2.46	2.31	2.19	2.10	2.03	1.98	1.93	1.89	1.85	1.82	1.79	1.77	1.75	1.75	1.71	1.69	1.68	1.52	1.45	1.39

Table 10.4 Percentage points of the F distribution – upper 2.5% points

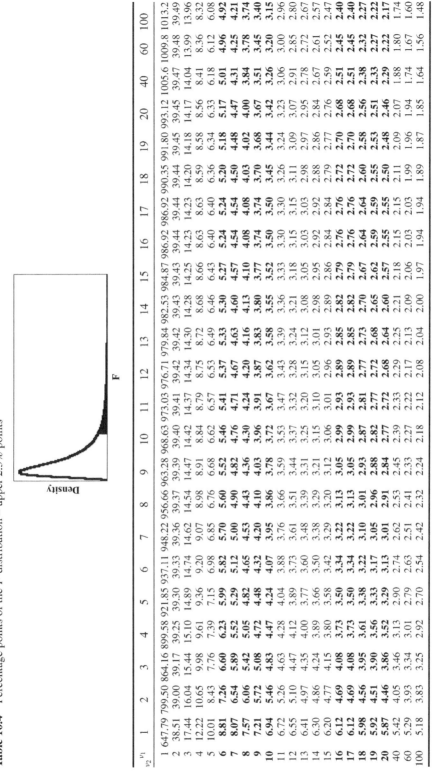

ν_2 \ ν_1	1	2	3	4	5	6	7	8	9	10	11	12	13	14	15	16	17	18	19	20	40	60	100
1	647.79	799.50	864.16	899.58	921.85	937.11	948.22	956.66	963.28	968.63	973.03	976.71	979.84	982.53	984.87	986.92	986.92	990.35	991.80	993.12	1005.6	1009.8	1013.2
2	38.51	39.00	39.17	39.25	39.30	39.33	39.36	39.37	39.39	39.40	39.41	39.42	39.42	39.43	39.43	39.44	39.44	39.44	39.45	39.45	39.47	39.48	39.49
3	17.44	16.04	15.44	15.10	14.89	14.74	14.62	14.54	14.47	14.42	14.37	14.34	14.30	14.28	14.25	14.23	14.23	14.20	14.18	14.17	14.04	13.99	13.96
4	12.22	10.65	9.98	9.61	9.36	9.20	9.07	8.98	8.91	8.84	8.79	8.75	8.72	8.68	8.66	8.63	8.63	8.59	8.58	8.56	8.41	8.36	8.32
5	10.01	8.43	7.76	7.39	7.15	6.98	6.85	6.76	6.68	6.62	6.57	6.53	6.49	6.46	6.43	6.40	6.40	6.36	6.34	6.33	6.18	6.12	6.08
6	8.81	7.26	6.60	6.23	5.99	5.82	5.70	5.60	5.52	5.46	5.41	5.37	5.33	5.30	5.27	5.24	5.24	5.20	5.18	5.17	5.01	4.96	4.92
7	8.07	6.54	5.89	5.52	5.29	5.12	5.00	4.90	4.82	4.76	4.71	4.67	4.63	4.60	4.57	4.54	4.54	4.50	4.48	4.47	4.31	4.25	4.21
8	7.57	6.06	5.42	5.05	4.82	4.65	4.53	4.43	4.36	4.30	4.24	4.20	4.16	4.13	4.10	4.08	4.08	4.03	4.02	4.00	3.84	3.78	3.74
9	7.21	5.72	5.08	4.72	4.48	4.32	4.20	4.10	4.03	3.96	3.91	3.87	3.83	3.80	3.77	3.74	3.74	3.70	3.68	3.67	3.51	3.45	3.40
10	6.94	5.46	4.83	4.47	4.24	4.07	3.95	3.86	3.78	3.72	3.67	3.62	3.58	3.55	3.52	3.50	3.50	3.45	3.44	3.42	3.26	3.20	3.15
11	6.72	5.26	4.63	4.28	4.04	3.88	3.76	3.66	3.59	3.53	3.47	3.43	3.39	3.36	3.33	3.30	3.30	3.26	3.24	3.23	3.06	3.00	2.96
12	6.55	5.10	4.47	4.12	3.89	3.73	3.61	3.51	3.44	3.37	3.32	3.28	3.24	3.21	3.18	3.15	3.15	3.11	3.09	3.07	2.91	2.85	2.80
13	6.41	4.97	4.35	4.00	3.77	3.60	3.48	3.39	3.31	3.25	3.20	3.15	3.12	3.08	3.05	3.03	3.03	2.98	2.97	2.95	2.78	2.72	2.67
14	6.30	4.86	4.24	3.89	3.66	3.50	3.38	3.29	3.21	3.15	3.10	3.05	3.01	2.98	2.95	2.92	2.92	2.88	2.86	2.84	2.67	2.61	2.57
15	6.20	4.77	4.15	3.80	3.58	3.42	3.29	3.20	3.12	3.06	3.01	2.96	2.93	2.89	2.86	2.84	2.84	2.79	2.77	2.76	2.59	2.52	2.47
16	6.12	4.69	4.08	3.73	3.50	3.34	3.22	3.13	3.05	2.99	2.93	2.89	2.85	2.82	2.79	2.76	2.76	2.72	2.70	2.68	2.51	2.45	2.40
17	6.12	4.69	4.08	3.73	3.50	3.34	3.22	3.13	3.05	2.99	2.93	2.89	2.85	2.82	2.79	2.76	2.76	2.72	2.70	2.68	2.51	2.45	2.40
18	5.98	4.56	3.95	3.61	3.38	3.22	3.10	3.01	2.93	2.87	2.81	2.77	2.73	2.70	2.67	2.64	2.64	2.60	2.58	2.56	2.38	2.32	2.27
19	5.92	4.51	3.90	3.56	3.33	3.17	3.05	2.96	2.88	2.82	2.77	2.72	2.68	2.65	2.62	2.59	2.59	2.55	2.53	2.51	2.33	2.27	2.22
20	5.87	4.46	3.86	3.52	3.29	3.13	3.01	2.91	2.84	2.77	2.72	2.68	2.64	2.60	2.57	2.55	2.55	2.50	2.48	2.46	2.29	2.22	2.17
40	5.42	4.05	3.46	3.13	2.90	2.74	2.62	2.53	2.45	2.39	2.33	2.29	2.25	2.21	2.18	2.15	2.15	2.11	2.09	2.07	1.88	1.80	1.74
60	5.29	3.93	3.34	3.01	2.79	2.63	2.51	2.41	2.33	2.27	2.22	2.17	2.13	2.09	2.06	2.03	2.03	1.99	1.96	1.94	1.74	1.67	1.60
100	5.18	3.83	3.25	2.92	2.70	2.54	2.42	2.32	2.24	2.18	2.12	2.08	2.04	2.00	1.97	1.94	1.94	1.89	1.87	1.85	1.64	1.56	1.48

11
Chi-squared Goodness of Fit Test

11.1 INTRODUCTION

In Chapter 10, the chi-squared statistic was used to compare the observed and expected values of a variance. This distribution, however, has wider applications and can also be used to compare actual observations with those predicted by taking expectations from a claimed distribution. This is best demonstrated by an example.

Table 11.1 lists the number of processing errors that occurred annually within 387 transaction batches. If a model that fits the data can be identified, then predictions may be made as to the expected error rate for the coming year.

Table 11.1 Observed number of errors

Number of errors in a batch	Observed frequency (O_i)
0	200
1	126
2	44
3	15
4	2
5 or more	0
Total	**387**

Management considers that a Poisson distribution (see section 7.4) might provide a reasonable fit to this data, which has a mean of 0.69. Using this parameter, the expected frequencies displayed in Table 11.2 may be obtained using the equation

$$\text{Prob}(x;\lambda) = \frac{\lambda^x e^{-\lambda}}{x!}$$

where $\lambda = np$, from section 7.4. The final expected frequency, corresponding to 5 or more, is adjusted to ensure that the correct total is achieved (387).

Table 11.2 Expected number of errors assuming a Poisson distribution

Number of errors	Expected frequency (E_i)
0	194.12
1	133.93
2	46.20
3	10.63
4	1.83
5 or more	0.29
Total	**387**

To compare the observed and expected frequencies a chi-squared statistic is employed, where

$$\chi^2 = \sum_{i=1}^{6} \frac{(O_i - E_i)^2}{E_i}$$

with the proviso that each expected frequency is at least 5. It should not be used for any expected frequency below 5 since this may give a disproportionate result. To achieve this, the final three categories are combined into the single category 'three or more'. The resulting values are shown in Table 11.3, plus the contributions to the chi-squared value. In this instance the calculated value of chi-squared is 2.17.

Table 11.3 Contribution to the chi-squared statistic for errors assuming a Poisson distribution

Number of errors	Observed frequency (O_i)	Expected frequency (E_i)	$\dfrac{(O_i - E_i)^2}{E_i}$
0	200	194.12	0.18
1	126	133.93	0.47
2	44	46.20	0.10
3 or more	17	12.74	1.42
Total	**387**	**387**	**2.17**

The sole remaining problem is to calculate the degrees of freedom v. If m frequencies are left, having fitted a distribution with n parameters, estimated from the raw data then,

$$v = m - n - 1.$$

The factor of 1 arises since the grand total $\Sigma_i O_i$ which is 387, can also be found. Here $v = 4 - 1 - 1 = 2$ and since $\chi_2^2 (0.05) = 5.991$ (from Table 10.1), the hypothesis that the data comes from a Poisson distribution would be accepted since the critical value, from tables, exceeds the calculated value. It is reasonable to use the model, with the rate calculated above, to predict what might happen under other scenarios using the same conditions.

11.2 CONTINGENCY TABLES

Contingency tables use data as a series of individual counts. Typically this data can be presented in a table with r rows and c columns, appearing as a $r \times c$ table. The observed frequencies in row i and column j is denoted by O_{ij} and the probability associated with this cell by p_{ij}. Conventionally the various populations are stored in the rows and the categories stored in the columns.

Only the possibility that the categories and populations are independent is examined here. That is, could the observed table have arisen by chance? Here O_{i0} denotes the row totals and O_{oj} the column totals; the grand total is then O_{00}. The probability that an observation falls in row i is O_{i0}/O_{00}. Similarly, the probability that an observation falls in column j is O_{0j}/O_{00}. If the events are independent then the probability of an event falling in row i and column j is the product of these two probabilities $p_{ij} = (O_{i0}/O_{00}) \times (O_{0j}/O_{00})$, giving an expected frequency of $E_{ij} = O_{i0}O_{0j}/O_{00}$. These values give a set of expected cell frequencies.

To compare the observed and expected frequencies a chi-squared statistic is employed (see Table 10.1):

$$\chi^2 = \sum_{i=1}^{r} \sum_{j=1}^{c} \frac{(O_{ij} - E_{ij})^2}{E_{ij}}$$

which has $(r - 1) \times (c - 1)$ degrees of freedom. This follows since the row and column totals are kept fixed. Having selected the $(r - 1) \times (c - 1)$ values, the remaining $r + c - 1$ values may be found by ensuring that the row and column sums balance. Again it is advisable that all the expected frequencies exceed 5. If necessary categories are pooled to achieve this, since this reduces the number of frequencies, but keeps the total fixed.

Following some basic testing, employees are allocated to a physical (athletic, unfit) and a performance (high, average) category. The results are shown in Table 11.4.

Table 11.4   Observed categorisation of employees

	High performers	Average performers	Total
Athletic	745	727	1,472
Unfit	268	450	718
Total	**1,013**	**1,177**	**2,190**

Would it be true to say that these results are consistent with the hypothesis that the proportion of high-performance employees is the same for both athletic and unfit staff and that any difference could be due to chance?

On calculating the expected frequencies the values in Table 11.5 are obtained, and this leads to the contributions to the chi-squared value shown in Table 11.6.

Table 11.5   Expected categorisation of employees assuming independence

	High performers	Average performers	Total
Athletic	680.88	791.12	1,472
Unfit	332.12	385.88	718
Total	**1,013**	**1,177**	**2,190**

Table 11.6   Contributions to the chi-squared statistics for categorisation of employees

	High performers	Average performers	Total
Athletic	6.04	5.20	11.24
Unfit	12.37	10.65	23.02
Total	**18.41**	**15.85**	**34.26**

Therefore, the calculated chi-squared statistic is $\chi^2_{calc} = 34.26$. Since the table has two rows and two columns, it has one degree of freedom and the critical value is $\chi^2_1(0.05) = 3.84$

using Table 10.1. Since 34.26 > 3.84, the hypothesis that the proportion of high-performance employees is the same for both athletic and unfit staff and that any difference could be due to chance cannot be accepted. There appears to be a relationship between athleticism and performance. So in looking for improved performance it would be wise for the company to invest in gym memberships for staff.

11.3 MULTIWAY TABLES

The ideas introduced for two-way tables may be extended to multiway tables. For complete independence in a three-way table, the expected value in cell (i, j, k) is $O_{i00} O_{0j0} O_{00k} / O_{000}^2$. If the table has dimensions $r \times s \times t$, then the calculated chi-squared value is compared with a tabulated value having $(r - 1) \times (s - 1) \times (t - 1)$ degrees of freedom.

11.3.1 An example of a four by four table

A company has concerns about employees potentially damaging their eyes due to frequent use of terminal screens. It decides to test all 6,538 employees. The same test for each employee was carried out on the left eye (shown as columns) and the right eye (shown as rows). The data is presented in Table 11.7. For instance, 102 employees scored at the third level for the right eye and the highest (perfect vision) for the left.

Table 11.7 Observed results of eye tests

Right eye	Left eye				Total
	Highest	Second	Third	Lowest	
Highest	1,331	232	108	57	1,728
Second	204	1,324	378	68	1,974
Third	102	316	1,551	179	2,148
Lowest	31	71	156	430	688
Total	**1,668**	**1,943**	**2,193**	**734**	**6,538**

The company wishes to consider whether it would be true to say that the quality of the left eye is independent of that of the right. The expected frequencies, assuming independence, are shown in Table 11.8.

Table 11.8 Expected results of eye tests assuming independence

Right eye	Left eye				Total
	Highest	Second	Third	Lowest	
Highest	440.85	513.54	579.61	194.00	1,728
Second	503.61	586.64	662.13	221.61	1,974
Third	548.01	638.35	720.49	241.15	2,148
Lowest	175.53	204.46	230.77	77.24	688
Total	**1,668**	**1,943**	**2,193**	**734**	**6,538**

For the employees who scored at the third level for the right eye and the highest (perfect vision) for the right, the expected frequency would be

$$\frac{2,148 \times 1,668}{6,538} = 548.01$$

This leads to the contributions to the chi-squared value shown in Table 11.9.

Table 11.9 Contributions to the chi-squared statistics for eye tests

Right eye	Left eye				Total
	Highest	Second	Third	Lowest	
Highest	1,797.33	154.35	383.74	96.74	
Second	178.25	926.78	121.92	106.48	
Third	362.99	162.78	957.33	16.02	
Lowest	119.00	87.12	24.23	1,611.09	
Total					**7,106.15**

For the employees who scored at the third level for the right eye and the highest (perfect vision) for the left, the contribution to the chi-squared statistic is

$$\frac{(102 - 548.01)^2}{548.01} = 362.99$$

Therefore the calculated statistic is $\chi^2_{calc} = 7,106.15$. As Table 11.9 has four rows and four columns, it has nine degrees of freedom since $v = (r - 1)(c - 1) = (4 - 1)(4 - 1) = 9$ and the critical value is $\chi^2_9(0.05) = 16.92$ (using Table 10.1).

The hypothesis cannot be accepted because $7,106 > 16.92$. The above statistics make it very clear that there is some relationship between the quality of the right and left eyes. A simple inspection of the data is a wise precursor to analysis. In this case it is clear that the largest numbers are located down the diagonal of Table 11.9 (1,797, 927, 957 and 1,611). On calculating contributions to the chi-squared statistic, it is clear that almost every contribution exceeds the critical value. If a manual calculation is being attempted, it is sufficient to just consider the corner cell, which in this case is that the right and left eyes are at their highest, which is 1,797.

It is useful to compare the two sets of marginal totals from Table 11.7. In Table 11.10, it can be seen that the frequencies in each group are similar. In other words, similar proportions of the population have the same quality of left and right eyesight classification.

Table 11.10 Marginal totals for the eyesight data

	Highest	Second	Third	Lowest
Left eye	1,668	1,943	2,193	734
Right eye	1,728	1,974	2,148	688

12

Analysis of Paired Data

12.1 INTRODUCTION

Often within banking there is more than one model available that might be used in a particular area. In the case of derivatives pricing, for example, different models will actually come up with different results. The challenge then is how to compare the results of the two differing methods with differing assumptions inherent within them.

What we shall look at is a comparison between the two methods, A and B, to measure the mark-to-market value of a sample of credit derivatives. A sample of n credit derivatives is selected. Randomly half are evaluated according to method A with the remaining half being evaluated according to method B. The question you are trying to answer is whether the two methods appear to give, on balance, a consistent response – or is there something fundamentally different between the two methods that might render one, or both, unreliable.

This type of issue also arises when customer surveys are being analysed or when results obtained by more than one individual are compared. It can be applied to indicate whether some element of bias is being employed. For example, one of the reviewers may be drawing a different conclusion to the other on the implication of certain specific wording used in answer to an identical question. Such bias can potentially invalidate much of the research that has been commissioned.

12.2 t TEST

For the sample of credit derivatives, both models can be applied to come up with two different valuations, $x_i(A)$ and $x_i(B)$. Here the paired measurements are replaced by their difference $d = x_i(A) - x_i(B)$. This modelling technique then makes the assumption that these differences are a random sample from a normal distribution. If it is known that a normal distribution will not apply, then this test should not be used.

If the assumption of normality is valid, then a t test may be employed, at an appropriate level, to assess whether the mean is zero. In this case, the statistic has $n - 1$ degrees of freedom $t = \bar{d}/(s\sqrt{n})$, where the differences have a mean of $\bar{d}$ and a standard deviation of s. (See section 9.1, $(\bar{x} - \mu)/(s/\sqrt{n})$, where in this case the difference (d) becomes the variable of interest and we are testing if the population mean (μ) vanishes.)

If the normal distribution does have a mean of zero and if the differences are normally distributed, then there is every reason to believe that the two methods are both equally valid (or invalid). Were the mean to be significantly different from zero, it then would suggest that there is a difference between the two modelling techniques.

The data set in Table 12.1 records the values of two different sets of derivatives, both randomly selected from the same total population, with two different valuation bases being employed. The question is whether the two modelling techniques are consistent. The

Table 12.1   Paired data

Sample	1	2	3	4	5	6	7	8	9	10
A	26	25	38	33	42	40	44	26	43	35
B	44	30	34	47	35	46	35	47	48	34
Difference	−18	−5	4	−14	7	−6	9	−21	−5	1

mean difference is −4.8 and the standard deviation 10.35 leading to a calculated t statistic of −1.47

$$t = \frac{\bar{d}}{s/\sqrt{n}} = \frac{-4.8}{10.35/\sqrt{10}} = -1.47$$

which is compared with $t_9(0.025) = 2.262$, where the critical value is taken from Table 9.5. Since 1.47 is less than 2.262 there is no reason to believe that the two methods do produce systematically different answers.

12.3   SIGN TEST

The majority of the techniques employed so far have had an underlying assumption of normality. However, in many cases there is no chance of the data being normal. Consider a population made up of errors identified on deposit interest. The customers are likely to complain if they receive less interest than they expect, but are less likely to announce that they have received too much. Accordingly any distribution based on this data is unlikely to be normal. When the assumption of normality cannot be met, some form of non-parametric test will need to be employed. Here we discuss the commonly used sign test.

In the sign test it is assumed that the differences have a symmetric distribution. This means that any value is equally likely to fall above or below the median (see Figure 5.2). To enable you to test the hypothesis that the median takes a specific value (zero in the above example) replace any values falling above the median by a plus sign and any below by a minus. Should an observation equal the assumed median, it is ignored.

If any variation has arisen by chance, then the signs would be a random sample from a binomial distribution with sample size n and probability of occurrence $1/2$, because there is an equal chance of being above or below zero. The binomial distribution is described in section 7.3.

In the example in Table 12.1, there are four positive differences and six negative differences. Using the equations for probability from section 7.3 ($\text{Prob}(x) = {}_nC_x p^x q^{n-x}$, in this case $p = q = 1/2$ and $n = 10$), the probability that there will be six or more successes from a population of 10 is 0.377:

$$\text{Prob}\,(x \geq 6) = \binom{10}{6} p^6 (1-p)^4 + \binom{10}{7} p^7 (1-p)^3 + \binom{10}{8} p^8 (1-p)^2$$
$$+ \binom{10}{9} p^9 (1-p)^1 + \binom{10}{10} p^{10} (1-p)^0$$

$$= \left(\binom{10}{6} + \binom{10}{7} + \binom{10}{8} + \binom{10}{9} + \binom{10}{10} \right) \left(\tfrac{1}{2} \right)^{10}$$

since $p = 1 - p = \tfrac{1}{2}$

$$= (210 + 120 + 45 + 10 + 1) \left(\tfrac{1}{2} \right)^{10}$$

$$= 0.377$$

As you can see, the clauses actually look at the probability of 6 from 10, 7 from 10, 8 from 10, 9 from 10 and finally 10 from 10.

Since the choice of considering the pluses first was arbitrary, the overall probability is 0.754 (2×0.377) and the conclusion does not change (the value is within the body of the distribution). In other words, the probability is greater than 0.025 and less than 0.975 for 95% confidence. There is therefore no significant difference between the medians of the two distributions. For a large sample a normal approximation could be employed.

12.4 THE U TEST

This test is also called the Mann–Whitney test or the Wilcoxon test. Again using the data from Table 12.1, the data in this case is arranged in increasing order of magnitude, as if it arose from a single sample. This means that the values from the two models are shown together in one increasing list.

The data is initially sorted as one group. The values of rank and true rank, which allow for tied values, are calculated, as shown in Table 12.2. As two items are tied as being equal second, they are both shown as 2.5, being the average of ranks 2 and 3.

Table 12.2 Ranked data for groups A/B

Group	Data	Rank	True rank	True rank for A	True rank for B
B	48	1	1		1
B	47	2	2.5		2.5
B	47	3	2.5		2.5
B	46	4	4		4
A	44	5	5.5	5.5	
B	44	6	5.5		5.5
A	43	7	7	7	
A	42	8	8	8	
A	40	9	9	9	
A	38	10	10	10	
A	35	11	12	12	
B	35	12	12		12
B	35	13	12		12
B	34	14	14.5		14.5
B	34	15	14.5		14.5
A	33	16	16	16	
B	30	17	17		17
A	26	18	18.5	18.5	
A	26	19	18.5	18.5	
A	25	20	20	20	
Total		**210**	**210**	**124.5**	**85.5**

In the data column, there are three scores of 35 with ranks 11, 12 and 13. These are all assigned the 'true rank' of 12, the average of the three ranks. The rank totals are only included as a check, if $n = n_A + n_B$ then the sum of the ranks is $\frac{1}{2}n(n+1)$. If there are n_A items in sample A with rank sum S_A and n_B items with rank sum S_B for sample B, then a U statistic is calculated where:

$$U = n_A n_B + \tfrac{1}{2}n_A(n_A + 1) - S_A$$

Since the samples of derivatives come from the same population, U has a mean of $n_A n_B/2$ and a variance of $(n_A n_B(n_A + n_B + 1))/12$. If both n_A and n_B exceed 8, the distribution of U is assumed to be approximately normal and the variable of interest is

$$z = \frac{U - (n_A n_B/2)}{\sqrt{n_A n_B(n_A + n_B + 1)/12}}$$

This uses the equation for the normal distribution (see section 8.2, $z = (x - \mu)/\sigma$). If n_A and n_B are small, it is necessary to use additional statistical tables which, in practice, will be included as standard within your modelling software.

Calculating U for sample A or B will produce estimates which are equidistant from the mean. If the values are:

$$n_A = 10$$
$$n_B = 10$$
$$S_A = 124.5$$
$$S_B = 85.5$$

You can always cross check these calculations by ensuring that

$$S_A + S_B = \frac{(n_A + n_B)(n_A + n_B + 1)}{2}$$

Then again using the equation for U from above:

$$U = n_A n_B + \tfrac{1}{2}n_A(n_A + 1) - S_A$$

giving

$$U = 30.5 \text{ (for sample A)}$$
$$U = 69.5 \text{ (for sample B)}$$
$$\text{mean}(U) = 50$$
$$\text{variance}(U) = 175$$
$$\text{standard deviation}(U) = 13.23$$
$$z = -1.47$$
$$Z_{0.025} = 1.96$$

What all this means is that there is a 95% certainty that the models produce answers with the same median, and again our view of the data is unchanged.

12.4.1 An example of the use of the U test

In a test of professional competence, potential new recruits obtained the following marks

$$54, 97, 89, 76, 59, 78, 87, 56, 74, 70, 81, 68, 79, 53, 71,$$

while the employees had achieved the following results

$$75, 82, 67, 73, 72, 86, 55, 77, 94, 88, 52, 65$$

The question is whether there is a difference between the two sets of marks. The company is expecting the recruits to be less experienced then the employees and will therefore score lower on average. The data may be ranked, as shown in Table 12.3.

$$n_{New} = 15$$
$$n_{Emp} = 12$$
$$S_{New} = 212$$
$$S_{Emp} = 166$$
$$U = 88 \text{ (for the new recruits)}$$

Table 12.3 Ranked data for new recruits/employees

		Rank	True rank	True rank for new recruits	True rank for employees
New recruit	97	1	1	1	
Employee	94	2	2		2
New recruit	89	3	3	3	
Employee	88	4	4		4
New recruit	87	5	5	5	
Employee	86	6	6		6
Employee	82	7	7		7
New recruit	81	8	8	8	
New recruit	79	9	9	9	
New recruit	78	10	10	10	
Employee	77	11	11		11
New recruit	76	12	12	12	
Employee	75	13	13		13
New recruit	74	14	14	14	
Employee	73	15	15		15
Employee	72	16	16		16
New recruit	71	17	17	17	
New recruit	70	18	18	18	
New recruit	68	19	19	19	
Employee	67	20	20		20
Employee	65	21	21		21
New recruit	59	22	22	22	
New recruit	56	23	23	23	
Employee	55	24	24		24
New recruit	54	25	25	25	
New recruit	53	26	26	26	
Employee	52	27	27		27
Total		**378**	**378**	**212**	**166**

$$U = 92 \text{ (for the employees)}$$
$$\text{mean}(U) = 90$$
$$\text{variance}(U) = 420$$
$$\text{standard deviation}(U) = 20.49$$
$$z = -0.098$$
$$Z_{0.025} = 1.96$$

Therefore, there appears to be no significant difference between the two sets of marks and the test has not shown that the employees are at an advantage to the new recruits.

There is effectively a hierarchy for these tests.

1. If the data is unpaired and an underlying normal distribution may be assumed, employ a two-sample t test.
2. If the data is paired and an underlying normal distribution may be assumed, employ a t test.
3. If the data is unpaired and an underlying normal distribution may not be assumed, employ a U test.
4. If the data is paired and an underlying normal distribution may not be assumed, employ a sign test.

13

Linear Regression

13.1 INTRODUCTION

Regularly in business you will have two variables where it is thought there is some form of relationship between them. It could be the movement in an exchange rate and the base rate of the country, for example. Let us consider the time taken by a company to complete the processing of a batch of transactions. The time taken may be thought to depend on the number of transactions processed. Having obtained a series of n observations (transactions$_i$, time$_i$: $i = 1, \ldots, n$) the relationship can be investigated. The first step is to produce a scatter plot of the data (see section 1.2). This is simply the points plotted against a linear axis. The independent variable (time) is plotted on the horizontal axis and the dependent variable (number of transactions) on the vertical axis.

If a straight line could be drawn which passes close to most of the data points, then the data would appear to support a linear relationship. This would mean that, for example, a 20% increase in the number of transactions would increase processing time by 20%. If this is the case, then linear regression could be used to enable the time taken for any number of transactions to be estimated, provided that the number of transactions to be estimated is within the range of the accumulated data. It is always risky to attempt to extend results outside the range of the data observed.

13.2 LINEAR REGRESSION

If, when you have two variables x and y, a linear relationship is to be constructed that is consistent with n data points $(x_i, y_i : i = 1, \ldots, n)$, then this will be described by the equation

$$y = ax + b$$

where a is the gradient or slope of the line and b is the intercept with the vertical axis. If $x = 0$, then $y = b$, so the line starts initially with a value of b.

The parameters a and b can then be estimated by using the following equations and the data set:

$$\hat{a} = \frac{\left(\sum_{i=1}^{n} x_i y_i \right) - \frac{1}{n} \left(\sum_{i=1}^{n} x_i \right) \left(\sum_{i=1}^{n} y_i \right)}{\left(\sum_{i=1}^{n} x_i^2 \right) - \frac{1}{n} \left(\sum_{i=1}^{n} x_i \right)^2}$$

and

$$\hat{b} = \frac{1}{n} \sum_{i=1}^{n} y_i - \frac{\hat{a}}{n} \sum_{i=1}^{n} x_i$$

where the circumflex symbol stresses that we are only able to obtain estimates of the true values of the parameters from the experiment. In other words, the relationship we believe to be appropriate is $y = ax + b$. Since we only have limited data we are only able to estimate the gradient term a, and to make it clear that this is only an approximation, we write it as $\hat{a}$. Similarly, the intercept with the vertical axis, b, is approximated by $\hat{b}$. (See section 13.3.1 for an example of calculating these values.)

The denominator of $\hat{a}$ is effectively the variance of the x values and the numerator is a similar quantity, called the covariance ($\operatorname{cov}(x, y)$). The covariance is equal to the product of the differences from their respective means for the two variables.

So, from above we know that the gradient of the line is estimated by

$$\hat{a} = \frac{\left(\sum_{i=1}^{n} x_i y_i\right) - \frac{1}{n}\left(\sum_{i=1}^{n} x_i\right)\left(\sum_{i=1}^{n} y_i\right)}{\left(\sum_{i=1}^{n} x_i^2\right) - \frac{1}{n}\left(\sum_{i=1}^{n} x_i\right)^2}$$

This may be written in a more compact form since the variance (section 5.6) is

$$\operatorname{var}(x) = \frac{\left(\sum_{i=1}^{n} x_i^2\right) - \frac{1}{n}\left(\sum_{i=1}^{n} x_i\right)^2}{n - 1}$$

The covariance may be similarly written as:

$$\operatorname{cov}(x, y) = \frac{\sum_{i=1}^{n} (x_i - \bar{x})(y_i - \bar{y})}{n - 1} = \frac{\left(\sum_{i=1}^{n} x_i y_i\right) - \frac{1}{n}\left(\sum_{i=1}^{n} x_i\right)\left(\sum_{i=1}^{n} y_i\right)}{n - 1} \qquad (*)$$

We can then write the equation for the estimated gradient in a more compact form using this new notation:

$$\hat{a} = \frac{\operatorname{cov}(x, y)}{\operatorname{var}(x)}$$

13.3 CORRELATION COEFFICIENT

A closely related term to the covariance is the correlation coefficient ($r(x, y)$), which is simply

$$r(x, y) = \frac{\operatorname{cov}(x, y)}{\operatorname{std}(x)\,\operatorname{std}(y)}$$

where the standard deviation of x (section 5.6) is given by

$$\operatorname{std}(x) = \sqrt{\frac{\left(\sum_{i=1}^{n} x_i^2\right) - \frac{1}{n}\left(\sum_{i=1}^{n} x_i\right)^2}{n - 1}}$$

There would be a similar expression for y.

The correlation coefficient is a measure of the interdependence of two variables. The co-efficient ranges in value from -1 to $+1$, indicating perfect negative correlation at -1, absence of correlation at zero, and perfect positive correlation at $+1$. Two variables are positively correlated if the correlation coefficient is greater than zero and the line that is drawn to show a relationship between the items sampled has a positive gradient. If the correlation coefficient is negative, the variables are negatively correlated and the line drawn will have a negative gradient. The final option is that the correlation coefficient vanishes, and the gradient vanishes since $\hat{a} = 0$, in which case the variables are completely uncorrelated. This means that there is no relationship between the two variables. An example of this might be the time taken to process a batch of transactions and the movements in interest rates.

As a rough guide, $100r^2$ is the percentage of the total variation of the y population that is accounted for by their relationship with x. More precisely there is generally considered to be a significant correlation if the correlation coefficient, or r-value, exceeds the critical value (r_{crit}) at $n - 2$ degrees of freedom. This will be taken from standard statistical tables, or may be included within your existing modelling package.

Should the standard tables be unavailable, then a normal approximation may be employed to find the critical value for r (r_{crit}). This is defined by the following equation:

$$r_{\text{crit}} = \frac{X - 1}{X + 1} \quad \text{where} \quad X = \exp\left(\frac{2Z_{\alpha/2}}{\sqrt{n - 3}}\right).$$

Alternatively, and more precisely,

$$r_{\text{crit}} = r_v\left(\frac{\alpha}{2}\right) = \frac{t_{n-2}\left(\alpha/2\right)}{\sqrt{n - 2 + t_{n-2}^2\left(\alpha/2\right)}}$$

While this equation is more cumbersome it does provide a more accurate critical value. The following calculation shows the difference between the two equations.

If $n = 20$, and a 95% confidence level ($\alpha = 0.05$) is required then $Z_{\alpha/2} = 1.96$ (from Table 8.2 or Table 8.4).

Since

$$X = \exp\left(\frac{2Z_{\alpha/2}}{\sqrt{n - 3}}\right)$$

this equates to $\exp(2 \times 1.96/4.12)$, which gives $X = 2.59$. Now since $r_{\text{crit}} = (X - 1)/(X + 1)$, this becomes $1.59/3.59$ and therefore $r_{\text{crit}} = 0.44$.

Using the alternative and more precise equation above, since $t_{18}(0.025) = 2.11$ (see Table 9.5), and with $n = 20$, we obtain

$$r_v\left(\frac{\alpha}{2}\right) = \frac{t_{n-2}\left(\alpha/2\right)}{\sqrt{n - 2 + t_{n-2}^2\left(\alpha/2\right)}} = \frac{2.11}{\sqrt{20 - 2 + 2.11^2}} = 0.44$$

which gives $r_{18}(0.025) = 0.44$.

13.3.1 An example of examining correlation

A company has information on the weekly pay and age of its back office staff and is concerned whether staff are being remunerated for age rather than being a pure meritocracy (see Table 13.1). A perfect correlation with a correlation coefficient of $+1$ would indicate that staff are purely remunerated on the basis of age and that skills and performance have a lower impact.

Table 13.1   Weekly pay versus age for 20 back office staff

Person	Age (years) x_i	Weekly pay (£) y_i	$x_i y_i$	x_i^2	y_i^2
1	29	257	7,453	841	66,049
2	39	457	17,823	1,521	208,849
3	43	621	26,703	1,849	385,641
4	31	284	8,804	961	80,656
5	38	554	21,052	1,444	306,916
6	32	379	12,128	1,024	143,641
7	40	471	18,840	1,600	221,841
8	33	262	8,646	1,089	68,644
9	35	600	21,000	1,225	360,000
10	37	423	15,651	1,369	178,929
11	44	449	19,756	1,936	201,601
12	39	490	19,110	1,521	240,100
13	21	288	6,048	441	82,944
14	39	638	24,882	1,521	407,044
15	45	750	33,750	2,025	562,500
16	23	235	5,405	529	55,225
17	23	506	11,638	529	256,036
18	24	270	6,480	576	72,900
19	27	545	14,715	729	297,025
20	21	250	5,250	441	62,500
Total	**663**	**8,729**	**305,134**	**23,171**	**4,259,041**

Using the equations shown above, we use the totals to calculate the variances within the sample of ages (x) and salaries (y), and also to calculate both the covariance of x and y and the correlation coefficient.

Firstly, the variance of x is calculated using the equation (see section 5.6):

$$\text{var}(x) = \frac{\left(\sum_{i=1}^{n} x_i^2\right) - \frac{1}{n}\left(\sum_{i=1}^{n} x_i\right)^2}{n - 1}$$

The first term is the total of all of the x_i^2 terms, so that 23,171 from Table 13.1 replaces it. The first column shows that 20 people were sampled. n is therefore 20 and $n - 1$ becomes 19. The second column gives the total of the ages as 663, which is the sum of all of the x_i terms:

$$\text{var}(x) = \frac{23,171 - (663^2/20)}{19} = 62.77$$

Then the variance of y can be calculated in the same way, and again using the same equation:

$$\text{var}(y) = \frac{\left(\sum_{i=1}^{n} y_i^2\right) - \frac{1}{n}\left(\sum_{i=1}^{n} y_i\right)^2}{n - 1}$$

Now the final column of Table 13.1 gives the y_i^2 term, with weekly pay being shown in the third column (total 8,729) and the number of sample people remaining at 20. Therefore, the above equation becomes:

$$\text{var}(y) = \frac{4,259,041 - (8,729^2/20)}{19} = 23,645.73$$

Finally the covariance of x and y can be calculated using the starred equation from section 13.2:

$$\text{cov}(x, y) = \frac{\left(\sum_{i=1}^{n} x_i y_i\right) - \frac{1}{n}\left(\sum_{i=1}^{n} x_i\right)\left(\sum_{i=1}^{n} y_i\right)}{n - 1}$$

which gives

$$\text{cov}(x, y) = \frac{305,134 - [(663 \times 8,729)/20]}{19} = 829.88$$

These terms lead directly to the calculation of the correlation. In section 5.6 we explained that the standard deviation is in fact the square root of the variance, or mathematically, $\text{std}(x) = \sqrt{\text{var}(x)}$. Clearly a similar relationship would also apply to the standard deviation of y, which is the square root of the variance of y.

$$\text{corr}(x, y) = r = \frac{\text{cov}(x, y)}{\text{std}(x)\,\text{std}(y)}$$

$$r = \frac{829.88}{\sqrt{62.77 \times 23,645.73}} = 0.68$$

This then provides some evidence that the result from the linear regression will be valid, since:

$$r^2 = 0.68^2 = 0.46$$

This correlation is reasonably high, so the company can see that age is probably important in determining the level of increase in weekly pay, with performance therefore having a lesser impact.

Having decided that age is related to weekly pay the next step is to produce the linear equation, so that we can see the representation graphically and use this for prediction. The parameters for the appropriate fit are the estimated gradient $\hat{a}$ and the estimated intercept with the vertical axis $\hat{b}$.

Section 13.2 produced the following equation to represent the gradient:

$$\hat{a} = \frac{\left(\sum_{i=1}^{n} x_i y_i\right) - \frac{1}{n}\left(\sum_{i=1}^{n} x_i\right)\left(\sum_{i=1}^{n} y_i\right)}{\left(\sum_{i=1}^{n} x_i^2\right) - \frac{1}{n}\left(\sum_{i=1}^{n} x_i\right)^2}$$

Using the figures that we have calculated above and in Table 13.1, this gives:

$$\hat{a} = \frac{305,134 - ((663 \times 8,729)/20)}{23,171 - (663^2/20)} = \frac{829.88}{62.77} = 13.22$$

The intercept was also set out mathematically in section 13.2 as:

$$\hat{b} = \frac{1}{n}\sum_{i=1}^{n} y_i - \frac{\hat{a}}{n}\sum_{i=1}^{n} x_i$$

Again, using the information in Table 13.1 and the calculations above, this gives:

$$\hat{b} = \frac{8,729}{20} - \frac{13.22}{20}663 = -1.85$$

To draw the line two points are required. Typically x values near either end of the scale should be taken which appear to give a line that has an equal number of sample points above it and below it. The corresponding y values are computed using the fitted coefficients $(\hat{a}, \hat{b})$ as set out above. The fitted data with the line drawn is shown in Figure 13.1.

There are a number of ways of deriving the coefficients. You could use a formal mathematical approach, which minimises the distance between the point (x_i, y_i) and the corresponding point on the line $(x_i, \hat{a}x_i + \hat{b})$. Again, the way to solve this mathematically does involve knowledge of calculus, so in practice you may need to rely upon some form of modelling software to do this which will have calculus embedded within it.

While the line that is drawn in Figure 13.1 is helpful and can be used to produce values for intermediate points, it gives no indication of the level of accuracy of any estimate or of any uncertainty that has now been introduced as the sampled items are not all sitting on the line but are distributed around the line. The line has become an approximation to the model adopted to explain the data. To understand more about the level of uncertainty, we need to consider some further terms.

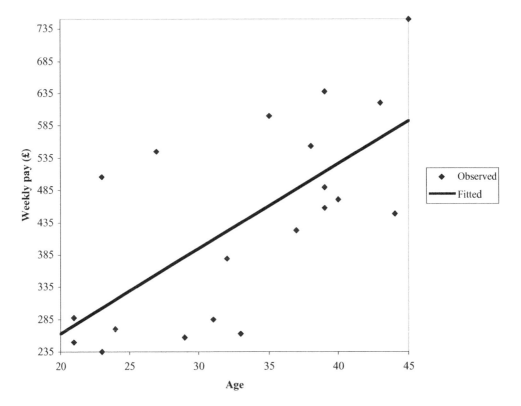

Figure 13.1 Weekly pay versus age for 20 back office staff.

13.4 ESTIMATION OF THE UNCERTAINTIES

What we want to know is by how much any observed y value might differ from that predicted by the straight line. The first step in examining this discrepancy is to calculate what is called the 'residual sum of the squares'.

The residual sum of squares (s^2) can be calculated using the equation

$$s^2 = \frac{\sum_{i=1}^{n}(y_i - \bar{y})^2 - \hat{a}\sum_{i=1}^{n}(x_i - \bar{x})(y_i - \bar{y})}{n - 2} = \frac{\sum_{i=1}^{n}y_i^2 - n\bar{y}^2 - \hat{a}\left(\left(\sum_{i=1}^{n}x_iy_i\right) - n\bar{x}\,\bar{y}\right)}{n - 2}$$

where we have n pairs of observed data x_i and y_i with means $\bar{x}$ and $\bar{y}$ (see section 5.2) respectively, while the estimated gradient of the fitted line is $\hat{a}$, as discussed above in section 13.2. Again, in practice, you will probably not actually see the equation, rather you will be asked to put a series of details into a modeller that will provide the answers, but the above equation will be embedded within the software.

It summarises how much each observed y value differs from that predicted by the straight line. This value can be used to predict the mean value of y corresponding to the value x by a confidence interval. This concept was introduced in Chapters 8 and 9, where we produced confidence intervals for the population mean. The aim there was to predict with 95% certainty an interval containing the population mean. The residual sum of squares can be used to predict the mean value of y corresponding to the value x with a confidence interval. As discussed below, it is a by-product of the analysis of the variance, being the error mean square term. Mathematically it can be expressed by the equation

$$\hat{a}x + \hat{b} \pm t_{n-2}(\alpha)s\sqrt{\frac{1}{n} + \frac{(x - \bar{x})^2}{\sum_{i=1}^{n}(x_i - \bar{x})^2}}$$

Often a two-tail statistic is employed to give the confidence level; in other words, the error could be either above or below the mean. The residual sum of the squares can also be used to predict the value of y corresponding to the value x by a prediction interval. Mathematically this is shown as:

$$\hat{a}x + \hat{b} \pm t_{n-2}(\alpha)s\sqrt{1 + \frac{1}{n} + \frac{(x - \bar{x})^2}{\sum_{i=1}^{n}(x_i - \bar{x})^2}}$$

where a two-tail statistic is employed to give the confidence level. It may be useful to have these equations plotted onto the graph to enable the user to understand the uncertainty inherent in the analysis.

The calculation for a given confidence interval will show the range for the population mean of all responses that correspond to the given value of the predictor. The calculation for a given prediction interval is the range taken for an individual observation. The confidence interval is appropriate for the data used in the regression (section 13.2).

It is necessary to assess the accuracy of the proposed line; for instance, are the parameters (a and b) significantly different from zero?

Table 13.2   A general ANOVA table for linear regression

Source	Sum of squares of deviations	Degrees of freedom	Mean square
Regression	$\sum (\bar{y} - \hat{y})^2$	1	$\dfrac{\sum (\bar{y} - \hat{y})^2}{1}$
Error	$\sum (y - \hat{y})^2$	$n - 2$	$\dfrac{\sum (y - \hat{y})^2}{n - 2}$
Total	$\sum (y - \bar{y})^2$	$n - 1$	

13.5   STATISTICAL ANALYSIS AND INTERPRETATION OF LINEAR REGRESSION

The previous sections have shown how to obtain parameter estimates when fitting the line $y = ax + b$ to the data $\{(x_1, y_1), (x_2, y_2), \ldots, (x_n, y_n)\}$. It is now necessary to work out whether the derived regression equation is statistically significant and can actually be used in practice with confidence. To do this, an analysis of variance (ANOVA) needs to be performed.

13.6   ANOVA FOR LINEAR REGRESSION

ANOVA for linear regression enables a comparison to be made between the variance explained by the regression and the error variance s_y^2, using an F test (see section 10.3). The hypothesis under test is that all the parameters estimated are zero, against the alternative that at least one of them is non-zero. If they are all zero, the sum of deviations due to the errors, $\Sigma(y - \hat{y})^2$, would be expected to be large; while $\Sigma(\bar{y} - \hat{y})^2$, the sum of deviations accounted for by the regression, would be small. The sum of the deviations due to the errors is small and the sum of the deviations accounted for by the regression is large, then at least one of the parameters is non-zero. If the gradient a vanishes then there is apparently no relationship between the variables.

There are various aids in calculating these values. For brevity write $S_{yy} = \Sigma(y - \bar{y})^2$ and $a^2 S_{xx} = \Sigma(\bar{y} - \hat{y})^2 = a^2 \Sigma(x - \bar{x})^2$. These are the key values that are entered in Table 13.2, with the highlighted cells being readily found by subtraction. In this case we have n pairs of observations. The final column is simply the ratio of the preceding two columns. A more concise presentation is shown in Table 13.3.

Table 13.3   A general ANOVA table for linear regression in terms of the basic parameters

Source	Sum of squares of deviations	Degrees of freedom	Mean square
Regression	$a^2 S_{xx}$	1	$a^2 S_{xx}/1$
Error	$\sum (y - \hat{y})^2$	$n - 2$	$\dfrac{\sum (y - \hat{y})^2}{n - 2}$
Total	S_{yy}	$n - 1$	

The analysis may be completed for the age versus weekly pay data that has been shown in Table 13.1, with the calculations from section 13.3.1:

$$S_{yy} = \Sigma(y - \bar{y})^2 = \Sigma y^2 - n\bar{y}^2 = 4{,}259{,}041 - 20 \left(\frac{8{,}729}{20} \right)^2 = 449{,}268.95$$

$$a^2 S_{xx} = a^2 \Sigma(x - \bar{x})^2 = a^2 \left(\Sigma x^2 - n\bar{x}^2 \right) = 13.22^2 \left(23{,}171 - 20 \left(\frac{663}{20} \right)^2 \right) = 208{,}476.61$$

Table 13.4   The ANOVA table for the regression of weekly pay versus age data

Source	Sum of squares of deviations	Degrees of freedom	Mean square
Regression	208,476.61	1	208,476.61
Error	240,792.34	18	13,377.35
Total	**449,268.95**	**19**	

We set out the calculation in full as Table 13.4. From the analysis we have already undertaken you can see that the highlighted section is found by subtraction, so $240,792.34 = 449,268.95 - 208,476.61$.

Degrees of freedom are a value based on the sample size and the number of variables in the model. In this case, since there are 20 pairs of observations, $n = 20$. The degrees of freedom for the regression are always taken to be 1.

For the error, $n - 2 = 18$ and for the total $n - 1 = 19$. The mean square values are the ratio of the sum of square to the degrees of freedom. Therefore the regression sum of squares of the deviations is given by:

$$\frac{208,476.61}{1} = 208,476.61$$

Similarly the error sum of squares of the deviations is given by:

$$\frac{240,792.34}{18} = 13,377.35$$

We are trying to find whether the gradient a is significantly different from zero. Taking the ratio of the entries in the final column (the mean square) as calculated above, gives:

$$F = \frac{208,476.61}{13,377.35} = 15.58$$

which should be compared with $F_{18}^1 (0.05) = 4.41$ (see Table 10.3). The degrees of freedom (1 for the numerator and 18 for the denominator) have been taken from the third column of Table 13.4.

Since the calculated value exceeds the critical value, it would appear that the coefficients are not all zero and therefore there would appear to be a linear equation that describes the data. However, we could also have the situation where the intercept b is non-zero while the gradient a actually vanishes. In this case our model would simply predict a constant b for all values of x.

If the ANOVA is satisfactory, then all the coefficients will not be zero, and a more detailed analysis may be considered necessary. The first question to be addressed is whether the gradient $\hat{a}$ is consistent with some theoretical value a, which might actually be zero. A value of zero would simply imply that there was in fact no relationship and the scatter plot would be essentially parallel to the x axis.

13.7   EQUATIONS FOR THE VARIANCE OF a AND b

In section 13.2 we defined the gradient a as:

$$\hat{a} = \frac{\left(\sum\limits_{i=1}^{n} x_i y_i\right) - \frac{1}{n}\left(\sum\limits_{i=1}^{n} x_i\right)\left(\sum\limits_{i=1}^{n} y_i\right)}{\left(\sum\limits_{i=1}^{n} x_i^2\right) - \frac{1}{n}\left(\sum\limits_{i=1}^{n} x_i\right)^2} = \frac{S_{xy}}{S_{xx}}$$

where, for example the numerator may be simplified to ease calculations as S_{xy}

$$S_{xy} = \left(\sum_{i=1}^{n} x_i y_i\right) - \frac{1}{n}\left(\sum_{i=1}^{n} x_i\right)\left(\sum_{i=1}^{n} y_i\right) = \left(\sum_{i=1}^{n} x_i y_i\right) - n\left(\frac{\sum\limits_{i=1}^{n} x_i}{n}\right)\left(\frac{\sum\limits_{i=1}^{n} y_i}{n}\right)$$

$$= \sum_{i=1}^{n} x_i y_i - n\bar{x}\,\bar{y}$$

with a similar expression for the denominator S_{xx}

$$S_{xx} = \left(\sum_{i=1}^{n} x_i^2\right) - \frac{1}{n}\left(\sum_{i=1}^{n} x_i\right)^2 = \left(\sum_{i=1}^{n} x_i^2\right) - n\left(\frac{\sum\limits_{i=1}^{n} x_i}{n}\right)^2 = \sum_{i=1}^{n} x_i^2 - n\bar{x}^2$$

These are the equations that we first saw in Table 13.3.

The basic assumption when performing the regression is that the independent variable $\{x_i\}$ is effectively without error. This is always a brave assumption and one that could potentially undermine the quality of the modelling. However, it is often made in practice, so the user should be aware of it, ideally highlighting this on any reports based on this assumption. It is necessary to obtain an estimate of the variance for the gradient a from the sample. This would be $s_a^2 = s_y^2/S_{xx}$, where s_y^2 is the variance about the regression line as opposed to the mean:

$$s_y^2 = \frac{\sum\limits_{i=1}^{n} (y_i - \hat{y}_i)^2}{n-2} = \frac{\sum\limits_{i=1}^{n} \left(y_i - \hat{a}x_i - \hat{b}\right)^2}{n-2} = \frac{\sum\limits_{i=1}^{n} y_i^2 - \hat{a}\sum\limits_{i=1}^{n} y_i x_i - \hat{b}\sum\limits_{i=1}^{n} y_i}{n-2}$$

where there are $n-2$ degrees of freedom since there are two constraints on the regression line $(\hat{a}, \hat{b})$.

To assess the intercept b its variance is also required. Its value is

$$s_b^2 = s_y^2\left(\frac{1}{n} + \frac{\bar{x}^2}{S_{xx}}\right)$$

These variance estimates may now be employed to assess the coefficients.

13.8   SIGNIFICANCE TEST FOR THE SLOPE

The aim is to test whether there is a significant difference between an actual gradient, **a**, and the value of a given by a regression line fitted to the sample. This will let us see how accurate the gradient is that we have drawn.

Since the population variance is not available, a t test (see section 9.2) is conducted on $|a - \mathbf{a}|$. This would be a two-tail test since the difference could be positive or negative, with the null hypothesis that $a = \mathbf{a}$ while the alternative is that $a \neq \mathbf{a}$. The value $\hat{a}$ is adopted as an estimate of a. The comparison is then made using $t = |a - \mathbf{a}| / s_a$ with the critical value having $n - 2$ degrees of freedom (see section 9.2). Another way of looking at this is to consider that effectively we have some 'guess' as to the value of $\mathbf{a}$. The question is then whether $\mathbf{a}$ is consistent with a. What you do is to estimate a as $\hat{a}$ since you need a numerical value. You then estimate the variance of a as $s_a^2 = s_y^2 / S_{xx}$ and perform a t test to assess the original estimate.

Clearly if the actual value of t calculated using $t = |a - \mathbf{a}| / s_a$ exceeds the critical value, then you would conclude that there is a significant difference between $\hat{a}$ and $\mathbf{a}$.

When examining for a non-zero slope, the test statistic becomes $t = |\hat{a}| / s_a$ and the test described above is once again carried out. In this case, if a does not differ significantly from zero, x and y are independent and the constructed regression line is of no value. A similar test may be conducted on the intercept, $\mathbf{b}$, using the test statistic $t = |b - \mathbf{b}| / s_b$. In this case, if the intercept vanishes ($b = 0$) the line simply passes through the origin.

13.8.1   An example of slope analysis

Let us reconsider the weekly pay data from Table 13.1. To make the calculation easier the key equations have been summarised in Table 13.5. From the information presented in Table 13.1 and section 13.2, the values summarised in Table 13.6 may also be worked out.

The term S_{yy} is not needed at this stage but would be required to complete the ANOVA table as set out in Table 13.3. The most important of the values found may be conveniently summarised in Table 13.6. (Note that to avoid gross rounding errors $\hat{a}$ has been shown to four decimal places.)

Since $t_{18}(0.025) = 2.101$ (see Table 9.5) the gradient, $\hat{a}$, is significantly different from zero while the intercept, $\hat{b}$, is not. This suggests that a weekly pay of zero is consistent with age zero, which is also hardly surprising.

A second example relates the performance of 15 employees.

Table 13.5   Key equations relating to assessing the regression coefficients

n	The number of pairs of data	S_{xx}	$\sum_{i=1}^{n} x_i^2 - n\bar{x}^2$	$\bar{x}$	$\sum_{i=1}^{n} x_i/n$	s_y	$\sqrt{\dfrac{\sum_{i=1}^{n} y_i^2 - \hat{a}\sum_{i=1}^{n} y_i x_i - \hat{b}\sum_{i=1}^{n} y_i}{n-2}}$
$\sum x$	$\sum_{i=1}^{n} x_i$	S_{xy}	$\sum_{i=1}^{n} x_i y_i - n\bar{x}\,\bar{y}$	$\bar{y}$	$\sum_{i=1}^{n} y_i/n$	s_a	$\sqrt{s_y^2/S_{xx}}$
$\sum y$	$\sum_{i=1}^{n} y_i$	S_{yy}	$\sum_{i=1}^{n} y_i^2 - n\bar{y}^2$			t_a	$|\hat{a}|/s_a$
$\sum x^2$	$\sum_{i=1}^{n} x_i^2$			$\hat{a}$	S_{xy}/S_{xx}	s_b	$\sqrt{s_y^2\left(\frac{1}{n} + \frac{\bar{x}^2}{S_{xx}}\right)}$
$\sum xy$	$\sum_{i=1}^{n} x_i y_i$			$\hat{b}$	$\bar{y} - \hat{a}\bar{x}$	t_b	$|\hat{b}|/s_b$
$\sum y^2$	$\sum_{i=1}^{n} y_i^2$						

Table 13.6 Key figures related to the salary versus age data for 20 back office staff

n	20	S_{xx}	$23{,}171 - 20 \times 33.15^2$	$\bar{x}$	$663/20$	s_y	$\sqrt{\dfrac{4{,}259{,}041 - 13.2218 \times 305{,}134 + 1.8527 \times 8729}{18}}$
		S_{xx}	$1{,}192.55$	$\bar{x}$	33.15	s_y	115.66
$\sum x$	663	S_{xy}	$305{,}134 - 20 \times 33.15 \times 436.45$	$\bar{y}$	$8{,}729/20$	s_a	$\sqrt{115.66^2/1{,}192.55}$
		S_{xy}	$15{,}767.65$	$\bar{y}$	436.45	s_a	3.35
$\sum y$	8,729	S_{yy}	$4{,}259{,}041 - 20 \times 436.45^2$			t_a	$|13.22|/3.35$
		S_{yy}	$449{,}268.95$			t_a	3.95
$\sum x^2$	23,171			$\hat{a}$	$15{,}767.65/1{,}192.55$	s_b	$\sqrt{115.66^2\left(\dfrac{1}{20} + \dfrac{33.15^2}{1{,}192.55}\right)}$
				$\hat{a}$	13.2218	s_b	114.00
$\sum xy$	305,134			$\hat{b}$	$436.45 - 13.2218 \times 33.15$	t_b	$|-1.8527|/114.00$
$\sum y^2$	4,259,041			$\hat{b}$	-1.8527	t_b	0.02

Table 13.7 Key summary coefficients estimates

Predictor	Coefficient	Standard deviation	t Ratio
Constant	−1.85	114.00	0.02
Gradient	13.22	3.35	3.95

13.8.2 A further example of correlation and linear regression

In Table 13.8 the performance of 15 employees is analysed, comparing the number of invoices processed by each employee in a month to the losses on average per transaction. The analysis attempts to investigate if these quantities are related and whether the employee makes more errors as he or she undertakes more transactions.

The totals may be employed to calculate certain useful values following the approach in section 13.3.1. Since the variance of x is given by the equation

$$\text{var}(x) = \frac{\left(\sum\limits_{i=1}^{n} x_i^2\right) - \dfrac{1}{n}\left(\sum\limits_{i=1}^{n} x_i\right)^2}{n-1}$$

the information in Table 13.8 is then inserted into the equation to give

$$\text{var}(x) = \frac{26{,}601{,}173 - (17{,}317^2/15)}{14} = 472{,}090.98$$

Table 13.8 Number of invoices processed and losses per transaction for 15 employees

Employee	Number of invoices processed x_i	Losses per transaction (£) y_i	$x_i y_i$	x_i^2	y_i^2
1	1,561	14	21,854	2,436,721	196
2	2,500	6	15,000	6,250,000	36
3	213	15	3,195	45,369	225
4	458	17	7,786	209,764	289
5	835	14	11,690	697,225	196
6	1,342	11	14,762	1,800,964	121
7	2,189	2	4,378	4,791,721	4
8	1,342	8	10,736	1,800,964	64
9	1,500	3	4,500	2,250,000	9
10	518	11	5,698	268,324	121
11	1,416	10	14,160	2,005,056	100
12	660	16	10,560	435,600	256
13	1,331	10	13,310	1,771,561	100
14	1,352	14	18,928	1,827,904	196
15	100	20	2,000	10,000	400
Total	**17,317**	**171**	**158,557**	**26,601,173**	**2,313**

Similarly the variance of y can be calculated as:

$$\text{var}(y) = \frac{2,313 - (171^2/15)}{14} = 25.97$$

The covariance uses the following equation, that was given in section 13.3.1:

$$\text{cov}(x, y) = \frac{\left(\sum_{i=1}^{n} x_i y_i\right) - \frac{1}{n}\left(\sum_{i=1}^{n} x_i\right)\left(\sum_{i=1}^{n} y_i\right)}{n - 1}$$

Again inserting the information from above, this gives:

$$\text{cov}(x, y) = \frac{158,557 - ((17,317 \times 171)/15)}{14} = -2,775.49$$

The correlation equation can now be used as follows:

$$\text{corr}(x, y) = r = \frac{\text{cov}(x, y)}{\text{std}(x)\,\text{std}(y)}$$

Since we now know the standard deviation and covariance for x and y, these may be inserted to give:

$$\text{corr}(x, y) = \frac{-2,775.49}{\sqrt{472,090.98 \times 25.97}} = -0.79$$

Finally we can take the square of this, as follows:

$$r^2 = -0.79^2 = 0.63$$

Since $r_{13}(0.05) = 0.51$ is exceeded by the value for r, this provides support for the proposition that some form of linear relationship does in fact exist. Therefore any line will provide a reasonable fit to the data and present a negative relationship. The fitting coefficients may now be calculated. The gradient may be found by using the equation:

$$\hat{a} = \frac{\left(\sum_{i=1}^{n} x_i y_i\right) - \frac{1}{n}\left(\sum_{i=1}^{n} x_i\right)\left(\sum_{i=1}^{n} y_i\right)}{\left(\sum_{i=1}^{n} x_i^2\right) - \frac{1}{n}\left(\sum_{i=1}^{n} x_i\right)^2}$$

which gives a value of $\hat{a} = -0.0059$. Similarly, we can calculate the intercept by using the equation:

$$\hat{b} = \frac{1}{n}\sum_{i=1}^{n} y_i - \frac{\hat{a}}{n}\sum_{i=1}^{n} x_i$$

to give a value of $\hat{b} = 18.19$. This may be shown graphically as set out in Figure 13.2.

Therefore, we can see that if an employee processes more invoices, then the losses per invoice actually decrease – and so they appear to be actually becoming more efficient. The upper and lower confidence limits for the mean value of y are presented in Table 13.9 and plotted in Figure 13.3 using the calculations shown in section 13.4. For instance, to complete

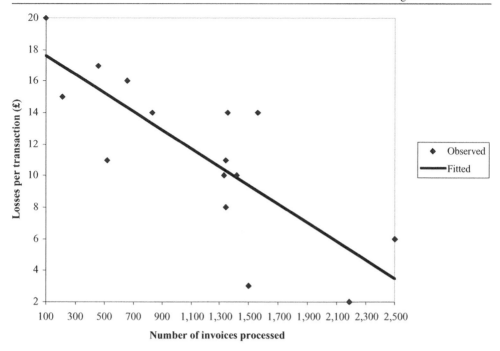

Figure 13.2   Number of invoices processed and losses per transaction for 15 employees.

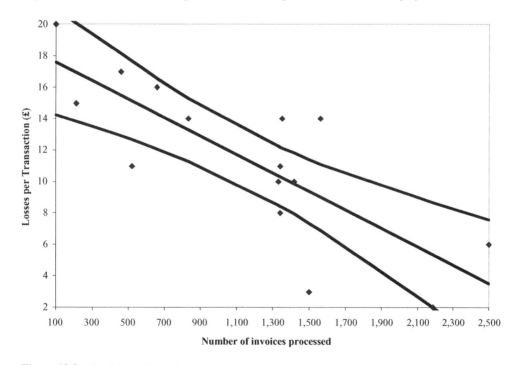

Figure 13.3   Confidence limits for number of invoices processed and losses per transaction.

the second row, the following equation from section 13.4 is used

$$\hat{a}x + \hat{b} \pm t_{n-2}(\alpha)s \sqrt{\frac{1}{n} + \frac{(x - \bar{x})^2}{\sum_{i=1}^{n}(x_i - \bar{x})^2}}$$

Here the gradient is $\hat{a} = -0.0059$ and the intercept is $\hat{b} = 18.19$.
   Since we are interested in the second row of Table 13.9

$$x = 213$$

and the fitted line is:

$$\hat{a}x_i + \hat{b} = -0.0059 \times 213 + 18.19 = 16.94$$

From Table 9.5 the appropriate value is:

$$t_{13}(0.025) = 2.16$$

To derive the confidence limits the following list of values are required:

$$\bar{x} = \frac{17,317}{15} = 1,154.47$$

$$\bar{y} = \frac{171}{15} = 11.40$$

$$s^2 = \frac{\sum_{i=1}^{n} y_i^2 - n\bar{y}^2 - \hat{a}\left(\sum_{i=1}^{n} x_i y_i\right) - n\bar{x}\,\bar{y}}{n - 2}$$

$$= \frac{2,313 - 15 \times 11.40^2 + 0.0059\,(158,557 - 15 \times 1,154.47 \times 11.40)}{13} = 10.40$$

Alternatively s^2 may be found from the ANOVA shown later as Table 13.11, since it is the mean square error.

$$s = 3.22$$

$$\sum_{i=1}^{n}(x_i - \bar{x})^2 = \sum_{i=1}^{n} x_i^2 - n\bar{x}^2 = 6,609,273.73$$

$$(x - \bar{x})^2 = 886,359.48$$

These values provide all the values required in the equation. So finally:

$$t_{n-2}(\alpha)s \sqrt{\frac{1}{n} + \frac{(x - \bar{x})^2}{\sum_{i=1}^{n}(x_i - \bar{x})^2}} = 2.16 \times 3.22 \sqrt{\frac{1}{15} + \frac{886,359.48}{6,609,273.73}} = 3.12$$

So for this point the limits are $16.94 \pm 3.12 = [13.82, 20.06]$. In other words, if we process 213 invoices we can be 95% certain that losses per transaction would be between £13.82 and £20.06 (see Figure 13.3).

   Often the original actual observations will not be shown, but they are of interest. You can see that some of the observations are outside the 95% confidence levels shown here, but that is the nature of the analysis – on average 5% of the transactions will be outside the tolerances set. What we are doing is trying to fit the data to enable intermediate readings to be taken and conclusions to be drawn.

This procedure must always be used with care. You must consider whether the data has been collected accurately and from sources that were reliable. Extrapolation outside the range of the data may also be unreliable and should be used with care.

This type of analysis is used when there is a series of observations of a pair of variables. As always, the more assumptions made, the higher the risk of the result being inappropriate. Obviously it makes sense to implement the procedures on a computer, if only for the superior graphics. Another warning is that it makes no sense to try to relate variables that in reality are totally unrelated.

To complete the analysis the figures shown in Table 13.9 are further combined to provide the key figures in Table 13.10.

The completed ANOVA calculation (see section 13.6) is presented in Table 13.11.

Taking the ratio of the entries in the final column gives $F = 21.97$, which should be compared with $F_{13}^1 (0.05) = 4.67$ (see Table 10.3). Since the calculated value exceeds the critical value

Table 13.9 Confidence limits for number of invoices processed and losses per transaction

				Confidence limits	
i	x_i	y_i	Fit $\hat{a}x_i + \hat{b}$	Upper	Lower
1	100	20	17.60	20.98	14.22
2	213	15	16.94	20.06	13.82
3	458	17	15.49	18.10	12.89
4	518	11	15.14	17.63	12.65
5	660	16	14.31	16.55	12.06
6	835	14	13.28	15.27	11.28
7	1,331	10	10.36	12.22	8.50
8	1,342	11	10.30	12.17	8.43
9	1,342	8	10.30	12.17	8.43
10	1,352	14	10.24	12.12	8.36
11	1,416	10	9.86	11.80	7.93
12	1,500	3	9.37	11.40	7.34
13	1,561	14	9.01	11.12	6.90
14	2,189	2	5.32	8.65	1.99
15	2,500	6	3.49	7.55	−0.58

Table 13.10 Key figures related to the number of invoices processed and losses per transaction

n	15	S_{xx}	6,609,273.73	$\bar{x}$	1,154.47	s_y	3.22
$\sum x$	17,317	S_{xy}	−38,856.80	$\bar{y}$	11.40	s_a	0.00
$\sum y$	171	S_{yy}	363.60			t_a	−4.69
$\sum x^2$	26,601,173			$\hat{a}$	−0.0059	s_b	1.67
$\sum xy$	158,557			$\hat{b}$	18.19	t_b	10.89
$\sum y^2$	2,313						

Table 13.11   The ANOVA table for the regression of number of invoices processed and losses per transaction

Source	Sum of squares of deviations	Degrees of freedom	Mean square
Regression	228.44	1	228.44
Error	135.16	13	10.40
Total	**363.60**	**14**	

Table 13.12   Key summary coefficients estimates

Predictor	Coefficient	Standard deviation	t-Ratio
Constant	18.19	1.67	10.89
Gradient	−0.006	0.001	4.69

it would appear that the coefficients are not all zero and the linear fit may be employed with confidence.

The most important of the values found may be conveniently summarised in Table 13.12.

Since $t_{13}(0.025) = 2.16$ (Table 9.5), the gradient $\hat{a}$ and intercept $\hat{b}$ are both significantly different from zero, confirming the validity of the derived equation.

14
Analysis of Variance

14.1 INTRODUCTION

Chapters 8 and 9 explained how you should compare the means of two populations. This concluded that if the underlying variances are known, a normal statistic could be employed. Similarly, a t statistic is required if this information is not available, or the sample sizes are too small. The next problem would be how to compare the means of more than two populations.

Given a large number of populations, it would be inefficient to run t tests on all possible pairs of means to try to pick up the individual correlations. If, for example, 10 populations were under consideration, then 45 ($_{10}C_2 = 45$) tests would be required. In addition, if we are trying to prove that the means are not significantly different ($\mu_1 = \mu_2 = \ldots = \mu_{10}$), say, at the 95% level, then the probability of each of the 45 samples being correct is $0.95^{45} = 0.0094$.

Therefore there is a large probability ($1 - 0.0994 = 0.9006$, or in excess of 90%) of actually rejecting a valid hypothesis and claiming that there is a difference when in fact none actually exists. This level of significance is far greater than the 5% that would be required. This anomaly arises since all that should really be tested is $\mu_{(1)} = \mu_{(2)} = \ldots = \mu_{(10)}$ for the ranked means ($\mu_{(1)} \leq \mu_{(2)} \leq \ldots \leq \mu_{(10)}$).

In order to avoid the problems outlined above, the significance of the difference between k populations needs to be tested, assuming that there are more than two populations that need to be tested simultaneously. This procedure is known as the analysis of variance, or ANOVA. The procedure is to partition the total variation into variations that may be assigned to specific causes and those attributable purely to chance. The latter group includes all of the variances caused by uncontrollable factors. The general mathematical formulation assumes that n items are sampled from each of the k populations.

14.2 FORMAL BACKGROUND TO THE ANOVA TABLE

Let y_{ij} denote the ith measurement taken from the jth specific cause. The means may be calculated for the k causes ($\bar{y}_1, \bar{y}_2, \ldots, \bar{y}_k$), using the techniques explained in Chapter 13. The overall mean, $\bar{y}$, can also then be calculated. Next the total sum of squares of the deviations, denoted by SST, is calculated using the following equation:

$$\text{SST} = \sum_{j=1}^{k}\sum_{i=1}^{n}(y_{ij} - \bar{y})^2 = \sum_{j=1}^{k}\sum_{i=1}^{n}y_{ij}^2 - \frac{1}{kn}\left(\sum_{j=1}^{k}\sum_{i=1}^{n}y_{ij}\right)^2 \tag{A}$$

since the average is calculated for the k causes and the n repeated measurements. The sum of squares for the causes, SSC, is the part of the total sum of squares that may be assigned to the causes themselves. The error sum of squares, SSE, is the sum of squares due to random or chance error. Therefore:

$$\text{SST} = \text{SSC}_1 + \text{SSC}_2 + \ldots + \text{SSC}_k + \text{SSE} = \text{SSC} + \text{SSE}$$

This means that you can modify equation (A) above to give:

$$\text{SSC} = \sum_{j=1}^{k} n\left(\bar{y}_j - \bar{y}\right)^2 = \frac{1}{n}\sum_{j=1}^{k}\left(\sum_{i=1}^{n} y_{ij}\right)^2 - \frac{1}{kn}\left(\sum_{j=1}^{k}\sum_{i=1}^{n} y_{ij}\right)^2$$

$$\text{SSE} = \sum_{j=1}^{k}\sum_{i=1}^{n}\left(y_{ij} - \bar{y}_j\right)^2$$

However, it is not always necessary to evaluate all of these expressions from first principles, since the ANOVA table must balance. When you divide the sums of squares by their degrees of freedom, the values for the mean square causes (MSC) and mean square errors (MSE) can then be calculated since:

$$\text{MSC} = \frac{\text{SSC}}{k-1} \quad \text{and} \quad \text{MSE} = \frac{\text{SSE}}{k(n-1)}$$

The appropriate values are displayed in an ANOVA as Table 14.1.

Table 14.1   General ANOVA table for k means

Source of variation	Sum of squares	Degrees of freedom ν	Mean square
Between causes	SSC	$k-1$	$\text{SSC}/(k-1)$
Within causes	SSE	$k(n-1)$	$\text{SSE}/(k(n-1))$
Total	**SST**	$\mathbf{kn-1}$	

14.3   ANALYSIS OF THE ANOVA TABLE

Using a formal statistical framework, the null hypothesis becomes $H_0: \mu_1 = \mu_2 = \ldots = \mu_k$. This is taken against the alternative hypothesis H_a, which is that one or more of the means will in fact differ. This would suggest that one type of cause differs.

The mean square error term (MSE) estimates the variability, σ^2, in the data regardless of whether H_0 is true or not. However, MSC estimates σ^2 only if H_0 is actually true. If H_a is accepted, the cause means appear to differ and MSC would then be the sum of two components, σ^2, plus a factor that represents these differences. In this case MSC > MSE, so the result of this is that the test reduces to just examining the two mean square values.

Using section 10.3, we know that an F statistic is appropriate for comparing variances, therefore:

$$F_{\text{calc}} = \frac{\text{MSC}}{\text{MSE}} \quad \text{is compared to} \quad F_{k(n-1)}^{k-1}(\alpha)$$

As outlined above, MSC will exceed MSE when H_0 is false and H_a is then rejected at a significance level α, when:

$$F_{\text{calc}} > F_{k(n-1)}^{k-1}(\alpha)$$

So this has simplified the problem into something that can be managed, which is what most statistical packages will choose to do. While you will not actually see the equations, these should be embedded within the package. There is a risk, however, that these equations will not actually have been accurately transposed and, consequently, some level of additional review is also required.

14.4   COMPARISON OF TWO CAUSAL MEANS

In the event that the null hypothesis is rejected – and we therefore conclude that cause differences cannot be explained as an effect due to chance fluctuations – it would be useful to locate the cause(s) whose mean(s) appear inconsistent. To locate a significant difference in the cause, the means are placed in numerical order.

As set out in Chapter 9, the appropriate test is a two-sample t test. Taking s_P^2 as the total population variance, then since we are comparing two means with the same variance, we pool them as set out in Chapter 9. The pooled variance is therefore given by:

$$s^2 = \frac{s_P^2}{n} + \frac{s_P^2}{n} = \frac{2s_P^2}{n}$$

From section 14.3 we can estimate the population variance from the estimate from our sample. Therefore, an estimate for s_P^2 is provided by MSE. This will enable us to assess if any two causal means are significantly different. Our objective is to locate causes whose means appear inconsistent with the remainder of the population. Then the least significant difference is given by:

$$t_{k(n-1)}(\alpha)s = t_{k(n-1)}(\alpha)\sqrt{\frac{2\text{MSE}}{n}}$$

Then since $s^2 = 2s_P^2/n$

$$s_P^2 = \text{MSE}$$

therefore,

$$s^2 = \frac{\text{MSE}}{n}$$

If we are asking whether $a \neq b$, then we use a one-tail test; however, since here we are asking whether $a > b$ or alternatively $a < b$, a two-tail test would be used.

This will become clearer when you consider the following practical example.

14.4.1   An example of extinguisher discharge times

A company is considering four different types of fire extinguisher to replace the existing systems after an office refit. The company decides to measure the efficiency of five examples of each extinguisher by comparing the length of time that each takes to discharge. The measurements are presented in Table 14.2. All the manufacturers have told the company that their two-litre extinguisher should discharge in 16 seconds.

In addition, the sum of squares is required. These figures are presented in Table 14.3 where 5,178 is the grand total of the times squared since

$$19^2 + \cdots + 15^2 = 361 + \ldots + 225 = 5,178$$

Table 14.4 contains the key values need to form the ANOVA table and the resulting ANOVA table is presented in Table 14.5

Table 14.2 Extinguisher discharge times

Samples	Causes 1	2	3	4	Sum
1	19	12	19	12	
2	13	17	15	10	
3	24	10	21	12	
4	16	20	11	13	
5	21	16	16	15	
Sum	**93**	**75**	**82**	**62**	**312**
Sum^2	**8,649**	**5,625**	**6,724**	**3,844**	**24,842**

Table 14.3 Extinguisher discharge times squared

Samples	Causes 1	2	3	4	Sum
1	361	144	361	144	
2	169	289	225	100	
3	576	100	441	144	
4	256	400	121	169	
5	441	256	256	225	
					5,178

Table 14.4 Summary values for extinguisher discharge times

4	k (number of types of extinguisher reviewed) columns
5	n (number of extinguishers sampled) rows
312	sum of all observations (from Table 14.2)
24,842	sum of squares of cause sums (from Table 14.2)
5,178	sum of all observations squared (from Table 14.3)

sum of squares of deviations

310.80
$$\text{SST} = \sum_{j=1}^{k}\sum_{i=1}^{n} y_{ij}^2 - \frac{1}{kn}\left(\sum_{j=1}^{k}\sum_{i=1}^{n} y_{ij}\right)^2$$

$$\text{SST} = 5{,}178 - \frac{1}{4 \times 5} 312^2$$

sum of squares for sample means

101.20
$$\text{SSC} = \frac{1}{n}\sum_{j=1}^{k}\left(\sum_{i=1}^{n} y_{ij}\right)^2 - \frac{1}{kn}\left(\sum_{j=1}^{k}\sum_{i=1}^{n} y_{ij}\right)^2$$

$$\text{SSC} = \frac{24{,}842}{5} - \frac{1}{4 \times 5} 312^2$$

Table 14.5   ANOVA for extinguisher discharge times

Source	SS	v	MS
Between samples	101.20	3	$33.73 = 101.20/3$
Within samples	209.60	16	$13.10 = 209.60/16$
Total	**310.80**	**19**	

As before, the highlighted values are found by subtraction ($209.60 = 310.80 - 101.20$). For the degrees of freedom, $3 = k - 1$ while $19 = kn - 1$ (see Table 14.1), the 16 being found by subtraction.

You are then able to compare $F_{calc} = 33.73/13.10 = 2.58$ with $F_{16}^3(0.05) = 3.24$ from section 10.3. Since 2.58 is less than 3.24, the means do not appear to differ statistically. There is apparently no difference between the discharge times for any of the extinguishers being tested, so the final decision will need to be made on the basis of other factors, such as price or availability.

As a double check on the calculations, a t test may be conducted on the causal means (see Chapter 9). In this case the critical value is $t_{16}(0.025) = 2.12$ (from Table 9.5) if you employ a two-tail test at 95% confidence. This leads to the conclusion that the least significant difference $(t_{k(n-1)}(\alpha)\sqrt{2MSE/n})$ is calculated by $2.12\sqrt{(2 \times 13.10)/5} = 4.85$, so any difference that is below this level will not matter. The sorted means are presented in Table 14.6.

Since all the differences are less than the least significant value (4.85), it is believed that the fire extinguishers are broadly the same. Another example will further highlight what we are seeking to achieve.

Table 14.6   Sorted means for extinguisher discharge times

Cause	4	2	3	1
Mean	12.4	15.0	16.4	18.6
Difference		2.6	1.4	2.2

14.4.2   An example of the lifetime of lamps

A company utilise a great number of lamps to illuminate the work place. To decide which of five suppliers is most appropriate, four bulbs are selected from each and tested to destruction. The lifetimes and required sums are shown in Table 14.7. Typically, lamps with LED bulbs are said to be bright, efficient, have a long lifetime (about 10,000–12,000 hours), and emit low heat, which means that there will be a saving in air-conditioning costs.

In addition, the sum of squares is required. The figures are presented in Table 14.8.

Here we have calculated the grand total of the observations squared,

$$11,753^2 + \cdots + 11,194^2 = 138,133,009 + \cdots + 125,305,636 = 2,426,619,850.$$

Table 14.9 contains the key values needed to form the ANOVA table, and the resulting ANOVA table is presented in Table 14.10. The remaining values, which are highlighted in Table 14.10, are found by ensuring that the table totals balance.

Table 14.7 Lamp lifetimes

Samples	Causes					Sum
	1	2	3	4	5	
1	11,753	10,701	10,141	11,750	11,609	
2	11,120	10,423	10,495	12,100	11,118	
3	11,124	10,635	10,285	11,818	10,356	
4	10,911	10,772	10,212	11,473	11,194	
Sum	**44,908**	**42,531**	**41,133**	**47,141**	**44,277**	**219,990**
Sum^2	**2,016,728,464**	**1,808,885,961**	**1,691,923,689**	**2,222,273,881**	**1,960,452,729**	**9,700,264,724**

Table 14.8 Lamp lifetimes squared

Samples	Causes					Sum
	1	2	3	4	5	
1	138,133,009	114,511,401	102,839,881	138,062,500	134,768,881	
2	123,654,400	108,638,929	110,145,025	146,410,000	123,609,924	
3	123,743,376	113,103,225	105,781,225	139,665,124	107,246,736	
4	119,049,921	116,035,984	104,284,944	131,629,729	125,305,636	
						2,426,619,850

Table 14.9   Summary values for lamp lifetimes

5	k (number of causes) columns
4	n (number of samples) rows
219,990	sum of all observations
9,700,264,724	sum of squares of cause sums
2,426,619,850	sum of all observations squared
6,839,845	sum of squares of deviations
5,286,176	sum of squares for sample means

Table 14.10   ANOVA table for lamp lifetimes

Source	SS	v	MS
Between samples	5,286,176	4	1,321,544.00
Within samples	1,553,669	15	103,577.93
Total	**6,839,845**	**19**	

Finally $F_{calc} = 12.76$ is compared with $F_{15}^{4}(0.05) = 3.03$ from Table 10.3 and we can conclude that in this case there is a difference and that one product would appear to be longer lasting than another.

To locate the mean or means that are different, a t test (Chapter 9) should be conducted on the product means. In this case the critical value is $t_{15}(0.025) = 2.13$, from Table 9.5, employing a two-tail test, since again we could get over- or under-statements, at a 95% confidence level. This leads to the least significant difference being 484.73, as shown below:

$$t_{k(n-1)}(\alpha)\sqrt{\frac{2MSE}{n}} = 2.13\sqrt{\frac{2 \times 103,577.93}{4}} = 484.73$$

This metric will then be used to see if there is any significant difference in the data. To do this the sorted means are required, and these should be compared to the least significant difference (484.73). Only those values that exceed this value will be considered significant. The sorted means are presented in Table 14.11.

Table 14.11   Sorted means for lamp lifetimes

Cause	3		2		5		1		4
Mean	10,283.25		10,632.75		11,069.25		11,227.00		11,785.25
Difference		349.50		436.50		157.75		558.25	

Since the only difference that exceeds the least significant value is between 1 and 4, the analysis has proved to be extremely useful. Not only do the means differ, but also one is significantly greater than the rest. It would be appropriate to select supplier 4 if this were the only criterion to be considered. If the company were to review in excess of 20 causes, then the procedure would become even more important since differences would be even harder to assess.

15
Design and Approach to the
Analysis of Data

15.1 INTRODUCTION

The preceding chapters have considered the analysis available when you have sampled data. However, in other cases, a company may need to develop an approach to the analysis prior to the data actually being sampled. The choice of the correct methodology is crucial since this will potentially improve both the effectiveness and efficiency of the data analysis that is to be conducted. Decisions will still need to be made at the outset, which will make use of management's experience, the financial impact of the decisions and prior knowledge of the variability of the expected results.

The following issues need to be addressed at the outset.

1. *The problem must be well defined.* Without knowing what you are trying to achieve you will not know how to achieve it. In practice, it is failure to identify the problem that often lets down the analysis. It results in an analysis methodology or approach being adopted that is either inconsistent with the objectives, or inconsistent with the data. Also, analysis can be undertaken where a crucial element could have been collected, but was not collected as it was not considered. In practice this can be both annoying and expensive.
2. *The size of the sample must be chosen.* In choosing the sample size you are taking a view on the level of resources you are willing to put into the project. Further resources will, of course, be required during the data analysis and consolidation phases. However, you are also taking a view as to the level of precision you require. Clearly if you sample a larger number of items you will achieve a greater level of accuracy, and therefore confidence in your conclusions.
3. *Decide how the data is to be collected.* Your objective is to collect data from a cross-section of the population. You need to assess whether all the information is in one place, or is in some other databases. If this is the case how are you intending to ensure that there is no bias in your population sampling technique, which would potentially invalidate your conclusions? Further, you need to make sure that all the data you need is collected at this stage.

This chapter falls into two distinct, but related, parts. Initially, we discuss some ways of designing tests that will need to be considered in practice. Then the chapter moves on to look at more general forms of analysis, which are then applied to some specific test designs. As always we use practical examples to enable you to use these techniques in practice.

15.2 RANDOMISED BLOCK DESIGN

It is essential that any investigation into a problem should be designed such that any errors that might occur within the analysis will be both unbiased and, where possible, minimised. Errors will often occur during the data collection or translation process. The data may be partially incomplete or simple processing or transposition errors could have been made. Alternatively a source for the data may be unreliable or omitted entirely. The technique that will be selected should be capable of dealing with random errors that might occur within the sampling population without undermining the results of the analysis. However, were a systematic error to be present within the sampling population then this would be likely to invalidate the analysis. It is therefore important to ensure that any systematic error is identified. To do this you should consider using a randomised block design. This is best demonstrated by an example.

15.2.1   An example of outsourcing

A company is considering outsourcing transaction processing. They need to make a comparison between the efficiency of processing transactions, by reviewing the performance of four different potential outsourced processing suppliers. In addition, the amount of time and money available will only allow the company to undertake four tests per supplier. Here each test, which is a group of individual selections, will be referred to as a block and the outsourced suppliers as causes.

The objective of the randomised block approach is to eliminate any form of bias from the analysis. For example, this could arise from the order in which the outsourced suppliers are tested, due to increased familiarity of the tester with the outsourcing market. It is assumed that the elements selected in each block are more homogeneous than would have been the case had the sample selection been made from the total population.

Given this assumption, any difference between the blocks, or samples, may be identified when conducting the analysis of the variances. The test error resulting from the application of this approach should be lower than that generated when using a completely randomised selection from the total population. Therefore, in a completely randomised design, to compare p suppliers means (see section 5.2.1) that the suppliers are randomly assigned to the test units. In other words, independent random samples are drawn from each of the p populations. This means that each of the blocks will include tests drawn from each of the outsourced suppliers.

The p (in this case four) outsourced suppliers are assigned, randomly, to the positions within each block, with one test being assigned per supplier. How this would potentially look for the outsourcing problem outlined above is shown in Table 15.1.

Here each supplier has a test occurring within each block, the order having been randomised. It is also important to see that some of the tests are not actually used at all. For example, when reviewing the first outsourced supplier, the results of tester B are not actually selected at all.

This becomes clearer when we consider another example. A company is considering what software to purchase and wants to see how long it will take to load the software onto a set

Table 15.1   A randomised block design

| Block | Outsourced supplier | | | |
	1	2	3	4
1	D	C	A	B
2	A	D	B	C
3	A	B	C	D
4	C	B	A	D

of PCs prior to going for a global product implementation. The company is intending to test three types of software on 10 PCs, with a standard and identical test being conducted in each case. Treating the PCs as blocks and using a randomised block design, 10 PCs are required to obtain 10 software implementation measurements. However, a completely randomised design would require $3 \times 10 = 30$ PCs to achieve the same level of information. This demonstrates that the use of a randomised block design significantly reduces the amount of resources needed to conduct the test.

For a completely randomised design the blocking term is omitted. However, in some cases blocking will be considered to be impractical, or management may just not believe that it can provide the benefits that we have set out. In these cases a further approach could be considered.

15.3   LATIN SQUARES

In a 1782 paper, Euler started by stating the problem of the 36 officers. This problem asks for an arrangement of 36 officers of six ranks and from six regiments in a square formation of size six by six. Each vertical and each horizontal line of this formation is to contain one and only one officer of each rank and one and only one officer from each regiment. Euler denoted the six regiments by the Latin letters **a, b, c, d, e, f** and the six ranks by the Greek letters α, β, γ, δ, ε, ζ. He further remarked that the two letters, one Latin and the other Greek, determined the characteristic of an officer and that the problem consists of arranging the 36 combinations of two letters in a square in such a manner that every row and every column contains the six Latin as well as the six Greek letters. This was the origin of the term 'Greco-Latin Square'. Euler observed that the first step was to arrange the Latin letters in a square so that no letter was missing either from any row or from any column. He called this square a Latin square.

Taking this idea into a commercial situation, a company is conducting an investigation to test five computers from an available test population of 25 computers. The problem is that only five tests can be performed on any day due to time constraints and management have decided that they do not want to partition the samples into blocks. To avoid variations that may arise from testing being conducted on different days, each daily selection of five items is treated as a block. Then tests are assigned randomly to each day and to one of the five computers (A, B, C, D, E). There is an additional constraint that each of the five computers must be tested on each day. A further factor that might be allowed for is to take account of the time of day when the test was commenced. This can also be introduced into the design, as shown in Table 15.2.

Clearly on any day (row) and at any time (column) each test occurs only once. The procedure gets its name since the number of items tested is the square of the number of objects being

Table 15.2   A Latin squares design

	17:00	18:30	19:00	20:30	21:00
Day 1	A	B	C	D	E
Day 2	E	A	B	C	D
Day 3	D	E	A	B	C
Day 4	C	D	E	A	B
Day 5	B	C	D	E	A

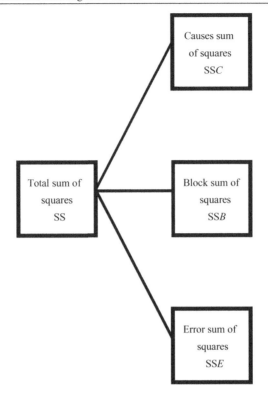

Figure 15.1   Partition of the total sum of squares (1).

tested. In this case it is $5^2 = 25$. The analysis will partition the total sum of squares along the lines displayed in Figure 15.1.

More complex problems can also be dealt with in this way. For instance, a two-factor model with some overlap between the properties of each factor would lead to the partition of the sum of squares displayed in Figure 15.2.

15.4   ANALYSIS OF A RANDOMISED BLOCK DESIGN

As we move towards looking at practical applications of these ideas, we first need to look at a series of mathematical notation that we actually use later in this chapter. When we are seeking to analyse the block design, the key parameters are:

b = number of measurements for a single object

p = number of measurements in a single block

n = total number of measurements in the complete investigation ($n = bp$)

The observations may be combined to give the following totals:

$T_1, \ldots, T_p$ the object totals, each summing b measurements for a single object

$B_1, \ldots, B_b$ the block totals, each summing p measurements for a single block

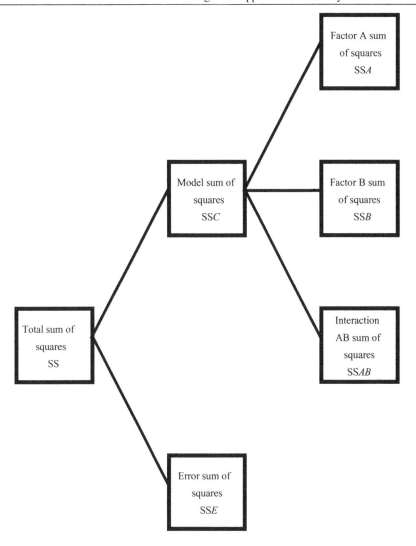

Figure 15.2   Partition of the total sum of squares (2).

These totals are further combined to give the key variables:

$$A = \sum_{i=1}^{n} y_i \quad \text{the sum of all measurements taken}$$

$$B = \sum_{i=1}^{n} y_i^2 \quad \text{the sum of squares of all measurements taken}$$

$$C = \frac{1}{n} \left(\sum_{i=1}^{n} y_i \right)^2 = \frac{A^2}{n} \quad \text{the mean correction term}$$

Table 15.3   ANOVA table for a randomised block design

Source	Sum of squares	v	Mean square	F statistic
Causes	SSC	$p-1$	$MSC = SSC/(p-1)$	MSC/MSE
Blocks	SSB	$b-1$	$MSB = SSB/(b-1)$	MSB/MSE
Error	SSE	$n-b-p+1$	$MSE = SSE/(n-b-p+1)$	
Total	**SS**	$n-1$		

The required sums of squares are

$$SS = \sum_{i=1}^{n} y_i^2 - C = B - C \quad \text{the total sum of squares}$$

$$SSC = \frac{1}{b} \sum_{i=1}^{p} T_i^2 - C \quad \text{the sum of squares for causes}$$

$$SSB = \frac{1}{p} \sum_{i=1}^{b} B_i^2 - C \quad \text{the sum of squares for blocks}$$

$$SSE = SS - SSC - SSB \quad \text{the error sum of squares}$$

Using these equations we can devise an equation for the required mean square values:

$$MSC = \frac{SSC}{p-1} \quad \text{the mean square for causes}$$

$$MSB = \frac{SSB}{b-1} \quad \text{the mean square for blocks}$$

$$MSE = \frac{SSE}{n-p-b+1} \quad \text{the error mean square}$$

The summary ANOVA tabulation is presented in Table 15.3, which immediately suggests two possibilities since there are two F statistics.

(1) *Is there a difference between the p object means?*
   The null hypothesis H_0 is that all the means are apparently the same, whereas the alternative hypothesis H_a is that at least two of the means differ. Together these cover all possibilities and are shown mathematically as:

H_0: $\mu_1 = \mu_2 = \ldots = \mu_p$
H_a: at least two of the cause means differ

Using the test statistic from section 10.3, the test statistic becomes:

$$F_{\text{calc}} = \frac{MSC}{MSE}$$

This is then compared to:

$$F_{n-p-b+1}^{p-1}(\alpha)$$

This then has a rejection region for $F > F(\alpha)$.

(2) *Is there a difference between the b block means?*

Similar to the above in respect of the blocks, the null hypothesis H_0 is that all the means are apparently the same, whereas the alternative hypothesis H_a is that at least two of the means differ. Together these cover all possibilities and are shown mathematically as:

H_0: $v_1 = v_2 = \ldots = v_b$

H_a: at least two of the block means differ

In this case the test statistic becomes:

$$F_{\text{calc}} = \frac{\text{MSB}}{\text{MSE}}$$

This is then compared to:

$$F_{n-p-b+1}^{b-1}(\alpha)$$

The rejection region in this case is now $F > F(\alpha)$.

If required, the confidence intervals may be constructed for the population means. Therefore, using the equation from section 14.4 for the objects, the confidence interval is:

$$\left(\bar{T}_i - \bar{T}_j\right) \pm t_{n-b-p+1}\left(\frac{\alpha}{2}\right)\sqrt{\frac{2\text{MSE}}{b}}$$

while for the block means, the confidence interval is given by:

$$\left(\bar{B}_i - \bar{B}_j\right) \pm t_{n-b-p+1}\left(\frac{\alpha}{2}\right)\sqrt{\frac{2\text{MSE}}{p}}$$

15.5 ANALYSIS OF A TWO-WAY CLASSIFICATION

The key parameters are

a = number of levels of independent factor 1

b = number of levels of independent factor 2

r = number of measurements for each pair of levels of factors 1 and 2

$n = a \times b \times r$ the total number of measurements taken.

The observations may be combined to give the following totals.

$A_1, \ldots, A_a$ the total of all measurements of factor 1 at levels $1, \ldots, a$

$B_1, \ldots, B_b$ the total of all measurements of factor 2 at levels $1, \ldots, b$

AB_{ij} the total of all measurements of factor 1 at level $i(i = 1, \ldots, a)$ and factor 2 at level $j(j = 1, \ldots, b)$.

These have the following associated averages:

$\bar{A}_i = \dfrac{A_i}{br}$ the mean of measurements for factor 1 at levels $i = 1, \ldots, a$

$\bar{B}_i = \dfrac{B_i}{ar}$ the mean of measurements for factor 2 at levels $i = 1, \ldots, b$

These totals should then be further combined to give the following key variables:

$$A = \sum_{i=1}^{n} y_i \quad \text{the sum of all measurements taken}$$

$$B = \sum_{i=1}^{n} y_i^2 \quad \text{the sum of squares of all measurements taken}$$

$$C = \frac{1}{n} \left(\sum_{i=1}^{n} y_i \right)^2 = \frac{A^2}{n} \quad \text{the mean correction term}$$

Then you can calculate the sums of squares that are now required, using the following equations:

$$SS = \sum_{i=1}^{n} y_i^2 - C = B - C \quad \text{the total sum of squares}$$

$$SSA = \frac{1}{br} \sum_{i=1}^{a} A_i^2 - C \quad \text{the sum of squares for factor 1}$$

$$SSB = \frac{1}{ar} \sum_{i=1}^{b} B_i^2 - C \quad \text{the sum of squares for factor 2}$$

$$SSAB = \frac{1}{r} \sum_{i=1}^{a} \sum_{j=1}^{b} AB_{ij}^2 - SSA - SSB - C \quad \begin{array}{l} \text{the sum of squares for the interaction of} \\ \text{both factors} \end{array}$$

$$SSE = SS - SSA - SSB - SSAB \quad \text{the error sum of squares}$$

Since we always divide the sum of squares by their degrees of freedom to get the mean square, which will then be summarised in the ANOVA table, this leads to the mean square values, which are now required, as follows:

$$MSA = \frac{SSA}{a - 1} \quad \text{the mean square for factor 1}$$

$$MSB = \frac{SSB}{b - 1} \quad \text{the mean square for factor 2}$$

$$MSAB = \frac{SSAB}{(a - 1)(b - 1)} \quad \text{the mean square for the interaction between causes } A \text{ and } B$$

$$MSE = \frac{SSE}{ab(r - 1)} \quad \text{the error mean square}$$

The summary ANOVA table is presented in Table 15.4. The comparative F values are then obtained from Tables 10.2, 10.3 and 10.4.

Table 15.4   ANOVA table for a two-way classification

Source	Sum of squares	v	Mean square	F statistic
Factor A	SSA	$a - 1$	$MSA = SSA/(a - 1)$	MSA/MSE
Factor B	SSB	$b - 1$	$MSB = SSB/(b - 1)$	MSB/MSE
Factor AB	SSAB	$(a - 1)(b - 1)$	$MSAB = SSAB/((a - 1)(b - 1))$	$MSAB/MSE$
Error	SSE	$ab(r - 1)$	$MSE = SSE/(ab(r - 1))$	
Total	**SS**	$abr - 1$		

This may all seem a rather lengthy exercise, but the equations do enable you to solve the kind of problems that you will face in practice and will improve the quality of the analysis that you conduct.

There are three different hypotheses that would need to be addressed in this type of problem:

1. *Is there any interaction between the two factors A and B?*

   H_0: This is the assumption that the two factors are completely independent and there is no interaction between factors A and B

   H_a: This is the assumption that there is some interaction between the two factors and so they are not completely independent.

   To use the model we consider the F test statistic $F = MSAB/MSE$, which is compared to $F_{ab(r-1)}^{(a-1)(b-1)}(\alpha)$, with a rejection region $MSAB/MBE > F(\alpha)$.

2. *Is there a difference between the means for factor A?*

   H_0: $\mu_1 = \mu_2 = \ldots = \mu_a$

   H_a: at least two of the factor A means differ

   The test statistic becomes $F = MSA/MSE$, which is compared to $F_{ab(r-1)}^{a-1}(\alpha)$, with a rejection region for $F > F(\alpha)$.

3. *Is there a difference between the means for factor B?*

   H_0: $v_1 = v_2 = \ldots = v_b$

   H_a: at least two of the factor B means differ

   The test statistic becomes $F = MSB/MSE$, which is compared to $F_{ab(r-1)}^{b-1}(\alpha)$, with a rejection region for $F > F(\alpha)$.

Again, if required, confidence intervals may be constructed for the population means. This is achieved by knowing that for the specific cell (i, j) the interval is:

$$\bar{y}_{ij} \pm t_{ab(r-1)}\left(\frac{\alpha}{2}\right)\sqrt{\frac{MSE}{r}}$$

If you have a pair of cell means, the interval is:

$$(\bar{y}_1 - \bar{y}_2) \pm t_{ab(r-1)}\left(\frac{\alpha}{2}\right)\sqrt{\frac{2MSE}{r}}$$

since there were two factors. To show how this might work in practice, let us consider three detailed examples.

15.5.1   An example of two-way analysis

A company wish to investigate the influence of illumination type and background music on the errors generated by their employees. Three background music styles were chosen and two illumination types were also selected. Limitations on resources only permitted three selections to be taken of each combination, with each sampled item being returned to the total population after selection so that it might be selected again. The resulting numbers of daily errors are shown in Table 15.5.

To analyse the results of this investigation, an ANOVA table should be constructed. From this you will be able to obtain evidence on the interaction between the illumination type and the type of background music and, more importantly, how these affect the errors generated.

To assist in following the calculations the data is presented as a series of sorted columns (Tables 15.6 and 15.7). For brevity, illumination type is referred to as factor A and background music as factor B.

Table 15.5 Two-way analysis of daily error reports

		Background music		
Illumination type	Selections	1	2	3
1	1	3	10	4
	2	4	6	9
	3	6	3	12
2	1	9	10	13
	2	7	9	10
	3	6	9	9

Table 15.6 Sorted values from daily error reports

A	B	Data	Data^2	Cumulative sum for A	A sum^2
1	1	3	9	3	
1	1	4	16	7	
1	1	6	36	13	
1	2	10	100	23	
1	2	6	36	29	
1	2	3	9	32	
1	3	4	16	36	
1	3	9	81	45	
1	3	12	144	57	3,249
2	1	9	81	9	
2	1	7	49	16	
2	1	6	36	22	
2	2	10	100	32	
2	2	9	81	41	
2	2	9	81	50	
2	3	13	169	63	
2	3	10	100	73	
2	3	9	81	82	6,724
Sum		**139**	**1,225**		**9,973**
n		**18**	**18**		**2**

Table 15.7 Sums required of resorted daily error reports

A	B	Data	Cumulative sum for B	B sum²	Cumulative sum for AB	AB sum²
1	1	3	3		3	
1	1	4	7		7	
1	1	6	13		13	169
2	1	9	22		9	
2	1	7	29		16	
2	1	6	35	1,225	22	484
1	2	10	10		10	
1	2	6	16		16	
1	2	3	19		19	361
2	2	10	29		10	
2	2	9	38		19	
2	2	9	47	2,209	28	784
1	3	4	4		4	
1	3	9	13		13	
1	3	12	25		25	625
2	3	13	38		13	
2	3	10	48		23	
2	3	9	57	3,249	32	1,024
Sum				**6,683**		**3,447**
n				**3**		**6**

The key values are

$a = 2$
$b = 3$
$r = 3$
$n = abr = 18$

We then need to use the following equations, which are all taken from section 15.5.

$$A = \sum_{i=1}^{n} y_i = 139$$

$$B = \sum_{i=1}^{n} y_i^2 = 1{,}225$$

$$C = \frac{1}{n}\left(\sum_{i=1}^{n} y_i\right)^2 = \frac{A^2}{n} = \frac{139^2}{18}$$

The following sum of squares may then be calculated, again using the equations from above:

$$SSA = \frac{1}{br}\sum_{i=1}^{a} A_i^2 - C = \frac{9{,}973}{3 \times 3} - \frac{139^2}{18} = 34.72$$

$$SSB = \frac{1}{ar}\sum_{i=1}^{b} B_i^2 - C = \frac{6{,}683}{2 \times 3} - \frac{139^2}{18} = 40.44$$

Table 15.8   ANOVA table for daily error reports

Source	Sum of squares	ν	Mean square	F statistic
Factor A	34.72	1	34.72	5.48
Factor B	40.44	2	20.22	3.19
Factor AB	0.44	2	0.22	0.04
Error	76.00	12	6.33	
Total	**151.61**	**17**		

$$SSAB = \frac{1}{r}\sum_{i=1}^{a}\sum_{j=1}^{b}AB_{ij}^2 - SSA - SSB - C = \frac{3,447}{3} - \frac{139^2}{18} - 34.72 - 40.44 = 0.44$$

$$SS = B - C = 1,225 - \frac{139^2}{18} = 151.61$$

The ANOVA table can now be constructed, and is displayed in Table 15.8.

There is now enough information to enable the required analysis to be completed and the problem solved. The first question is whether the two factors are actually totally independent.

The calculated value is $F = 0.04$, which is compared with $F_{12}^2(0.05) = 3.89$ from Table 10.3. Therefore, the two factors do appear to be independent, and the effect of light and noise are apparently unrelated.

Assuming that the types of illumination (factor A) were selected at random, then the effect of illumination type (factor B) may also be examined. The calculated value in this case is:

$$F = \frac{34.72}{0.22} = 156.25$$

which is much more than $F_2^1(0.05) = 18.51$ from Table 10.3. This therefore provides strong evidence that illumination type does affect the frequency of errors generated.

For the background music (effect B), the calculated value is $F = 3.19$, which is less than $F_{12}^2(0.05) = 3.89$, again taken from Table 10.3. Therefore it would appear that, with a 95% confidence level, the background music does not appear to affect the errors generated.

Finally, if the illuminations (effect A) were chosen specifically, rather than at random, then the illumination type could also be examined. The calculated value now becomes $F = 5.48$ which is more than $F_{12}^1(0.05) = 4.75$ from Table 10.3, so there is evidence that the illumination type does affect the number of errors generated.

15.5.2   An example of a randomised block

A company intends to conduct an investigation to find out what is the ideal workplace temperature for maximum business efficiency. They decide that this will be measured by reviewing the number of tasks completed. Processing an invoice or answering a call would both be considered as tasks for this purpose. Five slightly increasing temperatures have been selected as being suitable for testing, the lowest being referred to as 1 and the highest, 5. Four blocks are then made up from selections for each of the different temperatures. The data are presented in Table 15.9.

Table 15.9   Randomised block for completed tasks and temperature

Block	Temperature level				
	1	2	3	4	5
1	165	165	206	202	223
2	154	161	194	185	219
3	151	179	182	219	221
4	149	164	183	201	208

Table 15.10   Sums required of completed tasks

B	R	Data	Data^2	Cumulative sum for B	B sum^2
1	1	165	27,225	165	
1	2	154	23,716	319	
1	3	151	22,801	470	
1	4	149	22,201	619	383,161
2	1	165	27,225	165	
2	2	161	25,921	326	
2	3	179	32,041	505	
2	4	164	26,896	669	447,561
3	1	206	42,436	206	
3	2	194	37,636	400	
3	3	182	33,124	582	
3	4	183	33,489	765	585,225
4	1	202	40,804	202	
4	2	185	34,225	387	
4	3	219	47,961	606	
4	4	201	40,401	807	651,249
5	1	223	49,729	223	
5	2	219	47,961	442	
5	3	221	48,841	663	
5	4	208	43,264	871	758,641
Sum		**3,731**	**707,897**		**2,825,837**
n		20	20		20

An ANOVA table is then constructed to aid in assessing the effect that the temperature has on the number of tasks completed. In addition, the company will want to know what can be stated about the uniformity of the original samples.

To assist in following the calculations, the data is presented as a series of sorted columns (see Tables 15.10 and 15.11). For brevity the temperature blocks are referred to as B and the items to be tested as R.

The key values are

$B = 5$
$R = 4$
$n = BR = 20$

Table 15.11 Sums required of sorted completed tasks

B	R	Data	Cumulative sum	R sum^2
1	1	165	165	
2	1	165	330	
3	1	206	536	
4	1	202	738	
5	1	223	961	923,521
1	2	154	154	
2	2	161	315	
3	2	194	509	
4	2	185	694	
5	2	219	913	833,569
1	3	151	151	
2	3	179	330	
3	3	182	512	
4	3	219	731	
5	3	221	952	906,304
1	4	149	149	
2	4	164	313	
3	4	183	496	
4	4	201	697	
5	4	208	905	819,025
Sum				**3,482,419**
n				**20**

All the following equations are again taken from section 15.5:

$$A = \sum_{i=1}^{n} y_i = 3,731$$

$$B = \sum_{i=1}^{n} y_i^2 = 707,897$$

$$C = \frac{1}{n}\left(\sum_{i=1}^{n} y_i\right)^2 = \frac{A^2}{n} = \frac{3,731^2}{20}$$

The following sum of squares may then be calculated

$$SSA = \frac{1}{R}\sum_{i=1}^{B} A_i^2 - C = \frac{2,825,837 \times 5}{20} - \frac{3,731^2}{20} = 10,441.20$$

$$SSR = \frac{1}{B}\sum_{i=1}^{R} B_i^2 - C = \frac{3,482,419 \times 4}{20} - \frac{3,731^2}{20} = 465.75$$

$$SS = B - C = 707,897 - \frac{3,731^2}{20} = 11,878.95$$

The ANOVA table is now constructed in Table 15.12.
    The required tests may now be performed.

Table 15.12 ANOVA table for completed tasks

Source	Sum of squares	ν	Mean square	F statistic
Blocks	104,41.20	4	2,610.30	32.23
Tests	465.75	3	155.25	1.92
Error	972.00	12	81.00	
Total	**11,878.95**	**19**		

For the blocks, the F statistic (see Table 15.12) is 32.23, which is then compared with $F_{12}^4(0.05) = 3.26$ (from Table 10.3). The implication from this is that temperature does appear to affect the number of tasks completed.

For the test repetitions we have an F statistic of 1.92, which is less than $F_{12}^3(0.05) = 3.49$. There would therefore appear to be nothing that suggests that the samples themselves are unreasonable. However, notice that everything has been calculated at a 95% confidence level, which will certainly be sufficient for most management decisions of this type. It means that one time in 20 an incorrect conclusion will be drawn from the analysis. If you were trying to look at something where a higher level of certainty was required, then a confidence level of perhaps 99% or even 99.9% should be selected.

As always in mathematical analysis, the results are only as good as the data, the modelling and the assumptions. Any assumptions that have been made (for example, that work will be conducted at a 95% confidence level) should be clearly set out on any reports that are provided to management so that they can assess whether they are content with this assumption.

15.5.3   An example of the use of the Latin square

Consider a company that is seeking to change the computers in a processing area. There is any number of products available, so they decide to undertake a test on a series of potential products. The question they are trying to assess is whether monitor and keyboard type in itself affects the rate of data processing. If it does, it will provide another factor to be considered in conjunction with price, reliability and availability.

The experiment was conducted using six operators (A, B, C, D, E, F), chosen at random, working at six different monitor types with six different keyboard styles for one hour. The data recording the number of transaction forms completed are recorded in Table 15.13.

Table 15.13 Latin square of completed transactions for selected monitor/keyboard

Monitor type	Keyboard type											
	1		2		3		4		5		6	
1	A	12	E	10	D	8	C	12	B	13	F	16
2	D	10	A	8	C	11	E	15	F	14	B	16
3	E	11	C	9	B	12	F	13	D	14	A	15
4	C	9	F	6	E	9	B	11	A	15	D	14
5	F	7	B	10	A	7	D	15	E	15	C	14
6	B	9	D	6	F	8	A	12	C	13	E	16

The three factors can all be reviewed:

- the type of keyboard
- the type of monitor
- the operator.

Once again the first thing to do is to set the data out in a series of sorted columns as in Tables 15.14, 15.15 and 15.16.

Table 15.14   Data sorted by monitor type

Monitor	Keyboard	Operator	Data	Data^2	Cumulative sum	Monitor sum^2
1	1	A	12	144	12	
1	2	D	10	100	22	
1	3	E	11	121	33	
1	4	C	9	81	42	
1	5	F	7	49	49	
1	6	B	9	81	58	3,364
2	1	E	10	100	10	
2	2	A	8	64	18	
2	3	C	9	81	27	
2	4	F	6	36	33	
2	5	B	10	100	43	
2	6	D	6	36	49	2,401
3	1	D	8	64	8	
3	2	C	11	121	19	
3	3	B	12	144	31	
3	4	E	9	81	40	
3	5	A	7	49	47	
3	6	F	8	64	55	3,025
4	1	C	12	144	12	
4	2	E	15	225	27	
4	3	F	13	169	40	
4	4	B	11	121	51	
4	5	D	15	225	66	
4	6	A	12	144	78	6,084
5	1	B	13	169	13	
5	2	F	14	196	27	
5	3	D	14	196	41	
5	4	A	15	225	56	
5	5	E	15	225	71	
5	6	C	13	169	84	7,056
6	1	F	16	256	16	
6	2	B	16	256	32	
6	3	A	15	225	47	
6	4	D	14	196	61	
6	5	C	14	196	75	
6	6	E	16	256	91	8,281
Sum			**415**	**5,109**		**30,211**
n			**36**	**36**		**6**

Table 15.15   Sums required of data sorted by keyboard type

Monitor	Keyboard	Operator	Data	Cumulative sum	Keyboard sum^2
1	1	A	12	12	
2	1	E	10	22	
3	1	D	8	30	
4	1	C	12	42	
5	1	B	13	55	
6	1	F	16	71	5,041
1	2	D	10	10	
2	2	A	8	18	
3	2	C	11	29	
4	2	E	15	44	
5	2	F	14	58	
6	2	B	16	74	5,476
1	3	E	11	11	
2	3	C	9	20	
3	3	B	12	32	
4	3	F	13	45	
5	3	D	14	59	
6	3	A	15	74	5,476
1	4	C	9	9	
2	4	F	6	15	
3	4	E	9	24	
4	4	B	11	35	
5	4	A	15	50	
6	4	D	14	64	4,096
1	5	F	7	7	
2	5	B	10	17	
3	5	A	7	24	
4	5	D	15	39	
5	5	E	15	54	
6	5	C	14	68	4,624
1	6	B	9	9	
2	6	D	6	15	
3	6	F	8	23	
4	6	A	12	35	
5	6	C	13	48	
6	6	E	16	64	4,096
Sum					**28,809**
n					**6**

The key values are

monitor $= 6$
keyboard $= 6$
operators $= 6$
$n \qquad = 36$

Table 15.16 Data sorted by operator

Monitor	Keyboard	Operator	Data	Cumulative sum	Operator sum^2
1	1	A	12	12	
2	2	A	8	20	
6	3	A	15	35	
5	4	A	15	50	
3	5	A	7	57	
4	6	A	12	69	4,761
5	1	B	13	13	
6	2	B	16	29	
3	3	B	12	41	
4	4	B	11	52	
2	5	B	10	62	
1	6	B	9	71	5,041
4	1	C	12	12	
3	2	C	11	23	
2	3	C	9	32	
1	4	C	9	41	
6	5	C	14	55	
5	6	C	13	68	4,624
3	1	D	8	8	
1	2	D	10	18	
5	3	D	14	32	
6	4	D	14	46	
4	5	D	15	61	
2	6	D	6	67	4,489
2	1	E	10	10	
4	2	E	15	25	
1	3	E	11	36	
3	4	E	9	45	
5	5	E	15	60	
6	6	E	16	76	5,776
6	1	F	16	16	
5	2	F	14	30	
4	3	F	13	43	
2	4	F	6	49	
1	5	F	7	56	
3	6	F	8	64	4,096
Sum					**28,787**
n					**6**

All the following equations are again required and are taken from section 15.5:

$$A = \sum_{i=1}^{n} y_i = 415$$

$$B = \sum_{i=1}^{n} y_i^2 = 5,109$$

$$C = \frac{1}{n}\left(\sum_{i=1}^{n} y_i\right)^2 = \frac{A^2}{n} = \frac{415^2}{36}$$

Table 15.17 ANOVA table for completed transactions

Source	Sum of squares	ν	Mean square	F statistic
Monitor	251.14	5	50.23	23.61
Keyboard	17.47	5	3.49	1.64
Operators	13.81	35	2.76	1.30
Error	42.56	20	2.13	
Total	**324.97**	**35**		

The following sum of squares then need to be calculated:

$$SS_{monitor} = \frac{1}{monitor} \sum_{i=1}^{monitor} A_i^2 - C = \frac{30,211}{6} - \frac{415^2}{36} = 251.14$$

$$SS_{keyboard} = \frac{1}{keyboard} \sum_{i=1}^{keyboard} A_i^2 - C = \frac{28,809}{6} - \frac{415^2}{36} = 17.47$$

$$SS_{operators} = \frac{1}{operators} \sum_{i=1}^{operators} A_i^2 - C = \frac{28,787}{6} - \frac{415^2}{36} = 13.81$$

$$SS = B - C = 5,109 - \frac{415^2}{36} = 324.97$$

You can then construct the ANOVA table as set out in Table 15.17.

We now have sufficient information for the required investigation to be performed. For the monitor, the F statistic is 23.61, whereas for the keyboard the figure is 1.64 and for the operators 1.30. Each of these should then be compared to $F_{20}^5(0.05) = 2.71$ (see Table 10.3). Therefore, since only the monitor F test is a lot larger than the crucial amount, the other choices are then down to other factors, for example reliability, price and availability. However, in the case of the monitors, it is clear that there is a significant difference (with a 95% confidence level) in the results from their usage.

By examining the sorted means (Table 15.18) for the six monitor types it is clear that they fall into two groups. Monitor 6 appears to be superior, although compromise models would be model 5 and model 4.

Table 15.18 Mean rates of data processing by monitor

Monitor	Mean rates of data processing
2	8.17
3	9.17
1	9.67
4	13.00
5	14.00
6	15.17

16

Linear Programming: Graphical Method

16.1 INTRODUCTION

Typically in business when you are trying to make a decision there will be a range of restrictions and constraints that you will need to consider, for example:

- the price of the solution
- the length of time the solution will take to implement
- the human resources required to implement the solution
- the credit quality of the solution to the vendor.

All these issues will need to be taken into consideration. Typically what you need to do is change the problem into something that you can solve mathematically effectively changing a practical problem into a series of linear expressions. Using these equations as a framework you can then locate an optimal solution by using graphical techniques. Indeed, in practice, this is what the systems you will be using are actually doing; although the mathematics will be embedded and therefore almost invisible.

16.2 PRACTICAL EXAMPLES

Your challenge is to find out how to express the problem as a mathematical model, with the elements of the problem becoming variables in a series of linear equations or inequalities.

16.2.1 An example of an optimum investment strategy

A fund manager has a small high-risk portfolio that needs to be fully invested and at present £50,000 is sitting in a cash deposit account. The fund manager is keen to change the mix of investments in the fund and has identified two different asset classes that could add value to the portfolio. The first is to invest some or all of the £50,000 in a one-year fixed income debenture paying a rate of 7%. The alternative is to invest in a venture capital transaction with a partial guarantee backing, providing a certain return of 4%, but with the potential of earning a 12% return. The fund manager's objective is to invest the minimum amount necessary to achieve a potential return of £3,000 and a guaranteed return of at least £1,500. The question is how little can be invested in these investments to provide maximum cash for the fund manager for additional investments that may come forward in the future.

Denoting the amount invested in the debenture as 'debenture' and that invested in the venture capital transaction as 'VC', then the key values are summarised in Table 16.1.

For the purpose of this example we are considering the debenture rate as being guaranteed and are ignoring credit risk. Since the total budget is limited, it follows that the amount invested

Table 16.1 A summary of the key figures for an optimum investment strategy

	Debenture	VC	Limit
Cost	1	1	50,000
Guarantee	7%	4%	1,500
Potential	7%	12%	3,000

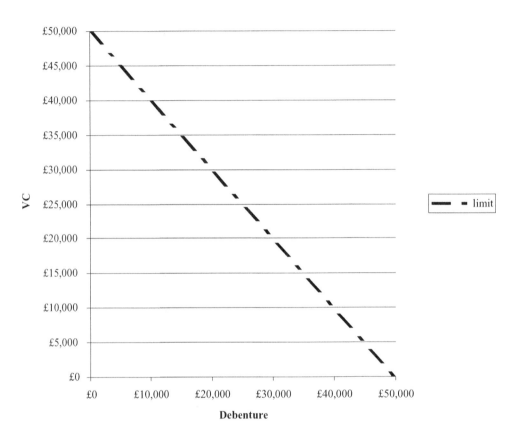

Figure 16.1   The upper limit on the investment.

in the debenture, when added to the amount invested in venture capital, must be less than or equal to £50,000

$$\text{Debenture} + \text{VC} \le 50{,}000$$

This limiting condition is shown graphically in Figure 16.1.

The line plotted represents a border; acceptable options lie to one side of this partition and inappropriate options on the other. The simplest way to deduce which region is acceptable is to check a typical point. For example, would (0,0) be consistent with the equation? Clearly by making no investments at all, then less than £50,000 has actually been spent. Therefore, the feasible region is contained in the triangle bounded by the axes and the diagonal line representing the maximum investment that could be made.

You can then look to changing the guarantees into some form of equation. The debenture will yield 7% so, ignoring credit risk issues, this becomes certain. Likewise a 4% return on the venture capital investment is guaranteed, again ignoring credit risk. Finally a return of at least £1,500 is required. This can then be turned into the following equation:

$$0.07 \times \text{Value invested in debenture} + 0.04$$
$$\times \text{Value invested in venture capital} \geq 1,500$$

In terms of the potential returns, the debenture can only offer the certain return of 7%, again ignoring credit risk, whereas the venture capital investment is estimated, potentially, to have a 12% return. The boundary criterion is that the investments could achieve a return in excess of £3,000. The equation to show this then becomes:

$$0.07 \times \text{Amount invested in debenture} + 0.12$$
$$\times \text{Amount invested in venture capital} \geq 3,000$$

This is then added to the original criteria set out in Figure 16.1 and the result is shown in Figure 16.2.

So now we have a lot of lines to understand. We are looking for the area on the graph where everything is achievable. This will represent that area containing all of the possible positions

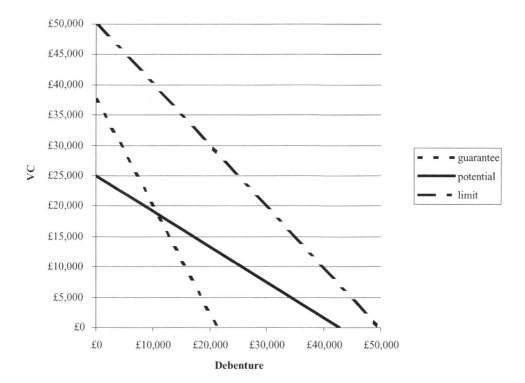

Figure 16.2   All the limit bounds for the investment.

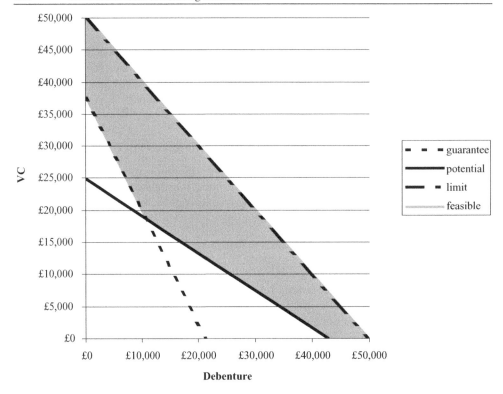

Figure 16.3 The feasibility polygon.

that are consistent with all of the constraints being met. This is known as the feasibility polygon, within which the acceptable solution must lie.

We know that the budget limit provides an upper bound since there is only £50,000 to invest. Similarly, the guaranteed and potential return lines provide lower limits. Once again, to check that what we are looking at makes sense, check the zero investment option and we can see that it fails to meet the required criteria. The area that meets all of the criteria is shaded in Figure 16.3.

The problem now is to decide which of the many points in the feasible region provide the best solution.

In this case, the cost is simply the investment in the two options; in other words the amount invested is equal to the amount invested in debentures plus the amount invested in the venture capital project.

$$\text{Cost} = \text{Debenture} + \text{VC}$$

This may also be plotted onto the graph by making the venture capital investment the subject of the equation. Unfortunately, the actual amount invested at this stage remains an unknown variable. A number of plausible values for the investment (£35,000, £40,000 and £45,000)

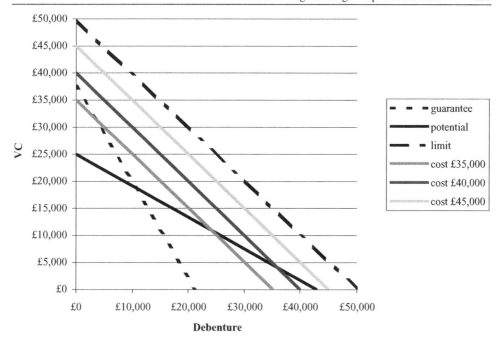

Figure 16.4 Superimposing of cost lines.

could be considered by also adding these lines to the diagram. The result of doing this is shown in Figure 16.4.

Clearly all the different total investment cost lines are parallel, and as the investment increases the lines move towards the budget limit line, which is £50,000 in this example. To minimise the investment the lines must be forced as near to the origin as possible, without leaving the feasibility polygon. In general, the solution for maximising or minimising must lie at a corner of the feasibility polygon. The only exception to this general rule would be if the cost lines were parallel to a boundary of the feasible region. In which case every point on the boundary would also have to enter into our consideration.

For the problem considered here, the estimates and investment associated with each corner of the polygon shaded in Figure 16.3 are summarised in Table 16.2. The optimum investment strategy is therefore to invest £10,714 in the 7% debentures and a further £18,750 in the

Table 16.2 Cost at corners of the feasibility polygon

Debenture	VC	Investment		Surplus
0	50,000	50,000		0.00
50,000	0	50,000		0.00
10,714	18,750	29,464	◄	20,536
42,857	0	42,857		7,142
0	37,500	37,500		12,500

venture capital investment, leaving a surplus of £20,536, which would be available for other investments. This maximises the investment available for future uses while meeting all the required criteria.

A second example is considered, which deals with a case in which there is an additional constraint.

16.2.2   An example of the optimal allocation of advertising

Full-page advertisements in the weekday editions (Monday–Saturday) of a newspaper cost £3,000, whereas on Sunday a full-page advertisement costs £7,500. The daily circulation figure is 40,000 on weekdays and 70,000 on Sundays. A company has a monthly advertising budget of £100,000. An experienced advertising executive feels that both weekday and Sunday newspaper advertisements are important, therefore the aim is to pay for at least three weekdays and at least one Sunday advertisement during the month. The objective is to maximise the cumulative total exposure (as measured by circulation) for the month. A standard month is considered which has 31 days, four Sundays and 27 weekdays. The key figures are summarised in Table 16.3.

Table 16.3   A summary of the key figures for an optimal allocation of advertising

	Weekday	Sunday	Maximum
Minimum	3	1	
Maximum	27	4	
Cost	3,000	7,500	100,000
Circulation	40,000	70,000	

Denoting the number of weekday advertisements as 'Weekday' and those on a Sunday as 'Sunday', a number of limiting equations may then be constructed, as follows:

$$\text{Weekday} \times 3,000 + \text{Sunday} \times 7,500 \leq 100,000$$

- Weekday ≤ 27 (since there cannot be more than 27 weekdays in the standard month)
- Sunday ≤ 4 (since there cannot be more than four Sundays in the standard month)
- Weekday ≥ 3 (since there must be at least three weekday advertisements)
- Sunday ≥ 1 (since there must be at least one Sunday advertisement)

These equations should then be drawn as lines, as shown in Figure 16.5.

So the challenge now is to identify all the candidate solutions, looking again at the corners of the feasibility polygon (Figure 16.6).

Finally, the total circulation, which the company wishes to maximise, needs to be introduced:

$$\text{Circulation} = \text{Number of weekdays} \times 40,000 + \text{Number of Sundays} \times 70,000$$

This is plotted on the same graph using values that might be considered appropriate for example, 500,000, 750,000 and 1,000,000 (see Figure 16.7).

In this instance the aim is to maximise exposure, therefore the exposure lines must move as far from the origin as possible. The optimum strategy must again occur at one of the corners of the feasibility polygon. All the corner values are presented in Table 16.4.

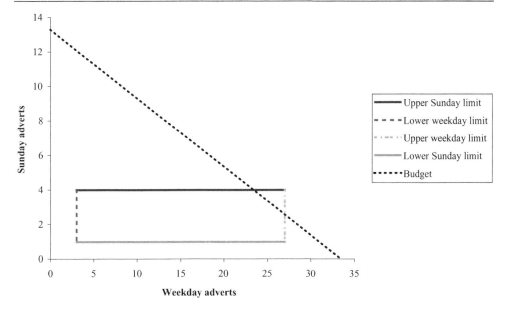

Figure 16.5   Limits on the optimal allocation of advertising.

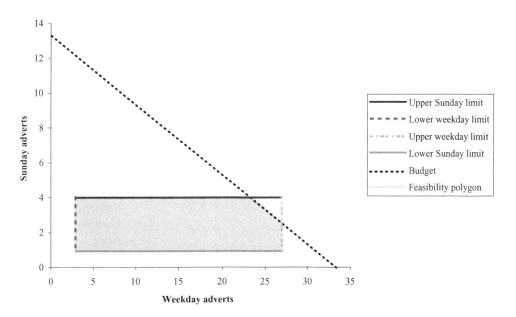

Figure 16.6   Feasibility polygon for the optimal allocation of advertising.

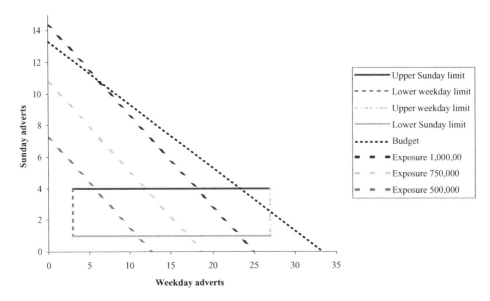

Figure 16.7 Exposure for the optimal allocation of advertising.

Table 16.4 Optimal allocation of advertising

Weekday	Sunday	Coverage
3	1	19,0000
3	4	400,000
23.3	4	1,213,333
27	2.5	1,257,333 ◄
27	1	1,150,000

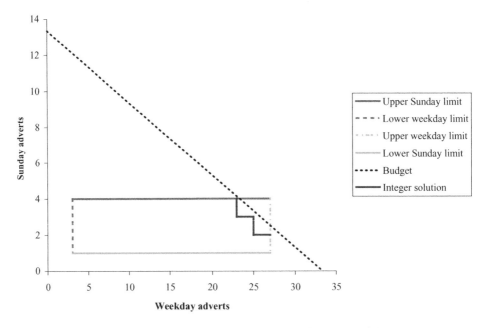

Figure 16.8 Modified feasibility polygon for the optimal allocation of advertising.

Table 16.5 Integer values for the optimal
allocation of advertising

Weekday	Sunday	Coverage
23	4	1,200,000
23	3	1,130,000
25	3	1,210,000
25	2	1,140,000
27	2	1,220,000

The ideal is to employ 27 weekday advertisements and 2.53 Sunday advertisements. Unfortunately, as posed, the criterion all relate to full-page advertisements. So the ideal is not attainable, instead it is necessary to modify the feasibility polygon to allow only integer solutions. This mainly affects the budget constraint, which is now almost redundant, as shown in Figure 16.8.

The same coverage equation is employed, and it must achieve its optimum at a corner of the feasibility polygon. The new values are collated in Table 16.5.

The new solution is to purchase 27 weekday advertisement and a further two on Sundays.

17

Linear Programming: Simplex Method

17.1 INTRODUCTION

Chapter 16 set out how a company should analyse problems where there are only two variables to consider. That means that any problem for which the solution has only two dependencies – for example, cost and time – has been addressed. Frequently, however, in business there is often the need to consider more than just two variables. Cases where four variables need to be considered – for example, interest rates, economic growth, costs and credit quality – are commonplace.

Since the two-variable approach from Chapter 16 cannot be easily extended to address problems with more than two variables, a company should instead adopt the simplex method to solve problems with in excess of two variables. This approach can cope with any number of variables and any number of constraining equations.

To start to analyse the problem the company must first change it into a standard form of notation that will facilitate the problem being solved. One possible solution is then initially identified from a review of this information and is used for the first phase of the analysis. This initial solution will then be improved upon through executing a sequence of operations aimed at providing a better estimate of the optimal solution. This sequence may be repeated using ever-improving estimates until either the result has converged to the optimal solution or a solution has been found that is acceptable to the company.

To use this procedure the company must undertake some algebraic manipulation of the constraining equations. If the company uses elementary arithmetic, this will generally work if there are not too many variables to deal with, but it does become cumbersome if there are more than, say, four variables. In situations where there are more than four variables a more systematic approach needs to be adopted.

To illustrate the procedure we shall consider a simple problem that could also have been solved by the two-variable approach discussed in Chapter 16. This will also enable the solution to be checked graphically.

17.2 MOST PROFITABLE LOANS

Consider the case of a bank that has only two products available: credit card loans and normal customer loans. Regardless of type, each loan must pass through two different processes: data input and risk assessment. Normal loan transactions take three times as long to input as credit card transactions, since for the latter most of the information is already available on the system. Regardless of the type of loan, the risk assessment will on average take the same amount of time. The profit from loan accounts is double that for credit cards for this institution. There are 138 man-hours of data input time available to the bank and a further 72 man-hours of risk assessment time available. These key figures are summarised in Table 17.1.

Table 17.1 Key figures for most profitable loans

Process	Product		Maximum time available
	Normal loans	Credit card	
	Processing time per unit		
Data input	3	1	138
Risk assessment	1	1	72
	Profit per unit		
	2	1	

Using mathematical notation we shall take x to represent the number of credit card loans, and y to represent the number of normal customer loans. We will then use A to denote the clerical input process and B to denote the risk assessment process. Finally P will be used to denote the profit. This then gives a profit equation shown by

$$P = 2x + 1y$$

This is then subject to the following constraints:

$$3x + y \leq 138 \quad \text{and} \quad x + y \leq 72$$

To solve this particular problem using the simplex approach, the company will need to work through four key stages.

Stage 1

All the equations need to be written as equalities through the introduction of slack variables (s_1 and s_2) that are used to represent any unused resources that might remain, in this case data input time and risk assessment time. If at any time during the analysis, all of the resources will have been fully used, then the slack variables will have been reduced to zero. The constraining equations, including the slack variables, become:

$$3x + y + s_1 = 138 \quad \text{and} \quad x + y + s_2 = 72$$

In addition, values (costs/profits) need to be chosen for the slack variables that will guarantee that these variables will not contribute to the function being optimised.

Stage 2

A summary matrix should then be constructed from the coefficients, which is displayed in Figure 17.1. Since there are two constraining equations, at most two non-zero variables can be expected, and these are shown as 'variable' and 'capacity' in the second and third columns of Figure 17.1, where the slack variables currently appear. The initial solution is found by taking values for the slack variables that satisfy the equations but include neither processing nor profit. This will mean that all of the utilisation will effectively fall into the slack variables, which then become $s_1 = 138$ and $s_2 = 72$. Under this scenario there is no processing, and therefore there is no profit. These are the simplest values to adopt as a starting point.

Process	Variable	Capacity	x	y	s_1	s_2
A	s_1	138	3	1	1	0
B	s_2	72	1	1	0	1
P			2	1	0	0
	Opportunity profit		2	1	0	0

Figure 17.1 Initialisation of the simplex procedure.

The x column in Figure 17.1 shows that processing one unit of x will reduce s_1 by 3 and s_2 by 1. This will result in a profit of £2. There is a gain of one unit of x and a loss of three of s_1 and one of s_2, which were not yielding any profit in any case since they are just the slack variables. Similar calculations for the remaining three columns reveal profits of £1, £0 and £0 respectively, again representing opportunity profits.

Stage 3

The next stage is to identify the column where the greatest opportunity for profit has been identified. This will be referred to as the pivotal column and is shown by the symbol (↑) in Figure 17.2. The capacity column is then divided, term-by-term by this pivotal column. Now it is time to identify the pivotal row, which is denoted by the symbol (←). This will contain the smallest value of capacity when divided by the figures in the pivotal column. The value common to the pivotal row and the pivotal column is referred to as the pivotal factor or pivot and is denoted by an asterisk (*).

This procedure shows that product x, normal loans, makes the greatest contribution to increasing profits. However, any increase in profits from normal loans is limited by the capacity of data input resources available, which will only enable 46 such loans to be processed.

If instead of considering a strategy to maximise the variable you are considering a minimisation strategy, then the column with the least strictly negative opportunity profit (cost) is identified. This will become the pivotal column. The pivotal row will, however, still correspond to the lowest value obtained on dividing the capacity column by the pivotal column.

Process	Variable	Capacity	x	y	s_1	s_2	
Data input	s_1	138	3*	1	1	0	← $\frac{138}{3} = 46$
Risk assessment	s_2	72	1	1	0	1	$\frac{72}{1} = 72$
Profit			2 ↑	1	0	0	
	Opportunity profit		2	1	0	0	

Figure 17.2 Identification of the first pivotal value.

Stage 4

A new table now needs to be constructed by dividing all the coefficients in the pivotal row by the pivotal factor, which in this case is 3, as shown in Figure 17.2. This includes dividing the capacity value, which is assigned to the variable corresponding to the pivotal column, also by the pivotal value.

All the remaining rows then need to be recalculated. For a specific row you need to locate the entry in the pivotal column, which for the second row has the value 1. You then need to subtract the product of the new pivotal row, and this value (1) from the row that is then being considered. This effectively eliminates from the equation the variable corresponding to the pivotal column. These operations are displayed in Figure 17.3.

Now that s_1 takes the value zero, it is replaced in the capacity column by x, which has effectively taken up all the slack processing available. All the available capacity for data input has now been accounted for. These calculations ensure that the pivotal value becomes 1 and is the only non-zero value in the current pivot column.

The opportunity profits can now be calculated. For a unit of y, $\frac{1}{3}$ of a unit of x and $\frac{2}{3}$ of a unit of s_2 are required. Since there are no opportunity profits from the slack variable s_2, this leads to a value of $1 - (\frac{1}{3} \times 2) = \frac{1}{3}$. Similar calculations need to be carried out for the remaining variables to give, for s_1 a value of $-\frac{2}{3}$. The value for s_2 is zero since there are no x transactions (loan accounts) available and the only other alternative is itself a slack variable. The results of this are displayed in Figure 17.4. At this stage the profit has increased to 92.

Now y, the number of credit card transactions, becomes the new pivotal column. The corresponding scaled capacity values are now $46/\frac{1}{3} = 138$ and $26/\frac{2}{3} = 39$ and the lower

Process	Variable	Capacity	x	y	s_1	s_2	
Data input	x	$\frac{138}{3} = 46$	$\frac{3}{3} = 1$	$\frac{1}{3}$	$\frac{1}{3}$	0	←
Risk assessment	s_2	$72 - 46 = 26$	$1 - 1 = 0$	$1 - \frac{1}{3} = \frac{2}{3}$	$0 - \frac{1}{3} = -\frac{1}{3}$	1	
Profit			2 ↑	1	0	0	

Figure 17.3   Evaluation of the first capacity value.

Process	Variable	Capacity	x	y	s_1	s_2
Data input	x	46	1	$\frac{1}{3}$	$\frac{1}{3}$	0
Risk assessment	s_2	26	0	$\frac{2}{3}$	$-\frac{1}{3}$	1
Profit			2	1	0	0
Opportunity profit			0	$\frac{1}{3}$	$-\frac{2}{3}$	0

Figure 17.4   Re-initialisation of the simplex procedure.

Process	Variable	Capacity	x	y	s_1	s_2	
Data input	x	46	1	$\frac{1}{3}$	$\frac{1}{3}$	0	138
Risk assessment	y	26	0	$\frac{2}{3}^*$	$-\frac{1}{3}$	1	← 39
Profit			2	1	0	0	
Opportunity profit			0	$\frac{1}{3}$	$-\frac{2}{3}$	0	
				↑			

Figure 17.5 New pivotal values for the simplex procedure.

Process	Variable	Capacity	x	y	s_1	s_2	
Data input	x	$46-39\times\frac{1}{3}=33$	1	$\frac{1}{3}-\frac{1}{3}=0$	$\frac{1}{3}-\frac{1}{3}\left(-\frac{1}{2}\right)=\frac{1}{2}$	$-\frac{1}{3}\left(\frac{3}{2}\right)=-\frac{1}{2}$	
Risk assessment	y	$\frac{26}{2/3}=39$	0	$\frac{2/3}{2/3}=1$	$\frac{-1/3}{2/3}=-\frac{1}{2}$	$\frac{1}{2/3}=1.5$	←
Profit			2	1	0	0	
				↑			

Figure 17.6 New pivotal values for the simplex procedure.

value now gives the pivot row. The relevant pivotal row, column and values are set out in Figure 17.5.

Now you need to return to the beginning of this stage and repeat the previous exercise, as shown in Figure 17.6.

The top row has had $\frac{1}{3}$ times the new pivotal row subtracted from it. It is now necessary to recalculate the opportunity profits. In both the case of x and that of y, the inclusion of an additional unit requires a unit to be deleted, so the profit is zero. In the case of s_1, the value is:

$$-\tfrac{1}{2} \times 2 + \tfrac{1}{2} \times 1 = -\tfrac{1}{2}$$

Similarly for s_2 we have:

$$\tfrac{1}{2} \times 2 - \tfrac{3}{2} \times 1 = -\tfrac{1}{2}$$

Since all the opportunity profits are now either negative or zero, there is no point in progressing further. The optimum strategy that has been reached is therefore $x = 33$ and $y = 39$ as shown in Figure 17.6, with a profit of 105. This result is supported by the graphical analysis shown in Figure 17.7.

An examination of the corners of the feasibility polygon will give candidates that may produce a solution to the problem, in the same way that we solved problems in Chapter 16. Such possible candidates are shown in Table 17.2.

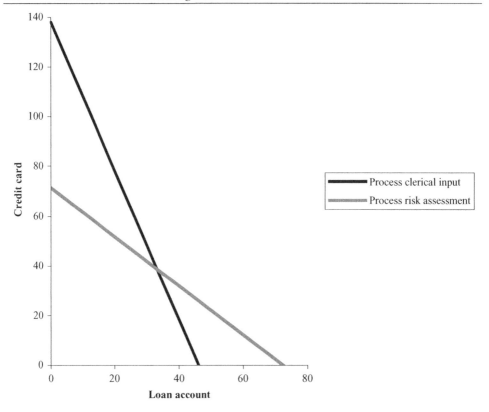

Figure 17.7   Graphical analysis of the loan problem.

Table 17.2   Candidate solutions from the feasibility polygon

Loan account	Credit card	Profit
0	0	0
46	0	92
0	72	72
33	39	105

In this case we have reached a solution that has integer values. There is nothing in the procedure that will ensure that this will happen. Introducing an additional constraint can modify the procedure. However, this requires an additional level of mathematics that is beyond the scope of this book.

We now extend the analysis to consider three variables.

17.2.1   An example of finance selection

A bank has three product lines: trade finance, project finance and loan finance. The average returns per £1,000 loan are £65, £75 and £55 respectively. The necessary time resources in terms of sales effort and processing time to achieve these returns are shown in Table 17.3.

Table 17.3 Project resources

	Trade	Project	Loan
Sales	2	3	4
Processing	4	3	2

The bank only has 6,000 man-hours of salesperson time available and also has a limit of 5,000 processing hours available. Assuming there is an unlimited demand for each product, what should the optimum strategy be? In producing the solution to this example we will only present the final values at each stage.

The three constraining equations are:

$$65 \text{ trade} + 75 \text{ project} + 55 \text{ loan} = P$$
$$2 \text{ trade} + 3 \text{ project} + 4 \text{ loan} \leq 6,000$$
$$4 \text{ trade} + 3 \text{ project} + 2 \text{ loan} \leq 5,000$$

Stage 1

The first stage is to introduce the two slack variables to pick up any excess capacity, as follows:

$$2 \text{ trade} + 3 \text{ project} + 4 \text{ loan} + s_1 = 6,000$$
$$4 \text{ trade} + 3 \text{ project} + 2 \text{ loan} + s_2 = 5,000$$

s_1 and s_2 again represent the slack variables. The remaining successive stages are displayed in Figures 17.8 to 17.12.

Process	Variable	Capacity	Trade	Project	Loan	s_1	s_2
Sales	s_1	6,000	2	3	4	1	0
Processing	s_2	5,000	4	3	2	0	1
P			65	75	55	0	0
Opportunity profit			65	75	55	0	0

Figure 17.8 Stage 2.

Process	Variable	Capacity	Trade	Project	Loan	s_1	s_2
Sales	s_1	6,000	2	3	4	1	0
Processing	s_2	5,000	4*	3	2	0	1	←
P			65	75	55	0	0
Opportunity profit			65	75	55	0	0
				↑			

Figure 17.9 Stage 3.

Process	Variable	Capacity	Trade	Project	Loan	s_1	s_2
Sales	s_1	1,000	−2	0	2	1	−1
Processing	Project	1,666.66	1.33	1	0.67	0	0.33
P			65	75	55	0	0
Opportunity profit			−35	0	5	0	−25

Figure 17.10   Stage 4.

Process	Variable	Capacity	Trade	Project	Loan	s_1	s_2	
Sales	s_1	1,000	−2	0	2*	1	−1	←
Processing	Project	1,666.66	1.33	1	0.67	0	0.33	
P			65	75	55	0	0	
Opportunity profit			−35	0	5	0	−25	
					↑			

Figure 17.11   Stage 5.

Process	Variable	Capacity	Trade	Project	Loan	s_1	s_2
Sales	Loan	500	−1	0	1	0.5	−0.5
Processing	Project	1,333.33	2	1	0	−0.33	0.67
P			65	75	55	0	0
Opportunity profit			−30	0	0	−2.5	−22.5

Figure 17.12   Final stage.

If you divide the capacity column by the pivotal column in Figure 17.9, the values will be:

$$6,000/3 = 2,000$$
$$5,000/3 = 1,667$$

Now the final row is the pivotal row. For stage 4 the profit is 125,000.

The solution to the problem is therefore to make sales of 500 units of loans and to ensure that you process 1,333.33 units of project finance at a profit of 127,500.

The approach that we have set out so far in this chapter is adequate for the type of problems that we have considered. If more complex problems arise then there are general rules that should be applied and will cover all situations.

17.3   GENERAL RULES

Firstly, any equations must be standardised to ensure that the right-hand side is positive. This is discussed in section 17.3.1. Then there will be the requirement to add additional slack variables, which is explained in section 17.3.2. An initial solution needs to be adopted as considered in section 17.3.3.

17.3.1   Standardisation

If a constraining equation has a negative right-hand side, simply multiply through by -1 to get an equivalent equation with a positive right-hand side. Therefore:

$$x_1 + 3x_2 - 2x_3 \geq -4 \equiv -x_1 - 3x_2 + 2x_3 \leq 4$$
$$x_1 + 3x_2 - 2x_3 \leq -4 \equiv -x_1 - 3x_2 + 2x_3 \geq 4$$
$$x_1 + 3x_2 - 2x_3 = -4 \equiv -x_1 - 3x_2 + 2x_3 = 4$$

What this achieves is to swap the sense of the inequality. It is therefore now possible to convert all the equations to equalities.

17.3.2   Introduction of additional variables

There are three basic rules that need to be followed to introduce the additional variables:

1. For each upper-bounded equation ($\leq$) introduce slack variables with 0 profit.
2. For each lower-bounded equation ($\geq$) subtract surplus variables with 0 profit.
3. For each lower-bounded equation ($\geq$) and all equalities ($=$) add an artificial variable. For minimisation problems the associated profit is M while for maximisation problems the associated profit becomes $-M$, for some large value M.

17.3.3   Initial solution

An initial estimate of the solution is always required. The best way to do this is to initially set all the original variables and all the surplus variables to zero. All the slack and artificial variables will then take on the values that will represent the initial solution.

To illustrate these concepts further we will consider an additional example.

17.3.4   An example to demonstrate the application of the general rules for linear programming

In this example, costs have been expressed in terms of four specific elements: people, process, systems and security. The aim is to minimise cost, subject to the time constraints that are summarised in Table 17.4. Generally in this example we have used mathematical equations to show the process that we are adopting since this will make the solution much shorter. In true business cases you will seek to replace the terms in the equations with the actual information that you are seeking to resolve.

Since all the variables are related to different aspects of costs, a mathematical equation may be created to address this issue, which would require the company to minimise the following terms:

$$x_1 + x_2 + x_3 + x_4$$

Table 17.4 Time constraints

Variable	People x_1	Process x_2	Systems x_3	Security x_4	Limit
Production	3	2	1	0	1,000
Assessment	1	3	4	6	1,000

From the information in the example, we are then able to construct the following constraints:

$$3x_1 + 2x_2 + x_3 \geq 1,000$$
$$x_1 + 3x_2 + 4x_3 + 6x_4 = 1,000$$

In this case we know that all the variables must be non-negative since you will not have negative costs. The second constraint is actually an equality since the objective is to utilise all the assessment time available. The analysis of this example is summarised in Figure 17.13, with successive steps shown in Figures 17.14 to 17.19. In this case we have used a_1 and a_2 to represent the artificial variables and s_1 to represent the surplus variable.

Current cost is calculated as follows (see Figure 17.15):

$$1,000 \, \text{cost}(a_1) + 1,000 \, \text{cost}(a_2) = 1,000 \times 999 + 1,000 \times 999 = 1998$$

Current cost is now calculated as follows (see Figure 17.16):

$$1,000 \, \text{cost}(a_2) + 166.67 \, \text{cost}(x_4) = 1,000 \times 999 + 166.67 \times 1 = 999,167$$

In this case the value remains unchanged from Figure 17.15, with the current value of cost still being 999,167 (see Figure 17.17). Now the current cost may be calculated as follows (see Figure 17.18):

$$333.33 \, \text{cost}(x_1) + 111.11 \, \text{cost}(x_4) = 333.33 \times 1 + 111.11 \times 1 = 444.44$$

Variable	Capacity	x_1	x_2	x_3	x_4	s_1	a_1	a_2
a_2	1,000	3	2	1	0	−1	0	1
a_1	1,000	1	3	4	6	0	1	0
Cost		1	1	1	1	0	999	999

Figure 17.13 Initialisation for minimising cost.

Variable	Capacity	x_1	x_2	x_3	x_4	s_1	a_1	a_2	
a_2	1,000	3	2	1	0	−1	0	1	∞
a_1	1,000	1	3	4	6*	0	1	0	← 167
Cost		1	1	1	1	0	999	999	
Opportunity cost		−3,995	−4,994	−4,994	−5,993	999	999	0.000	
					↑				

Figure 17.14 Identify first pivotal value for minimising cost.

Variable	Capacity	x_1	x_2	x_3	x_4	s_1	a_1	a_2
a_2	1,000	3	2	1	0	−1	0	1
x_4	166.67	0.17	0.5	0.67	1	0	0.17	0
Cost		1	1	1	1	0	999	999
Opportunity cost		−2,996	−1,998	−999	0	999	999	0

Figure 17.15   Employ first pivotal value for minimising cost.

Variable	Capacity.	x_1	x_2	x_3	x_4	s_1	a_1	a_2	
a_2	1,000	3*	2	1	0	−1	0	1	← 333
x_4	166.67	0.17	0.5	0.67	1	0	0.17	0	1,000
Cost		1	1	1	1	0	999	999	
Opportunity cost		−2,996	−1,998	−999	0	999	999	0	
		↑							

Figure 17.16   Identify second pivotal value for minimising cost.

Variable	Capacity	x_1	x_2	x_3	x_4	s_1	a_1	a_2
x_1	333.33	1	0.67	0.33	0	−0.33	0	0.33
x_4	111.11	0	0.39	0.61	1	0.06	0.17	−0.06
Cost		1.000	1.000	1.000	1.000	0.000	999	999
Opportunity cost		0	−0.06	0.06	0	0.28	999	999

Figure 17.17   Employ second pivotal value for minimising cost.

Variable	Capacity	x_1	x_2	x_3	x_4	s_1	a_1	a_2	
x_1	333.33	1	0.67	0.33	0	−0.33	0	0.33	500
x_4	111.11	0	0.39*	0.61	1	0.06	0.17	−0.06	← 286
Cost		1.000	1.000	1.000	1.000	0.000	999	999	
Opportunity Cost		0	−0.06	0.06	0	0.28	999	999	
			↑						

Figure 17.18   Identify third pivotal value for minimising cost.

Variable.	Capacity	x_1	x_2	x_3	x_4	s_1	a_1	a_2
x_1	142.86	1	0	−0.71	−1.71	−0.43	−0.29	0.43
x_2	285.71	0	1	1.57	2.57	0.14	0.43	−0.14
Cost		1.000	1.000	1.000	1.000	0.000	999	999
Opportunity cost		0	0	0.14	0.14	0.29	999	999

Figure 17.19 Employ third pivotal value for minimising cost.

Again at this stage the current cost is still unchanged from Figure 17.17 and is currently 444.44 (see Figure 17.19). The current cost can now be calculated as:

$$142.86 \, \text{cost}(x_1) + 285.71 \, \text{cost}(x_2) = 142.86 \times 1 + 285.71 \times 1 = 428.57$$

There are now no remaining negative opportunity costs, so the solution has variable 1 as 142.86 and variable 2 as 285.71 with the remaining variables no longer being used since they are now zero.

17.4   THE CONCERNS WITH THE APPROACH

In practice when you are inputting data into a system and then using some iterative process to try to find a better estimate of what is the best strategy, you are actually conducting the process laid out in this chapter – it is just that the actual work is normally embedded within a computer program. However, where possible there are real merits in carrying out the analysis in a manual form, not the least of which is the relative complexity of the software solutions currently available.

The key issue is always whether the right variables have been selected and whether any other factors have been ignored. A factor will often be omitted from the analysis because it is considered to be too difficult to measure, and omitting important information in this way would make it very difficult to create relationships in equation form. Further, ignoring an additional and significant variable will have the effect of potentially selecting an inappropriate conclusion to the analysis.

Also, some constraints may actually be truly linear. Considering time constraints, for example, it may be that at capacity either efficiency declines or error rates increase. If this is the case then using a simple linear approach will not be appropriate since it will be unable to take into account this type of information that is demonstrating a change in the relationship.

Once again this decreases the level of confidence you will have in the actual solution. However, it may well be that additional computer software could be obtained that is capable of dealing with these more complex and non-linear problems.

18

Transport Problems

18.1 INTRODUCTION

Transport problems typically deal with the action of shifting goods between a series of locations using a series of limited resources. In the wider business context the same methodology is used to look at the movement of transactions through a system, particularly where there are a limited number of servers or a limited amount of processing time available. The following is an illustration of how to solve this type of problem.

18.2 TRANSPORT PROBLEM

A company has undertaken an exercise and decided to outsource all of their transaction processing. The outsourced supplier has four locations available where processing can be undertaken and this provides a useful business continuity advantage to the company.

They currently have three different systems that produce information, each of which can be processed at any location, for example, System A can be processed at any one of the four possible locations. System A actually requires five hours of processing to enable its output to be produced. Each location has a set amount of time available for this piece of work and location A can only take on three hours of additional processing at this stage.

The challenge is to work out what would be the optimal processing strategy given the number of options that are available. The processing quantities available at each location and the differing system requirements are shown in Table 18.1.

Table 18.1 Processing supply and demand

System	Required	Location	Capacity
A	5	1	3
B	5	2	4
C	7	3	5
		4	5
Total	**17**		**17**

As we can see, the hours required for processing, at 17, is also the capacity, so in this case supply and demand balance. Were this not the case a slack variable would need to be introduced in the form of an additional system or location to absorb/generate the required excess. To solve the problem you will need to undertake a matrix-based approach, but this will need to consider other relevant factors, for example the cost of processing. These are the costs (time and money) that occur in moving a single unit from the production system to the processing location and are displayed in Table 18.2.

The objective for the outsourcing supplier is to undertake the processing for the three systems at the minimum cost.

Table 18.2   Processing costs (£)

System	Location			
	1	2	3	4
A	5	8	6	5
B	7	6	7	4
C	5	4	5	6

The procedure adopted is similar to the simplex method that is discussed in Chapter 17. In this case the process works by starting from the top left-hand corner of a supply/demand matrix. You first attempt to satisfy the processing demand by looking at the first location. The first location only has three hours available and this is less than the five hours required to process the output from System A. There will then be two hours of processing still required on the output from System A, which will now be processed at the second location. This process continues until all of the systems processing requirements have been accounted for. This provides the initial values for the analysis as shown in Table 18.3.

Table 18.3   Initial values: Cycle 1

System	Location				Available
	1	2	3	4	
A	3	2	0	0	5
B	0	2	3	0	5
C	0	0	2	5	7
Total	**3**	**4**	**5**	**5**	**17**

As you can see the way this has worked is to consider each of the locations in order. The resulting total processing cost can be calculated by using the information from the matrix given in Table 18.2. The total processing cost is therefore calculated as follows:

$$(3 \times £5) + (2 \times £8) + (2 \times £6) + (3 \times £7) + (2 \times £5) + (5 \times £6) = £104$$

However, this solution has only been reached by taking the four sites in an order that may not in fact be optimal. There is no reason to believe that it will be cost effective for the excess from processing System A to actually be processed by Location 2. It may be that Location 3 or 4 would be more appropriate, or that Location 1 should actually be processing something else altogether. It is therefore necessary to search for a lower cost solution.

To achieve this we need to introduce additional ghost costs. These imaginary costs are split into two parts, a component for each system and another for each location. Since only relative magnitudes are of interest, the first ghost cost is assigned the value zero. Only the unit costs of the cells used in the previous cost calculation (Table 18.2) are of interest. If the unit cost from system i to location j is C_{ij}, then ghost costs S_i and L_j need to be chosen such that $C_{ij} = S_i + L_j$. The resulting values are shown in Table 18.4.

The order in which the values are assigned is S_A(the ghost cost for System A), then the first location (L_1), followed by the second, L_2. The second ghost cost, for System B is then introduced, S_B, then successively L_3, S_C and L_4. We are assigning the value zero to S_A, since

Table 18.4   Allocation of the ghost costs: Cycle 1

System	\multicolumn{4}{c}{Location}				S_i
	1	2	3	4	
A	5	8			**0**
B		6	7		**−2**
C			5	6	**−4**
L_j	**5**	**8**	**9**	**10**	

$C_{A1} = 5$ and $C_{A2} = 8$. This gives $L_1 = 5$ and $L_2 = 8$. Since $C_{B2} = 6$ and $L_2 = 8$ this makes $S_B = -2$ and so on.

For the remaining cells, ghost costs $\tilde{C}_{ij} = S_i + L_j$ can be calculated. These values should then be compared to the true costs. Any differences, $C_{ij} - \tilde{C}_{ij}$, should then also be calculated. If any cell were showing a negative value then this would indicate that you have not yet reached the optimal solution and that further improvement can be achieved.

This difference gives an indication of the savings expected on employing the different processing allocation to the four sites. In practice you will normally adopt a presentational format using special notation designed to encapsulate all of this information. To achieve this you need to construct a new cell in the form shown in Figure 18.1 for each existing cell to show the relationship between the ghost and true costs.

Going back to the example shown in Table 18.4, for the cells that have already had a value allocated to them, the difference will be zero. This leads to the grid that is shown in Figure 18.2.

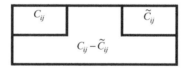

Figure 18.1   The relation between the ghost and true costs.

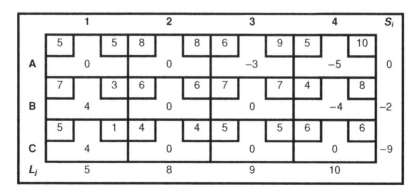

Figure 18.2   Ghost costs: cycle 1.

Table 18.5 Selection of initial values: Cycle 2

System	1	2	3	4	Available
			Location		
A	3	$2-x$	0	x	5
B	0	$2+x$	$3-x$	0	5
C	0	0	$2+x$	$5-x$	7
Total	**3**	**4**	**5**	**5**	

Since the number of non-zero cells will correspond to the number of system and location ghost costs that are required, the number of non-zero entries must be less than the number of ghost costs. Therefore, selecting too many cells in Table 18.3 will lead to an insoluble problem. The key is to initially use as few cells as possible.

Since there are still three negative values appearing in Figure 18.2, this is an indication that the optimal solution has not yet been reached. Since the cell A4 gives the largest negative value, it would make sense to see if we can increase its usage. Assume that the utilisation is increased by a value x, then this will create a capacity excess. One possible solution is shown in Table 18.5.

Since we need all of the values to be non-negative, the best that can be done is take x to be 2, since otherwise A2 would become negative. The expected savings are shown in Table 18.6, with the total savings being referred to as the improvement index.

There must be an even number of entries in the path and in this case the net saving is $5x$, which given that $x = 2$ is the highest possible value of x, means that the savings are 10. The new initial values are shown in Table 18.7.

At this stage the cost is 94, as expected, and an improvement has been achieved. The steps are now repeated to see if a further improvement can be achieved. For the ghost costs the values are shown in Table 18.8.

Table 18.6 Expected savings

Path	A4	C4	C3	B3	B2	A2	Total
Cost	5	6	5	7	6	8	
Change	x	$-x$	x	$-x$	x	$-x$	$-5x$

Table 18.7 Initial values: Cycle 2

System	1	2	3	4	Available
			Location		
A	3	0	0	2	5
B	0	4	1	0	5
C	0	0	4	3	7
Total	**3**	**4**	**5**	**5**	

Table 18.8   Allocation of the ghost costs: Cycle 2

System	Location 1	2	3	4	S_i
A	5			5	**0**
B		6	7		**3**
C			5	6	**1**
L_j	**5**	**3**	**4**	**5**	

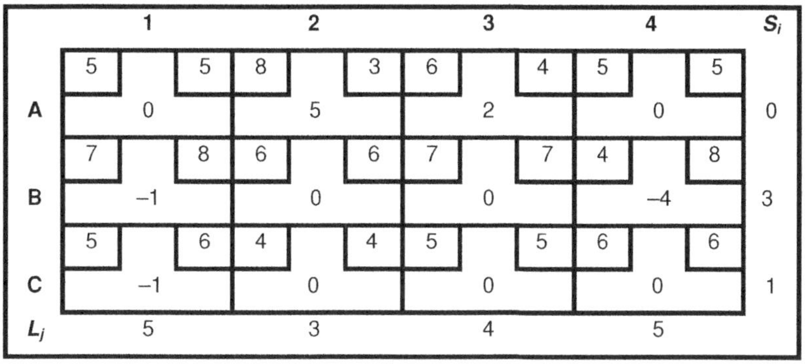

Figure 18.3   Ghost costs: cycle 2.

The order in which the values are assigned is S_A, L_1, L_4, S_C, L_3, S_B and finally L_2. The resulting difference grid is shown in Figure 18.3.

The most negative cell is now B_4. On assigning a further utilisation x to this system, the output available will give the results shown in Table 18.9, and the improvement index is shown in Table 18.10.

Table 18.9   Selection of initial values: Cycle 3

System	Location 1	2	3	4	**Available**
A	3	0	0	2	**5**
B	0	4	$1-x$	x	**5**
C	0	0	$4+x$	$3-x$	**7**
Total	**3**	**4**	**5**	**5**	

Table 18.10   Expected savings

Path	B4	B3	C3	C4	Total
Cost	4	7	5	6	
Change	x	$-x$	x	$-x$	$-4x$

Table 18.11   Initial values: Cycle 3

System	Location				Available
	1	2	3	4	
A	3	0	0	2	5
B	0	4	0	1	5
C	0	0	5	2	7
Total	3	4	5	5	

Table 18.12   Allocation of the ghost costs: Cycle 3

System	Location				S_i
	1	2	3	4	
A	5			5	0
B		6		4	−1
C			5	6	1
L_j	5	7	4	5	

The maximum allowed value for x is now only 1 since otherwise cell B3 would go negative. This therefore gives an expected improvement of −4. The initial values are now as shown in Table 18.11. The resulting cost is 90 with ghost costs shown in Table 18.12.

The order in which the values are assigned is S_A, L_1, L_4, S_C, S_B, L_3 and L_2. The resulting difference grid is shown in Figure 18.4.

You then continue to use the algorithm in a similar fashion until no further improvement is possible. After five cycles, since there are no negative cells, an optimal solution will have been obtained. This final solution is shown in Table 18.13. At this stage the cost has reduced to 78.

Therefore the optimal solution is for system A to send 3 hours of work to Location 1 and 2 hours to Location 3. System B should send 5 hours of work to Location 4 and System C should send 4 hours to Location 2 and 3 hours of work to Location 3.

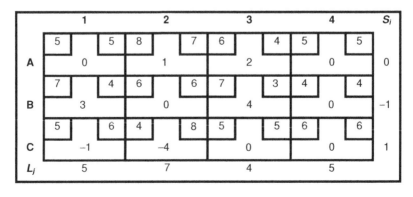

Figure 18.4   Ghost costs: cycle 3.

Table 18.13 Final values

System	Location 1	2	3	4	Available
A	3	0	2	0	5
B	0	0	0	5	5
C	0	4	3	0	7
Required	**3**	**4**	**5**	**5**	

In this instance the solution is unique.

While the adoption of the north-west corner as our starting point may be the simplest starting strategy, it is also rather naïve. A superior starting point is to select the minimum cost routes, in this case the starting guess actually corresponded to the final solution which was confirmed in one additional cycle.

When applying the approach to actual business problems there is a risk that a solution that is too simplistic will be adopted and that a number of important factors may be overlooked. There may be additional external constraints that need to be considered, including the training of staff required to undertake the work, or savings that may result from sending all the work from a single system to a single location.

This type of analysis can be easily applied to machine time and scheduling problems, including computer applications. The procedure could also be employed in reverse to decide the optimal number of locations or systems that meet a specific need. So the main concern is always to get your problem to fit into this type of analysis and then to make sure that all the constraints have been properly considered.

19 Dynamic Programming

19.1 INTRODUCTION

The aim of dynamic programming is to find the best solution to a problem posed, which may be set out as a series of alternatives. The idea behind this approach is to break down what is a complex problem into a series of sub-problems. The solution to the first sub-problem is then used to derive a solution to the next sub-problem and so on until the entire problem is solved.

The objective of undertaking the series of problem solutions is to reach an optimal solution to the entire problem.

19.2 PRINCIPLE OF OPTIMALITY

One key element of the dynamic programming approach is the basic principle of optimality. As stated above, the objective is to locate the optimal solution to the problem you are trying to solve. If an optimal set of decisions has been found, then clearly whatever the first decision is, the remaining decisions must still be optimal taking into account the results of the first decision. In total, they represent an optimal solution to the entire problem.

The procedure is displayed schematically on Figure 19.1. The solution identified at time t is shown as x_t and the selected action resulting as a_t, which results in a return of r_t.

x_0		x_1			x_{t-1}		x_t		x_{t+1}				x_n
	a_0		a_1	...		a_{t-1}		a_t		a_{t+1}	...	a_{n-1}	
	$\rightarrow$		$\rightarrow$			$\rightarrow$		$\rightarrow$		$\rightarrow$		$\rightarrow$	
r_0		r_1			r_{t-1}		r_t		r_{t+1}				r_n

Figure 19.1 Schematic of dynamic programming.

The aim is to optimise the total return for all the sub-projects:

$$R = \sum r_t$$

This is achieved by making an optimal choice of actions, which are shown as the various choices for a_t.

The optimum solution can be obtained by using what is referred to as backwards recursion. This operates by effectively applying a formula to the preceding terms. This is carried out from x_n using the scheme $t + 1 \rightarrow t$ as the analysis is first conducted on time $t + 1$ and then on the preceding item, t. The alternative approach would be to use forward recursion, where the procedure commences from x_0 using the scheme $t - 1 \rightarrow t$, where t represents time.

Whether you will select forward or backward recursion will depend on the problem under consideration. The first graphic example illustrates the two recursion approaches and the additional information you are able to generate concerning the problem.

19.3 EXAMPLES OF DYNAMIC PROGRAMMING

19.3.1 An example of forward and backward recursion

In this example (Figure 19.2) we have created a network, where the values shown represent the cost (time, distance or effort) in travelling along the adjacent edge. Each edge has a separate value. The aim of the analysis is to find the minimum cost in travelling from A to B.

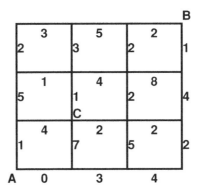

Figure 19.2   Graphic optimisation.

The cost in reaching each corner is displayed in Figure 19.3, where the route proceeds forwards from A. In each case the symbols (▼, ◄) indicate the selected optimal decision in terms of the direction in which to travel next. What this means is that at the starting corner, A in Figure 19.2, the challenge is to find the cheapest route forward to eventually reach position C. This will be the lower of the cost of the two routes available from this point. If you go right and then up, the cost will be 0 plus 7, which equals 7. If you go up then right, the cost will be 1 plus 4, which equals 5 and is cheaper. Therefore this route will be selected.

At each stage you can see the optimal choice you should make. Figure 19.4 displays the selected optimal path using forward recursion.

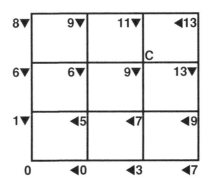

Figure 19.3   Graphic optimisation proceeding from A.

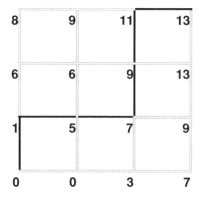

Figure 19.4   Graphic optimisation final solution proceeding from A (forward recursion).

The reverse strategy, backward recursion, may be presented commencing at vertex B. The cost in reaching each vertex and the selected decision is displayed in Figure 19.5, and Figure 19.6 displays the selected optimal path.

The overall solutions are, of course, identical since forward and backward recursion must give the same result. However, there is some additional useful information, which arises from looking at the results from the two approaches.

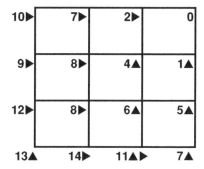

Figure 19.5   Graphic optimisation proceeding from B.

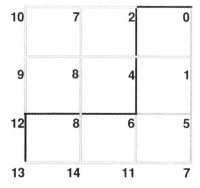

Figure 19.6   Graphic optimisation final solution proceeding from B (backward recursion).

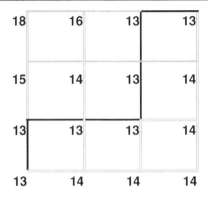

Figure 19.7   Graphic optimisation final solution optimal path from A to B.

On comparing the two final diagrams the corresponding pairs of values of the corners on the selected path always add to 13. In other words, proceeding backward to A, or forward to B, the total distance is 13. For all other routes, the total must either equal to or exceed 13.

Let us first consider the top left-hand corner of Figure 19.2. Here the shortest path from the corner to A is 8, while that to B is 10. This gives a total cost of 18. These totals for all nodes are displayed in Figure 19.7.

19.3.2   A practical example of recursion in use

A company is considering purchasing a series of portable air-conditioning units. Each unit costs £1,500 and the cost of maintaining the machine during its first three years of operation on average is £140 for the first year (m_1), £180 for the second year (m_2), £240 for the third year (m_3) and for all subsequent years.

A machine may be kept for up to three years before being sold, the second-hand value after the first year (s_1) being £1,000, declining to £800 in the second year (s_2) and £400 in the third year (s_3). After that point the resale value declines to zero. The company is proposing to use the mobile air-conditioning units for five years after purchase.

These costs may be summarised into a holding cost for the first year. Here there will be the original cost, £1,500, together with the repair costs for the first year of £140. At the end of the first year the unit has declined to a value of £1,000. Therefore the actual cost of use of the unit will be:

$$£1,500 + £140 - £1,000 = £640$$

The first year holding cost will be referred to as h_1.

The equivalent figure for two years of usage of the air-conditioning units, (h_2), will show two years of repair costs and also the declining resale value available at the end of the second year. This is therefore:

$$£1,500 + £140 + £180 - £800 = £1,020$$

The three year figure (h_3) is

$$£1,500 + £140 + £180 + £240 - £400 = £1,660$$

Table 19.1   Costs for the maintenance problem

$c_{01} = \underline{£640}$				
$c_{02} = \underline{£1,020}$	$c_{12} = £640$			
$c_{03} = \underline{£1,660}$	$c_{13} = £1,020$	$c_{23} = \underline{£640}$		
$c_{04} = $ n/a	$c_{14} = £1,660$	$c_{24} = £1,020$	$c_{34} = £640$	
$c_{05} = $ n/a	$c_{15} = $ n/a	$c_{25} = £1,660$	$c_{35} = \underline{£1,020}$	$c_{45} = £640$

The question the company will want to answer is: What is the best may to minimise costs over the five-year period?

Firstly, a full set of costs must be evaluated before commencing the optimisation. To simplify the procedure, an initial period 0 is introduced. Consider c_{ij}, the cost for a purchase of an air-conditioning unit at the start of period i with a subsequent sale at the end of period j. This step equates to constructing a map of the problem and the costs are displayed in Table 19.1.

To see how these individual cells are calculated, consider $c_{23} = £640$. This equates to an initial start up and equals c_{01} as shown above. Looking at another cell, $c_{35} = £1,020$ since this corresponds to a two-year figure and equals c_{02}.

The underlined figures in Table 19.1 have been calculated above. Now that the costs have been worked out, we can undertake some dynamic programming. If s_i is the cost at year i, using backward recursion:

$s_4 = c_{45} = 640$

$s_3 = $ the lower of c_{35} * and $c_{34} + s_4$. This equates to choosing between £1,020 and £1,280, so the lower value £1,020 is selected.

$s_2 = $ the challenge to find the lowest figure from c_{25} *, $c_{24} + s_4$ *, $c_{23} + s_3$ *. Since these values are all £1,660, £1,660 is chosen.

$s_1 = \min(c_{14} + s_4, c_{13} + s_3$ *, $c_{12} + s_2) = \min(£2,300, £2,040, £2,300) = £2,040$

$s_0 = \min(c_{03} + s_3$ *, $c_{02} + s_2$ *, $c_{01} + s_1$ *) = $\min(£2,680, £2,680, £2,680) = £2,680$

In each case the lowest cost has been selected and is denoted by an asterisk (*). From this you can find out a variety of equal cost strategies, which are summarised in Table 19.2. This shows the stage in the five-year cycle at which air-conditioning units are actually purchased, and demonstrates that the first solution is to buy the machines initially, then purchase additional new machines after years 1 and 3.

Table 19.2   Purchase schedules for the maintenance problem

Solution	Schedule		
1	0	1	3
2	0	2	3
3	0	2	4
4	0	2	
5	0	3	

As we have said, the first solution is to buy initially and then to purchase additional units after years 1 and 3. In this example there are a range of solutions which all cost £2,680. However when you are using this type of approach in the real world, you will tend to be working on more complex pricing strategies. In such cases you would only expect one solution to dominate as being the optimal solution.

19.3.3　A more complex example of dynamic programming

In this example a company requires its marketing department to supply marketing brochures over the next five quarters according to the schedule in Table 19.3, with each unit being 1,000 brochures.

Table 19.3　Production schedule

Period	1	2	3	4	5
Units	100	200	250	250	150

In this example it is assumed that the variable production costs for the brochures are the same regardless of the size of the batch being processed. However, it costs £500 to commission a production run of any size, and £1 per unit per period for additional storage. The marketing department needs to assess the production sequence that will minimise the total cost.

To solve this by a dynamic programming approach, you first need to introduce an initial production period 0, to generate the initial stock required. You will then define c_{ij} as being the cost incurred from the end of quarter i to the end of period j. Production will recommence at quarter $j + 1$, incurring a fresh start-up cost of £500.

A full set of costs must be evaluated before commencing the optimisation. All the production options are displayed in Table 19.4. In all cases, production occurs at time i and recommences at time $j + 1$.

Table 19.4　Production options

$P_{01} = 100$				
$P_{02} = 300$	$P_{12} = 200$			
$P_{03} = 550$	$P_{13} = 450$	$P_{23} = 250$		
$P_{04} = 800$	$P_{14} = 700$	$P_{24} = 500$	$P_{34} = 250$	
$P_{05} = 950$	$P_{15} = 850$	$P_{25} = 650$	$P_{35} = 400$	$P_{45} = 150$

The next stage is for the costs associated with the various strategies to be calculated. The costs associated with additional periods during which the brochures are held in storage need to be recorded. This is demonstrated in Table 19.5 where the relevant equations have been included. A summary of these values is shown in Table 19.6.

Table 19.5　Background to the costs for the production options

$c_{01} = 500$				
$c_{02} = c_{01} + 200$	$c_{12} = 500$			
$c_{03} = c_{02} + 2 \times 250$	$c_{13} = c_{12} + 250$	$c_{23} = 500$		
$c_{04} = c_{03} + 3 \times 250$	$c_{14} = c_{13} + 2 \times 250$	$c_{24} = c_{23} + 250$	$c_{34} = 500$	
$c_{05} = c_{04} + 4 \times 150$	$c_{15} = c_{14} + 3 \times 150$	$c_{25} = c_{24} + 2 \times 150$	$c_{35} = c_{34} + 150$	$c_{45} = 500$

Table 19.6   Costs for the production options

$c_{01} = 500$				
$c_{02} = 700$	$c_{12} = 500$			
$c_{03} = 1200$	$c_{13} = 750$	$c_{23} = 500$		
$c_{04} = 1950$	$c_{14} = 1250$	$c_{24} = 750$	$c_{34} = 500$	
$c_{05} = 2550$	$c_{15} = 1700$	$c_{25} = 1050$	$c_{35} = 650$	$c_{45} = 500$

Now that the costs have been ascertained, you can commence the dynamic programming procedure. If s_i is the cost at year i, using backward recursion:

$$s_4 = c_{45} = 500$$
$$s_3 = \min(c_{35}{}^*, c_{34} + s_4) = \min(650^*, 1{,}000) = 650$$
$$s_2 = \min(c_{25}{}^*, c_{24} + s_4, c_{23} + s_3) = \min(1{,}050^*, 1{,}250, 1{,}150) = 1{,}050$$
$$s_1 = \min(c_{15}, c_{14} + s_4, c_{13} + s_3{}^*, c_{12} + s_2)$$
$$= \min(1{,}700, 1{,}750, 1{,}400^*, 1{,}550) = 1{,}400$$
$$s_0 = \min(c_{05}, c_{04} + s_4, c_{03} + s_3, c_{02} + s_2{}^*, c_{01} + s_1)$$
$$= \min(2{,}550, 2{,}450, 1{,}850, 1{,}750^*, 1{,}900) = 1{,}750$$

Again, in each case the optimum solution selected is denoted by an asterisk (*). This shows that the best strategy is to produce 300 ($100 + 200$) units initially, shown as being after quarter 0, and 650 ($250 + 250 + 150$) after quarter 2 with a total cost of £1,750.

If it is later found that the storage cost is actually £2, then this will result in a radically different strategy. It is necessary to recalculate all the costs, then repeat the dynamic programming. The selected revised strategies are shown below.

$$s_4 = c_{45} = 500$$
$$s_3 = \min(c_{35}{}^*, c_{34} + s_4) = \min(800^*, 1{,}000) = 800$$
$$s_2 = \min(c_{25}, c_{24} + s_4, c_{23} + s_3{}^*) = \min(1{,}600, 1{,}500, 1{,}300^*) = 1{,}300$$
$$s_1 = \min(c_{15}, c_{14} + s_4, c_{13} + s_3{}^*, c_{12} + s_2{}^*)$$
$$= \min(2{,}900, 2{,}500, 1{,}800^*, 1{,}800^*) = 1{,}800$$
$$s_0 = \min(c_{05}, c_{04} + s_4, c_{03} + s_3, c_{02} + s_2{}^*, c_{01} + s_1)$$
$$= \min(4{,}600, 3{,}900, 2{,}700, 2{,}200^*, 2{,}300) = 2{,}200$$

So, if the storage costs are doubled, we come up with a radically different solution. In this case the best strategy is to produce 300 ($100 + 200$) units after quarter 0, 250 after quarter 2 and 400 ($250 + 150$) after quarter 3, with a total cost of £2,100.

19.3.4   The 'Travelling Salesman' problem

As a final dynamic programming example we consider the case of the travelling salesman. It is applicable to any problem that concerns something travelling by a 'circular' route. This approach is therefore suitable for any series of actions that commence and terminate at the same point and visit the remaining destinations once only.

In the traditional problem, a salesman must visit n customers. The question that the company will seek to answer is to identify the optimum order in which the visits should be made to minimise the total distance travelled.

Table 19.7   Inter-site distances

	A	B	C	D
B	5			
C	7	6		
D	9	13	8	
E	13	12	5	6

For three customers (A, B, C) there would be six possible options for the route that the salesman can travel (ABC, ACB, BAC, BCA, CAB, CBA), before the salesman returns home having completing the required circuit. While this appears rather simple, if there were 10 customers, there would in fact be 3,628,800 options, so a superior method would need to be employed.

Many different approaches may be considered to solve, or approximately solve, this type of problem. Here only the method of dynamic programming is used. This is best demonstrated by considering an example.

In this case a regional manager is planning a trip around five branches, labelled A, B, C, D and E. The distance between the five sites in miles is set out in Table 19.7. Since we are showing all of the distances between the branches, it will not matter at which branch the manager actually starts.

One simple approach would consist of ordering all of the distances and always picking the shortest available distance from the current site to the next available site. The shortest distances in order are E to C, D to E, C to A, B to D and A to B, which correspond to a final route commencing at A, then travelling to B, followed by travelling to D, then travelling to E, with C being the final port of call before finally returning to A. This route represents $5 + 13 + 6 + 5 + 7$, being the distance for each leg of the route, coming to a total distance of 36 miles.

This type of approach is inflexible since early decisions limit later available choices to quite a significant extent and can result in a choice in this case between two fairly large distances (B to D $= 13$). As a more advanced modelling approach could come up with a better solution, can an improved solution be obtained in this case?

To achieve this start by defining $g_k(i; t_1, \ldots, t_k)$ to be the minimum route from town i to the chosen destination, say A, passing through the k remaining towns $t_1, \ldots, t_k$ in any order. The process is conducted by successively calculating the set of values corresponding to g_1, g_2, g_3 and then finally g_4. Using forward recursion the successive terms are set out in Tables 19.8, 19.9 and 19.10.

In Table 19.8, d_{ij} is the distance between towns i and j. For example, $g_1(C; B)$ is the distance of the route from C via the one branch (B) to return home (A).

Table 19.8   First-order terms

$g_1(C; B) = d_{CB} + d_{BA} = 11$	$g_1(D; B) = d_{DB} + d_{BA} = 18$	$g_1(E; B) = d_{EB} + d_{BA} = 17$
$g_1(B; C) = d_{BC} + d_{CA} = 13$	$g_1(D; C) = d_{DC} + d_{CA} = 15$	$g_1(E; C) = d_{EC} + d_{CA} = 12$
$g_1(B; D) = d_{BD} + d_{DA} = 22$	$g_1(C; D) = d_{CD} + d_{DA} = 17$	$g_1(E; D) = d_{ED} + d_{DA} = 15$
$g_1(B; E) = d_{BE} + d_{EA} = 25$	$g_1(C; E) = d_{CE} + d_{EA} = 18$	$g_1(D; E) = d_{DE} + d_{EA} = 19$

Table 19.9 Second-order terms

	Sequence
$g_2(D; CB) = \min(d_{DC} + g_1(C; B)^*, d_{DB} + g_1(B; C)) = 19$	$D \to C \to B$
$g_2(E; CB) = \min(d_{EC} + g_1(C; B)^*, d_{EB} + g_1(B; C)) = 16$	$E \to C \to B$
$g_2(C; DB) = \min(d_{CD} + g_1(D; B)^*, d_{CB} + g_1(B; D)) = 26$	$C \to D \to B$
$g_2(E; DB) = \min(d_{ED} + g_1(D; B)^*, d_{EB} + g_1(B; D)) = 24$	$E \to D \to B$
$g_2(C; EB) = \min(d_{CE} + g_1(E; B)^*, d_{CB} + g1(B; E)) = 22$	$C \to E \to B$
$g_2(D; EB) = \min(d_{DE} + g_1(E; B)^*, d_{DB} + g_1(B; E)) = 23$	$D \to E \to B$
$g_2(B; CD) = \min(d_{BD} + g_1(D; C)^*, d_{BC} + g_1(C; D)) = 23$	$B \to C \to D$
$g_2(E; DC) = \min(d_{ED} + g_1(D; C)^*, d_{EC} + g_1(C; D)) = 21$	$E \to D \to C$
$g_2(B; EC) = \min(d_{BE} + g_1(E; C)^*, d_{BC} + g_1(C; E)) = 24$	$B \to E \to C$
$g_2(D; EC) = \min(d_{DE} + g_1(E; C)^*, d_{DC} + g_1(C; E)) = 18$	$D \to E \to C$
$g_2(B; ED) = \min(d_{BE} + g_1(E; D)^*, d_{BD} + g_1(D; E)) = 27$	$B \to E \to D$
$g_2(C; ED) = \min(d_{CE} + g_1(E; D)^*, d_{CD} + g_1(D; E)) = 20$	$C \to E \to D$

Table 19.10 Third-order terms

	Sequence
$g_3(E; DCB) = \min(d_{ED} + g_2(D; CB)^*, d_{EC} + g_2(C; DB), d_{EB} + g_2(B; CD)) = 25$	$E \to D \to C \to B$
$g_3(D; ECB) = \min(d_{DE} + g_2(E; CB)^*, d_{DC} + g_2(C; EB), d_{DB} + g_2(B; EC)) = 22$	$D \to E \to C \to B$
$g_3(C; EDB) = \min(d_{CE} + g_2(E; DB)^*, d_{CD} + g_2(D; EB), d_{CB} + g_2(B; ED)) = 29$	$C \to E \to D \to B$
$g_3(B; CED) = \min(d_{BE} + g_2(E; DC)^*, d_{BD} + g_2(D; EC), d_{BC} + g_2(C; ED)) = 26$	$B \to C \to E \to D$

In Tables 19.9 and 19.10 the selected route in each case has been denoted by an asterisk (*) and the optimum selection being recorded in the final column. For example, $g_2(D; CB)$ is the distance of the route from D via the two branches C and B (in any order) to return home (A). If C had been chosen as the second branch, then the remaining distance is $g_1(C; B)$. That is, the distance from C via B to reach A.

Finally for the fourth-order terms are calculated:

$$g_4(A; DECB) = \min(d_{AE} + g_3(E; DCB), d_{AD} + g_3(D; ECB)^*, d_{AC}$$
$$+ g_3(C; EDB), d_{AB} + g_3(B; CED)^*) = 31$$

The desired route is either A $\to$ D $\to$ E $\to$ C $\to$ B $\to$ A or A $\to$ B $\to$ C $\to$ E $\to$ D $\to$ A, one simply being the reverse of the other.

20

Decision Theory

20.1 INTRODUCTION

Throughout business, directors, managers and employees are required to make a series of decisions. These will vary from simple decisions such as the provider of electricity or the order in which a series of tasks should be conducted, to more complex decisions related to treasury management issues or strategic management. In this context a decision is simply the process that needs to be undertaken that will lead to the adoption of a specific course of action.

When making a decision, there are in practice a number of potential pitfalls that need to be addressed and if avoided will improve the general success of the decision-making process. The pitfalls include the following:

1. *Too little delegation*. In this case senior management makes all of the decisions, with little regard to the staff working in the business. This can mean that a decision is made that appears in principle to make good business sense, but in practice causes resentment, expense and future problems for business operations.
2. *Too few staff are authorised to make decisions*. When this applies there can often be decisions awaiting approval for lengthy periods of time. This can cause staff dissatisfaction and delay potentially important developments. Another problem that may occur is that the people making the actual decision either have insufficient knowledge and experience to make the decision or are too remote from the issue to fully appreciate the importance of the decision. Any of these problems will cause significant difficulties to a company and result in an inappropriate or sub-optimal decision being made.
3. *Poor communication*. In many cases a good decision can be let down by poor communication. The internal whispering structures tend to work much faster than the official internal communications structures. This can result in unnecessary concern over an issue that can potentially undermine staff morale. While getting the right decision is important – indeed the techniques set out in this book will assist with this process – communicating the message is also important. This requires training and, in particular, the use of tact, matters that are rarely addressed on internal training courses.
4. *Lethargy*. It is often easier to pass the decision making to someone else, or even better to a committee. This can often result in external factors meaning that the decision is now redundant – events have forced a single decision to be made. The resulting solution to the issue would probably not be the one that would have been chosen if a sensible modelling approach had been adopted, and is likely to result in a sub-optimal solution to the problems faced.
5. *Poor modelling*. Management can (a) choose to use a model that is either invalid or inappropriate for the specific scenario being considered, or can (b) use a model where the underlying parameters and assumptions are themselves no longer valid. They could use a simple model in a complex situation leading to a result with a low confidence level, or they could use

a complex modelling technique that no one understands when a simple technique would have been appropriate. All these factors are important for the company to consider since, if they follow a review process prior to modelling that establishes the selection of a valid approach using valid parameters and valid assumptions, they will significantly improve the likelihood of a successful modelling approach.

6. *Inappropriate confidence levels.* The person undertaking the analysis may have chosen to work at a 95% confidence level, for example. This means that there will be a 5% chance that the solution will be outside the bounds set by the modeller, and the answer will be effectively incorrect. If the management require the solution to be in a closer range with greater certainty, then the modeller will need to select a high confidence level (99% or even 99.9%) and undertake a greater level of analysis of the underlying information.

20.2   PROJECT ANALYSIS GUIDELINES

Prior to trying to make a decision, it is important that all the basic facts are obtained that are required to enable a complete analysis of the problem to be undertaken. It is generally recommended that a standard set of project analysis guidelines should be adopted which are both approved by senior management and utilised within the business. Further, a standard checklist should be completed every time a decision is required, to provide the solution to a problem that has been identified. The adoption of such a formal approach forces the management of the company to consider all the key aspects of the project management process prior to making a potentially incorrect or invalid decision.

The guidelines and checklists should require the following stages of decision making to be formally addressed:

1. Identify the problem.
   - Is it worth formally using a modelling technique?
   - Has the problem been solved before?
2. Identify the project sponsor
   - This is still a project and needs to be treated as such.
   - A project sponsor for the decision making needs to be appointed. The project sponsor will make most of the ultimate decisions.
   - The project sponsor needs to be sufficiently senior to be able either to make the decisions or to refer the material to the decision-making structure.
   - The project should be formally approved prior to the next stages being undertaken.
3. Gain a total overview of the problem.
   - The project sponsor will need to understand the issue that is being considered.
   - All the information necessary to undertake the evaluation will need to be obtained.
   - This will need to be segmented into key fields for further analysis.
4. Make a value judgement on the quality of the information obtained.
   - If the information obtained is of doubtful quality, then any analysis will also be of doubtful quality.
   - If you know that the input quality is poor – for example, in collecting loss data for capital modelling purposes – then you cannot realistically expect to come up with an answer to 99.9% confidence level. It is just unrealistic; the underlying data does not facilitate this level of accuracy.

Consider the modelling approach that is to be used. There are a series of modelling techniques and approaches available, and one that is suitable for the problem being considered needs to be selected.

- The simplest modelling technique – guesswork – is the one most commonly used.
- The technique suitable to the specific circumstances and the apparent data shape, volume and structure should be selected. At least if an incorrect decision is made, the analysis can now explain why.

5. Formally define your problem.
   - If a modelling approach is to be adopted then the problem needs to be analysed into its constituent parts.
   - These then need to be put into a form so that modelling software can deal with the issue concerned.
   - Prior to the final selection of the modelling technique it is always worth checking again that the assumptions on which the approach is based are either valid in the circumstances under consideration, or provides a sufficient level of confidence in the outcome.

6. Review the output of the modelling.
   - This should be verified independently to ensure that the output is accurate. Often modelling is undertaken outside the normal data entry control environment, so simple processing errors can occur which will totally invalidate the analysis.
   - A reasonableness test should always be conducted. When you are looking at the output, a high-level review of the key results will tell you if the answer is plausible, or whether it should be immediately rejected and the modelling should either be repeated or an alternative modelling technique selected.
   - The modelling should be formally signed off prior to any further actions being taken.

7. List the various alternative actions that could be adopted.
   - Modelling is only ever part of the solution. If there is a true problem that needs to be solved by the business, then there will consequently be business implications. Only some of these implications will be factors that will have been included within the actual project modelling that has been undertaken. Other issues are harder to define but could impact upon the selected solution. These should all be considered separately, for example is the solution that results from the modelling adopted right for the company at this time given the resources available to it?

8. Contrast the possible alternative actions available (time, cost, labour).
   - There will be a series of solutions on offer. The modeller will produce the optimal solution or solutions. Others can also still be evaluated which, although not optimal in general, may be optimal in terms of a specific resource.
   - Only through looking at the series of available options in this way will the analyst be comfortable, and be able to convince management, that the selected approach is in fact the best.

9. Adopt a specific course of action.
10. Obtain the necessary resources (time, money, labour).
11. Ensure that you have solved the problem you originally identified.
    - Another regular failing is that the analyst gets carried away with analysis and solves the problem that can be modelled rather than the problem that needs to be solved.
    - Management needs to guard against this and not be trapped into making a solution to a problem that did not exist just because it has been modelled, while the original problem is solved through lethargy, effectively making the decision for the company.

12. Obtain formal approval for the completion of the entire project.
13. Review the project to see if any lessons can be learned to improve the next similar project.

There are a number of tools that assist with this process. Two of these, Bayes' theorem and decision trees, were addressed in Chapter 4. Another common approach is the so-called Minimax Regret rule. This is also very easy to use and could be suitable for relatively simple problems.

20.3   MINIMAX REGRET RULE

Consider a case where the Board of a company is trying to decide which of three projects (A, B or C) to develop. Three possible scenarios have been identified and an estimate of the costs associated for each scenario for each of these three projects (1, 2 and 3) has been obtained. Therefore for each project the company has three possible costs, one for each scenario. The actual figures obtained are shown in Table 20.1.

Assuming that the projects will all return the same amount, which project should be selected? The Minimax Regret rule suggests that the company should minimise the costs and select the smallest worst result that could happen. This will represent the minimum cost solution. The appropriate values are produced as a final column in the following table. The strategy is to minimise the maximum cost as shown in Table 20.2. Selecting project B is the best in these circumstances.

For profits rather than costs a similar strategy may be adopted. Given that a company wishes to sell one of four products (A, B, C and D) and their profit will depend on customer reaction (scenarios 1, 2 and 3), the respective returns are shown in Table 20.3.

Reversing the previous strategy, Table 20.4 is constructed, where all of the minimums have been noted. The company will then select the largest minimum – this will be the assured profit since is it the smallest possible profit that must be earned through adopting any of the projects.

Table 20.1   Costs of three projects

	Cost		
Project	1	2	3
A	37	61	86
B	70	53	78
C	103	86	70

Table 20.2   Maximum costs of three projects

	Cost				
Project	1	2	3	Project maximum cost	
A	37	61	86	86	
B	70	53	78	78	Lowest
C	103	86	70	103	

Table 20.3 Profits of four projects

	Profit (Loss)		
Project	1	2	3
A	43	71	57
B	128	114	0
C	142	28	−14
D	28	157	71

Table 20.4 Minimum profits of four projects

	Profit/(Loss)				
Project	1	2	3	Project minimum Profit/Loss	
A	43	71	57	43	Maximum
B	128	114	0	0	
C	142	28	−14	−14	
D	28	157	71	28	

Table 20.5 Maximum profit for each outcome of four projects

	Profit		
Project	1	2	3
A	43	71	57
B	128	114	0
C	142	28	−14
D	28	157	71
Maximum	142	157	71

The maximum rule would select the highest minimum and project A would therefore be adopted. This strategy maximises the minimum profit. It does not, of course, maximise the possible profit.

This approach leaves a lot to be desired. What if scenario 1 occurred? If this were to actually happen then project C would have been a better choice. The return would have been improved by £99 over the Minimax Regret solution (£142 − £43). It could be said that £99 is a measure of the regret at accepting product A. The approach adopted should be to minimise the maximum regret that could arise from the selection of a specific product.

Using the same information, this time we select the maximum profit for each of the four possible outcomes. This is shown in Table 20.5.

As a first step in this process a table of regrets is constructed. This is done by taking the maximum for the first scenario and then systematically deducting each cell from it. The process is then repeated for the other two scenarios, with the solution being shown in Table 20.6. The

Table 20.6   Regrets of four projects

Project	Regret			Project maximum regret
	1	2	3	
A	99	86	14	99
B	14	43	71	71 Minimum
C	0	129	85	129
D	114	0	0	114

maximum regret for each product is shown in the table. The best choice is the project with the minimum maximum regret, which is B at £71.

These procedures are designed to avoid selecting the worst possible scenarios without taking into the account the full upside potential. They take no account of the different outcomes that might take place. In addition there is no possibility of rejecting all projects and doing nothing. Effectively it is a perfect low-risk accountant's tool.

21

Inventory and Stock Control

21.1 INTRODUCTION

A separate set of mathematical techniques has been designed that are of use to companies that have stock control issues to deal with. Typically, in a company, stock is in the form of raw materials, partially finished goods, completed goods or products awaiting shipment. The problem that the company has to deal with is to work out what is the level of stock that should be maintained to meet the anticipated demand without incurring unnecessary additional costs. Holding stock, or maintaining inventory, does result in a number of additional costs being incurred. These include, for example, interest costs on the investment in the stock and the physical costs of storage and maintenance.

This type of problem does occur in other areas of industry where stock or inventory in the classical sense are not held. In the securities industry, for example, an equities market maker will need to know how many securities to hold to ensure that they are able to meet the demands arising from quoted prices, while not holding more stock than is necessary.

Stock is held as an asset on the balance sheet at cost, including the costs incurred in bringing the stocks to their current state of readiness. The investment in stock has a future value since it is expected that at some stage in the future the goods will in fact be sold. However, the asset is not currently economically productive since no income is likely to be earned purely through holding stock in a warehouse.

With each stock item held there are a series of associated costs, only some of which will be included within the asset value of the stock as held in the balance sheet of the company. The accounting value of the stock will be made up from a combination of the original purchase price of the raw materials together with the costs that have been incurred in bringing the stock to its current state less any provision that is necessary to ensure that the stock is not held at a value that exceeds potential sales price net of sales expenses. The costs of storing and maintaining the stock items will not be included in the asset value and will immediately be expensed to profit and loss. Similarly any interest charges incurred through tying up capital in an asset that is currently unproductive will also be immediately expensed to profit and loss. The company has the objective of minimising the cost of holding inventory.

21.2 THE ECONOMIC ORDER QUANTITY MODEL

In the economic order quantity model we are seeking to establish the size of orders that should be made to meet expected demand for stock while minimising costs. This model converts all the costs involved in stock control into a mathematical representation. The economic order quantity model works fairly well despite a series of in-built assumptions. In particular, the model makes the following key assumptions:

1. Demand is known and is a constant.
2. The time between placing an order and receiving goods – the lead-time – is zero.

So here we have two simplifying assumptions. If they are either invalid or substantially invalid then any analysis undertaken based upon this model is likely to prove unreliable.

The model operates through assuming that associated with each item held within stock there are two basic costs. The first is the ordering cost that would cover such items as administration, postage and travel and are costs incurred each time an order is placed. The second cost is the holding cost which includes the cost of capital for maintaining the stock, together with the costs incurred in getting the stock to the current state, storage, insurance, deterioration and redundancy. The holding cost therefore covers all elements of the cost of keeping an item in stock.

21.2.1   An example of the use of the economic order quantity model

A company has a constant demand of 250 units per year for a particular product. The purchase cost per unit is £18. The cost of ordering, handling and delivering is known to be £27 per order and is assumed to be independent of the order size. The cost of holding items in stock is estimated to be 12.5% of the value of the stock held.

The company is seeking to establish the size of purchase order that would minimise the total inventory cost while ensuring that all orders could be met immediately.

Some mathematical notation is required to enable the problem to be solved. If Q is the quantity ordered on each occasion and D is the constant annual demand, then the stock level can be plotted as a function of time, see Figure 21.1.

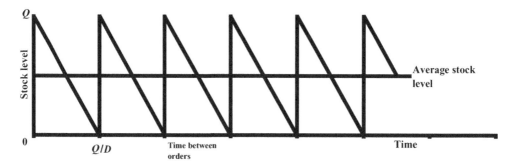

Figure 21.1   Stock level.

Initially there is an order for Q items. Since the lead-time is zero the stock held rises instantly from 0 to Q. The level then falls each year by the D units required. Therefore the stock ordered will last Q/D years.

In the example, D is 250 and if Q were 500, then the inventory level would fall to zero in two years. Alternatively, if the purchase order level Q were 125, the inventory level would fall to zero in $125/250 = 0.5$ years or 6 months.

The number of orders per year is D/Q and the last case considered above would require two deliveries each year (250/125). Since it is also assumed that the stock level is depleted uniformly, then the average stock level is $Q/2$ during the period of holding of the order. Costs should now be introduced into the model.

$$\text{Order cost} = \text{Cost per order} \times \text{Number of orders} = 27 \times \frac{D}{Q}$$

$$\text{Holding cost} = \text{Cost of holding an item} \times \text{Average number of items}$$

$$= \frac{12.5}{100} \times 18 \times \frac{Q}{2} = \frac{9Q}{8}$$

Clearly if no stock is held, then there will be no holding costs. In the example, the holding cost drops steadily from 12.5% (the estimated holding cost) of £18 (the original purchase price) for each of Q items to zero, when there is no stock held at all.

The company can exert control over the variable costs, which are the sum of the two costs defined above. An annual cost can also be computed by including the purchase cost. For the example this is shown in Figure 21.2, with total cost being shown in Figure 21.3.

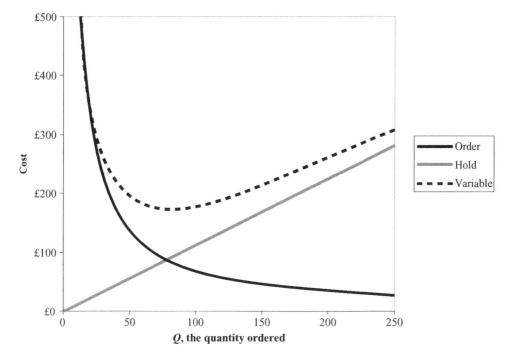

Figure 21.2   Cost functions.

Figure 21.3 shows the total annual cost, and to speed up the process of analysis, a trial and error approach is initially used to locate the lowest point of the graph, which corresponds to ordering 78 units of stock at each reordering event.

It is possible to use mathematical techniques to prove the same answer, recognising that:

$$\text{total}(Q) = \frac{27 \times 250}{Q} + 18 \times \frac{12.5}{100} \times \frac{Q}{2} + 250 \times 18$$

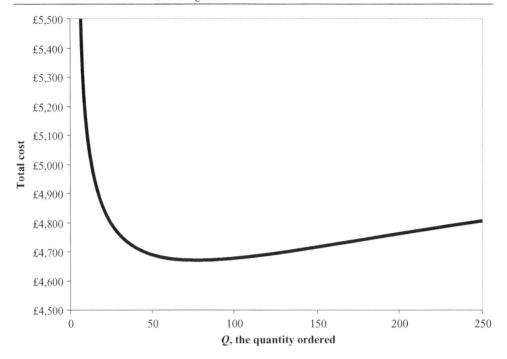

Figure 21.3   Total cost function.

If you take any a and b that are both positive, then basic calculus tells us that the minimum of $y(x) = ax + (b/x)$ occurs at $\sqrt{b/a}$. Then, using the above equation in our example, we know that the minimum corresponds to:

$$Q = \sqrt{\frac{27 \times 250 \times 2 \times 100}{18 \times 12.5}} = 77.46$$

As we can see, the actual mathematically calculated value is much the same as the approximate result that we had obtained by trial and error from the graph in Figure 21.3.

It is important to always bear in mind the simplifying assumptions built into the model.

- Demand is uniform over time.
- The lead-time for new deliveries is zero.
- Inventory is replenished when stock level is exactly zero.
- The entire order is received in one delivery.
- All costs are fixed over time.
- There is always sufficient storage space for the deliveries.

Clearly efficient inventory management will both save money and reduce the capital that is tied up by the business within inventory values. In practice, computer software is normally used to produce the graphs. However, the economic order quantity model is only a simple model and should always be used with care since in practice the assumptions are likely to be rather brave. If this model is adopted then the actual results that arise from actually following the model should be compared to those resulting from the theoretical use of the model in case this provides an indication that the model is not actually appropriate.

As set out above, the technique has changed a practical issue into a mathematical problem that can be solved. The aim of the analysis was to minimise cost, and this was achieved by locating the turning point in Figure 21.3. However, it must be appreciated that a small increase in Q, above this minimum, would lead to a minimal increase in cost. There may be sound reasons for adopting a larger order quantity despite the small penalty in terms of increased costs.

It may be the case that volume discounts are available from the supplier for larger orders. Taking advantage of such a discount has the effect of reducing the purchase cost and order cost while increasing the holding costs since the company will hold a greater level of stock. The economic order quantity model, employed above, may be modified to allow for this. If a discount of 5% is offered on orders of over 150 items then the solution is modified as set out in Figure 21.4.

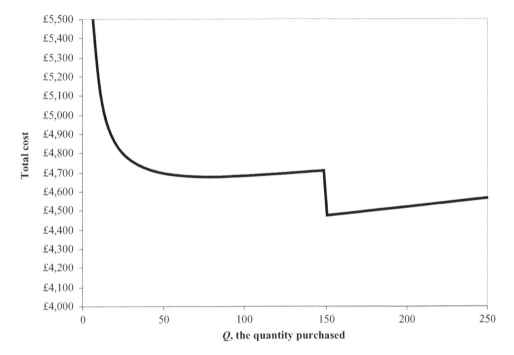

Figure 21.4   Discounted total cost.

Here we can see the discontinuity that has been created within the graph by the inclusion of the volume discount. Unsurprisingly, the minimum cost will now correspond to ordering 150 items, the minimum order value at which the discount is available, since this effectively skews the analysis.

21.3   NON-ZERO LEAD TIME

It would be more realistic to relax the assumption that we used in the above example that there is a zero lead time, since that is unlikely to be realistic in most cases. It is now necessary to calculate the point at which the order is placed, since this will determine when the stock will actually arrive. The amount of time prior to delivery that the order is made is referred to as the reorder point. We will use the same example and still assume a constant demand of 250 items per year. However, there will now be a lead time of one month between placing an order and actually receiving the goods. The monthly demand is given by:

$$250 \times \frac{1}{12} = 20.83 \approx 21$$

This means that when the stock level falls to 21 an order for 78 items must be placed to meet the expected demand since 21 items will be required in the month. The revised stock levels are shown in Figure 21.5.

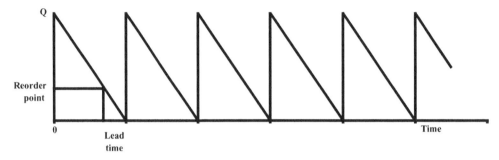

Figure 21.5   Stock level with non-zero lead time.

In reality, the actual demand will depend on some probabilistic distribution and is unlikely to be fixed unless there is an agreed supply contract in place. The reorder point will then depend upon the lead time (assumed fixed), the risk deemed acceptable of not meeting an order and the selected probabilistic demand function. The number of items held in stock when an order is placed will therefore depend on the risk accepted in failing to meet demand during the lead time.

21.3.1   An example of Poisson and continuous approximation

Let us assume that a Poisson distribution (see section 7.4) has been adopted to describe demand. In practice the analyst will look at what the demand has actually been over the last months and will then select the distribution that provides the best fit to the underlying data.

If we use the Poisson distribution then there will always be a risk that there will be insufficient stock available since the Poisson distribution has a long tail. The question then becomes: At what level should the reorder be set if management are willing to accept a risk of 5% that they will be unable to meet demand?

It was calculated in section 21.3 above that the monthly demand was 21, therefore for the Poisson distribution the probability of orders for x units is:

$$P(x) = \frac{\lambda^x e^{-\lambda}}{x!}$$

with $\lambda = 21$ (see section 7.4). Table 21.1 gives the appropriate cumulative Poisson probabilities for $\lambda = 21$.

Table 21.1   Cumulative poisson probabilities

x	Prob(x)	Prob(x or more)	x	Prob(x)	Prob(x or more)
0	0.000	1.000	19	0.083	0.616
1	0.000	1.000	20	0.087	0.529
2	0.000	1.000	21	0.087	0.442
3	0.000	1.000	22	0.083	0.360
4	0.000	1.000	23	0.076	0.284
5	0.000	1.000	24	0.066	0.218
6	0.000	1.000	25	0.056	0.162
7	0.000	1.000	26	0.045	0.117
8	0.001	0.999	27	0.035	0.083
9	0.002	0.997	28	0.026	0.056
10	0.003	0.994	29	0.019	0.037
11	0.007	0.987	30	0.013	0.024
12	0.012	0.975	31	0.009	0.015
13	0.019	0.957	32	0.006	0.009
14	0.028	0.928	33	0.004	0.006
15	0.040	0.889	34	0.002	0.003
16	0.052	0.837	35	0.001	0.002
17	0.064	0.773	36	0.001	0.001
18	0.075	0.698	37	0.000	0.001

If the adopted reorder level is 27 then

Prob(not being able to meet demand) = Prob(28 or more items per month) = 0.056 or 6%

If the adopted reorder level is 28 then

Prob(not being able to meet demand) = Prob(29 or more items per month) = 0.037 or 4%

Given that the level of risk of not being able to meet demand that is acceptable to management is 5%, the reorder level must be set at 28 items. In other words, when the stock falls to this level a new order must be placed.

As an approximation to the Poisson distribution a normal distribution (see Chapter 8), with appropriate parameters, may also be adopted. Using the notation from Chapter 8, it is then necessary to solve

$$\text{Prob}(z \geq z_c) = 0.05$$

from tables and as set out in Chapter 8, $z_c = 1.64$. If the order level x is assumed to be normal with mean λ and variance λ to match a Poisson distribution, then:

$$x_c = \lambda + z_c\sqrt{\lambda} = \lambda + 1.64\sqrt{\lambda} = 28.51$$

So the reorder level is now 29.

22

Simulation: Monte Carlo Methods

22.1 INTRODUCTION

In practice many of the issues that we have to deal with are too complex to enable them to be easily distilled into a simple mathematical equation or even for them to be governed by an underlying probabilistic structure. In such cases the approach that most companies will seek to adopt is Monte Carlo simulation.

22.2 WHAT IS MONTE CARLO SIMULATION?

Any variable that can be measured and can take on different values, such as the value of an equity portfolio over a given number of years, is commonly referred to as a random variable. The first type of probability structure that is normally created is called the *distribution function*, because it shows the frequency with which the random variable actually takes specific values within a certain range.

The second type of probability structure that might be created is called the *cumulative distribution function*. This displays the accumulated probability that the random variable falls below a certain value, effectively representing the total of the number of events that are below a value to the total number of observations.

Monte Carlo simulation takes the idea of using statistical trials to get an approximate solution that has been considered in previous chapters and enables this to be applied to a complex problem. There is a normally a process (such as the generation of an equity portfolio return) where some information is known, but other information that is required is not known with certainty. The expected return on an equity portfolio in 12 months' time is clearly not known with certainty, although we will know the historic returns that have been achieved.

Since these future values are not known exactly, many observations need to be made so that the uncertain values of the process can be estimated with increasing accuracy.

Prior to seeing Monte Carlo working in full we need to consider what happens when a company reorders stocks and seeks to meet demand from a standard reorder quantity.

22.2.1 An example of the use of Monte Carlo simulation: Theory of the inventory problem

A company sells computer software. Using mathematical notation, in a particular week a software reseller sells x units of computer software with probability, p_x. Historical data showing actual weekly demand over previous periods is collated in Table 22.1. Standard costs and order levels are summarised in Table 22.2.

The factor k is introduced to allow for contractual clauses, such as failing to fulfil orders for the delivery of software packages when a contract has been entered into that requires such a delivery; b has also been introduced to allow for additional factors such as the loss of reputation

Table 22.1   Probability of weekly demand

Demand (x)	0	1	2	3	4	5	6
Probability (p_x)	0.05	0.1	0.2	0.3	0.2	0.1	0.05

Table 22.2   Standard costs and order levels

S = Standard delivery amount in terms of units per week
A = Fixed cost
c = Unit cost per item ordered
h = Holding cost per unit per week
k = Penalty cost per unit of shortage
b = Backlog cost per item per week in shortage

that could result. Using this notation, the order cost becomes $A + cx$. For the remaining costs two cases must be considered.

What happens when demand is less than or equal to the standard delivery amount?

In this case supply exceeds or equals demand and the company will have an excess stock of software. The holding cost drops uniformly from the standard delivery amount S to $S - x$, where x is the actual demand. The costs are shown as reducing from Sh to $(S - x)h$ giving an average cost of $(Sh + (S - x)h)/2$. This situation is summarised in Figure 22.1.

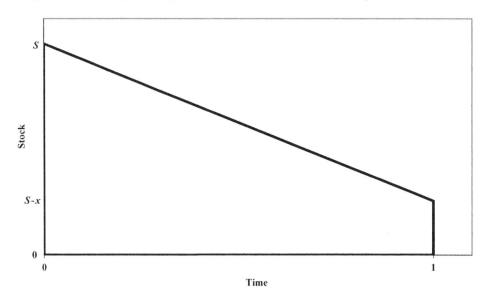

Figure 22.1   Stock when supply exceeds demand.

Demand is greater than or equal to supply

In this case demand exceeds or equates to the supply and the company will be unable to meet all the orders received from the single standard delivery amount. In this case the holding cost

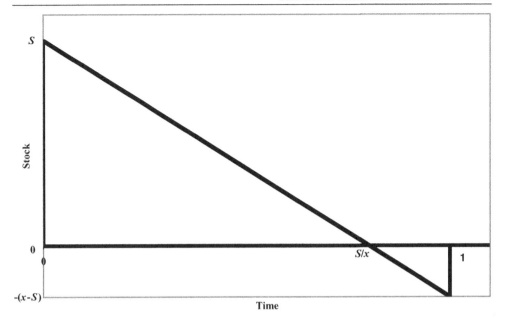

Figure 22.2   Stock when demand exceeds supply.

drops uniformly from Sh to zero in time S/x, giving an average cost of:

$$\frac{1}{2}Sh\frac{S}{x} = \frac{1}{2}S^2\frac{h}{x}$$

The shortage cost is a simple penalty and is evaluated as $k(x - S)$ since $x - S$ will represent the amount of the order that was not met. The backlog of unfilled orders rises from zero to $(x - S)$ between times S/x and 1. The order system is backlogged for time $1 - S/x$, giving an average cost of:

$$\frac{1}{2}b(x - S)\left(1 - \frac{S}{x}\right) = \frac{b(x - S)^2}{2x}$$

This situation is summarised in Figure 22.2.

   If $S = x$, the residual costs agree.

22.3   MONTE CARLO SIMULATION OF THE INVENTORY PROBLEM

The problem that the company is trying to solve is to determine the expected costs associated with a stock level, S. The weekly demand x has the probability distribution shown in Figure 22.3, which is just a bar chart (see Chapter 2) of the data in Table 22.1. The first step in the simulation is to generate a random number, y, which will be associated with a particular level of demand. The random number may be found from tables or from an appropriate package. They appear within Excel and are available on most calculators that are commonly purchased. Here it is assumed that the values of y are uniformly distributed over the interval $[0,1]$.

An x value is then associated with every y value generated ensuring that the correct proportion of the y's correspond to the probability of occurrence of a specific value of x. Effectively this amounts to stacking the bars from Figure 22.3 along a unit axis. The appropriate mapping is shown in Figure 22.4.

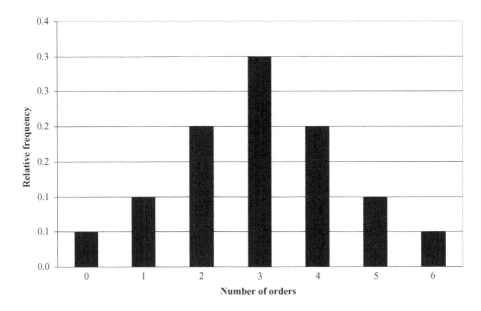

Figure 22.3   The probability of demand.

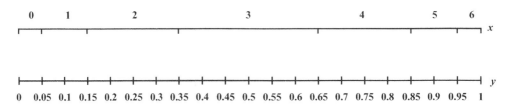

Figure 22.4   The probability of demand.

You can see that the length set aside for the three largest columns (two, three and four) still represent the largest part of the total distribution above. For the problem considered here the parameter values are as set out in Table 22.3.

Table 22.3   Numerical values for standard costs and order levels

S	2	Standard delivery amount
A	£5	Fixed cost
c	£20	Unit cost per item ordered
h	£5	Holding cost per unit per week
k	£10	Penalty cost per unit of shortage
b	£10	Backlog cost per item per week in shortage

Table 22.4   Cost and probabilities associated with order quantity

				x			
	0	1	2	3	4	5	6
Probability	0.05	0.1	0.2	0.3	0.2	0.1	0.05
Cumulative probability	0	0.05	0.15	0.35	0.65	0.85	0.95
Cost	£15	£32.50	£50	£80	£112.50	£146	£180
Expected cost	£0.75	£3.25	£10.00	£24.00	£22.50	£14.60	£9.00

If an Excel spreadsheet were used to produce the simulation, then the cumulative probabilities, which give the boundaries to the x intervals, would be needed for the 'lookup' function. Similar but different requirements exist for other types of spreadsheet. This is shown in Table 22.4 together with the associated total cost for the appropriate x value.

We have multiplied the cost by its associated probability and this is presented in the final row of the table. For example, looking at column two, the final figure shows £50 × 0.20 = £10.

On adding all these expected costs together, we obtain the following expected cost:

$$(0.75 + 3.25 + 10.00 + 24.00 + 22.50 + 14.60 + 9.00) = £84.10$$

After using 100 random numbers to carrying out 100 simulations, some of which are shown in Table 22.5, the observed costs are then averaged and give £87.14 as an expected cost resulting from the simulation. We have just shown the first 10 and final 6 simulations in this case and the random variable chosen from random number tables has been used in each case to set out the exact observation for the specific simulation.

Table 22.5   The simulations of cost associated with order quantity

Period	Random value	x	Initial inventory	Order quantity	Final inventory	Cost
1	0.8861	5	2	3	0	£146.00
2	0.0405	0	2	0	2	£15.00
3	0.1415	1	2	0	1	£32.50
4	0.6804	4	2	2	0	£112.50
5	0.9341	5	2	3	0	£146.00
6	0.1089	1	2	0	1	£32.50
7	0.8591	5	2	3	0	£146.00
8	0.7068	4	2	2	0	£112.50
9	0.0374	0	2	0	2	£15.00
10	0.8288	4	2	2	0	£112.50
95	0.1328	1	2	0	1	£32.50
96	0.0138	0	2	0	2	£15.00
97	0.7658	4	2	2	0	£112.50
98	0.3836	3	2	1	0	£80.00
99	0.6990	4	2	2	0	£112.50
100	0.5245	3	2	1	0	£80.00

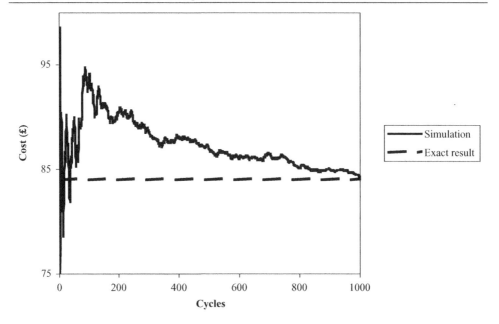

Figure 22.5   The simulation of 1,000 cycles of cost associated with order quantity.

As more simulations are conducted, the average of the transactions will slowly vary less and less, effectively converging to the final expected result.

You can see that the simulation (Figure 22.5) is slowly converging towards what is actually the exact result in this case. That is all Monte Carlo actually does – it takes a series of random numbers and then, through a series of linked probabilities, comes up with a converging solution. It effectively enables you to create order out of chaos.

22.4   QUEUING PROBLEM

To see how Monte Carlo techniques can add value in practice, let us consider a single server queue. In this case we assume that the service time is represented by an exponential distribution (see section 7.7) with parameter μ. This assumption is normally made because it is easier to simulate using the exponential distribution.

Therefore, there are μ services undertaken on average in a unit of time. The actual number of arrivals is assumed to follow a Poisson distribution (see section 7.4) since the distribution still leaves extreme values available.

Since the arrivals follow a Poisson distribution, the inter-arrival time will also be represented by an exponential distribution with parameter λ since this is a property of the Poisson distribution. Therefore, the average inter-arrival time is $1/\lambda$.

We define traffic intensity as $\rho = \lambda/\mu$. If the queue is to function adequately then $\lambda < \mu$ since, on average, there must be more server time available than there are arrivals. This is equivalent to the criterion that $\rho < 1$. If this were not the case then the server queue would grow indefinitely.

When you are doing Monte Carlo simulations you will generally be interested in the long-term behaviour of the queue, not in minor short-term fluctuations. It must also be believed that there is in fact some form of steady-state solution which adequately describes the system.

The following six useful quantities, describing the queue, can be obtained.

1. The probability of receiving instantaneous service is $p_0 = 1 - \rho$.
2. The probability of having to queue on arrival at the service point. This is equivalent to requiring that the service point is busy, which is ρ.
3. The average number of people in the system, including the current customer being served, is $\rho/(1 - \rho)$.
4. The average number of people in the queue is $\rho^2/(1 - \rho)$.
5. The average time spent in the queue is $\dfrac{\rho^2}{1 - \rho}\dfrac{1}{\lambda}$, since $1/\lambda$ is the average time between arrivals.
6. The average time spent in the system is a combination of the average time spent in the queue and the time being served, which is

$$\frac{\rho^2}{1 - \rho}\frac{1}{\lambda} + \frac{1}{\mu} = \frac{1}{\mu}\frac{1}{1 - \rho}$$

since $1/\mu$ is the average service time.

It is known that arrivals occur at a rate λ and that the server operates on μ occasions per unit of time. The probability of a service taking time x is therefore $(1/\mu)e^{-\mu x}$.

To perform the sort of mapping considered above, the cumulative distribution must now be produced. Using the notation that we have introduced, this is given by the equation:

$$F(z) = \int_0^z f(x)\,dx$$

which, in this case, gives $F(z) = 1 - e^{-\mu z}$. The density is shown in Figure 22.6 and the mapping is shown in Figure 22.7 for an occurrence rate of 24 services per unit time.

So given the graphs plotted, a transformation as described by Figure 22.7 from y (the uniform random number) to x may be made via the equation $y = 1 - e^{-\mu x}$, which was given above. This can be rearranged to give:

$$x = -\frac{1}{\mu}\ln(1 - y)$$

and provides an appropriate inter-arrival time or service time, depending on the choice of rate. So given the rate (λ or μ) and a random number (y), a time (x) may be calculated for either the inter-arrival time or the service time.

22.5   THE BANK CASHIER PROBLEM

Typically 12 customers arrive at a bank cashier's window every hour. The cashier, who on average is capable of processing 24 applications within an hour, staffs the window. The problem is to find the probability of a customer having to queue and also the average number of customers that will be in the system at any point of time.

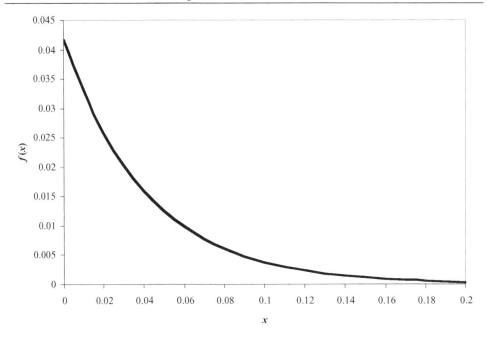

Figure 22.6   Exponential distribution rate (λ) 24.

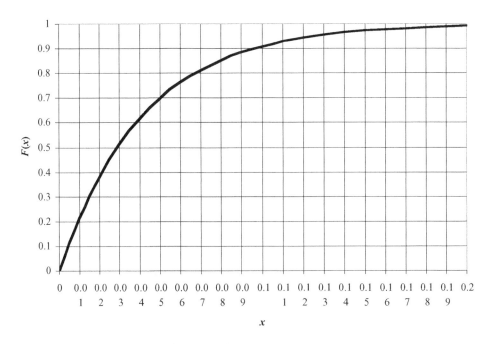

Figure 22.7   Cumulative exponential distribution rate (μ) 24.

Using the exact results given above,

- The parameters are $\lambda = 12$ and $\mu = 24$ so that:

$$\rho = \frac{12}{24} = 0.5$$

- The probability of queuing is therefore $\rho = 0.5$.
- The average time spent in the queue is:

$$\frac{\rho^2}{1-\rho}\frac{1}{\lambda} = 0.0417$$

- The average number of customers in the system is:

$$\frac{\rho}{1-\rho} = 1.0.$$

Now employing these parameters, we know that there is an arrival rate of 12 customers per hour, with the ability of the cashier to serve 24 customers in an hour. A simulation may now be readily implemented and a typical calculation is laid out in Table 22.6.

Table 22.6 Queue simulation

Customer number	Random value y_1	Inter-arrival time	Arrival time	Random value y_2	Service time	Start of service	Exit time	Idle time	Time in queue
1	0.89	0.1839	0.1839	0.47	0.0265	0.1839	0.2104	0.1839	0.0000
2	0.04	0.0034	0.1873	0.34	0.0173	0.2104	0.2277	0.0000	0.0231
3	0.14	0.0126	0.1999	0.14	0.0063	0.2277	0.2340	0.0000	0.0278
4	0.68	0.0950	0.2949	0.84	0.0764	0.2949	0.3712	0.0609	0.0000
5	0.93	0.2216	0.5165	0.67	0.0462	0.5165	0.5627	0.1452	0.0000
6	0.11	0.0097	0.5262	0.07	0.0030	0.5627	0.5657	0.0000	0.0365
7	0.86	0.1638	0.6900	0.86	0.0819	0.6900	0.7719	0.1243	0.0000
8	0.71	0.1032	0.7932	0.73	0.0546	0.7932	0.8477	0.0212	0.0000
9	0.04	0.0034	0.7966	0.15	0.0068	0.8477	0.8545	0.0000	0.0512
10	0.83	0.1477	0.9442	0.13	0.0058	0.9442	0.9500	0.0897	0.0000
11	0.28	0.0274	0.9716	0.68	0.0475	0.9716	1.0191	0.0216	0.0000
12	0.89	0.1839	1.1556	0.99	0.1919	1.1556	1.3474	0.1365	0.0000
13	0.42	0.0454	1.2010	0.4	0.0213	1.3474	1.3687	0.0000	0.1465
14	0.25	0.0240	1.2249	0.6	0.0382	1.3687	1.4069	0.0000	0.1438
15	0.76	0.1189	1.3439	0.38	0.0199	1.4069	1.4268	0.0000	0.0631

You can see where the random variables have been selected in columns two and five of Table 22.6. To show how this works, consider the second customer. The inter-arrival time is given by

$$-\frac{1}{12}\ln(1 - 0.04) = 0.0034$$

This is added to the arrival time for first customer, to give an arrival time for second customer of

$$0.1839 + 0.0034 = 0.1873 \text{ hours}$$

The service time for the second customer is given by

$$-\frac{1}{24}\ln(1 - 0.34) = 0.0173 \text{ hours}$$

The service can start at the maximum of the arrival of the second customer, or as the first customer leaves. Clearly if the second customer arrives after the first customer has left, then the teller will be waiting.

If the customer arrives before the first customer has completed the transaction, then the customer will have to wait. The exit time follows on, including the service time. The idle time is the difference between the start of the second customer service and the exit of the first customer. The time in the queue is the difference between the time of arrival of the second customer and the start of their service.

These times may be converted into the following useful measures:

1. 0.7834 hours is the total idle time, on summing the ninth column.
2. 55% is the proportion of idle time on comparing the idle time to the exit time of the last customer.
3. 0.1465 hours (the maximum number in column 10) is the maximum time spent in the queue.
4. 0.0328 is the average time spent in the queue, on averaging the times individuals spent in the queue.
5. 0.5333 is the probability of instantaneous service, since eight customers from a population of 15 received instant service (the zero values in column 10).

The theoretical values obtained above give 0.0417 as the average time spent in the queue and 0.5 as the probability of a customer receiving an instantaneous service. These results are remarkably close to those obtained from the very brief simulation conducted earlier.

22.6   MONTE CARLO FOR THE MONTY HALL PROBLEM

This problem was introduced at the conclusion of the probability section, within Chapter 4. The set of Monty Hall's game show *Let's Make a Deal* has three closed doors (A, B and C). Behind one of these doors is a car; behind the other two are goats. The contestant does not know where the car is, but Monty Hall does.

The contestant picks a door and Monty opens one of the remaining doors, one he knows does not hide the car. If the contestant has already chosen the correct door, Monty is equally likely to open either of the two remaining doors, since each would have a goat behind it.

After Monty has shown a goat behind the door that he opens, the contestant is always given the option to switch doors. What is the probability of winning the car if the contestant stays with his first choice? What if the contestant decides to switch?

The winning letter in the Monty Hall problem will represent a door, the position of which is always known to Monty. Let us assume it is A. The participant's initial choice is either A, B or C with equal probabilities. The cumulative probabilities are shown in Table 22.7 and these can be coupled with a random number to indicate the participant's first choice.

The next stage is to decide which letter the participant is shown. If the initial choice were A, then Monty is able to reveal B or C with equal likelihoods. However, if B or C is chosen, then Monty, respectively, must reveal C or B. These options are set out in Table 22.8.

Table 22.7   Cumulative initial probabilities for the Monty Hall problem

Choice	Probability	Cumulative probability
A	0.3333	0
B	0.3333	0.3333
C	0.3333	0.6666
		1

Table 22.8   Second event probabilities for the Monty Hall problem

Initial choice	Shown	Probability	Stick	Switch
A	B	0.5	A	C
A	C	0.5	A	B
B	C	1	A	B
C	B	!	A	C

Table 22.9   Simulation of the Monty Hall problem

Random variable	Initial choice	Random variable	Shown	Switch		Stick	
0.8444	C	0.8691	B	A	win	C	lose
0.1011	A	0.0009	B	C	lose	A	win
0.5444	B	0.4648	C	A	win	B	lose
0.9736	C	0.2184	B	A	win	C	lose
0.4440	B	0.7167	C	A	win	B	lose
0.2745	A	0.8878	C	B	lose	A	win
0.9083	C	0.4055	B	A	win	C	lose
0.6326	B	0.0617	C	A	win	B	lose
0.5568	B	0.9972	C	A	win	B	lose
0.6940	C	0.9833	B	A	win	C	lose

Table 22.10   Summary of a Monte Carlo simulation of the Monty Hall problem

	Switch	Stick
Win	1,320	680
Lose	680	1,320
Ratio	**0.66**	**0.34**

The player may either stick with the original choice or switch. This is equivalent to choosing the third letter option. A few simulations are displayed in Table 22.9. After 2,000 cycles the results are summarised in Table 22.10.

The probabilities of success agree reasonably with the exact values calculated previously (see Chapter 4). The best strategy is to switch, with a winning probability that is approximately 2/3. The convergence of successive estimates to this value is shown in Figure 22.8.

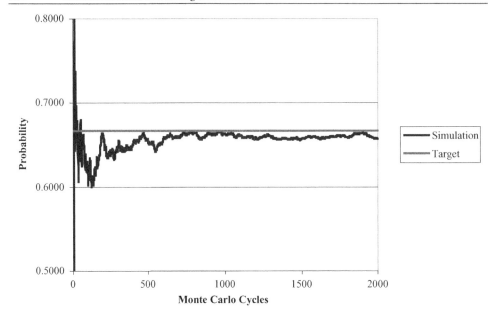

Figure 22.8   The simulation of 2,000 cycles of the switching probability.

22.7   CONCLUSION

Simulation is a very good technique when you need to bring together a lot of data and probabilities. Normally software solutions are used to show this. Indeed with both the simulators and computer capacity having grown, it is now possible to undertake very large simulations comparatively easily. However, even in large populations you will normally see that the simulation really has converged by the time you have done 250 simulations, although more can be conducted if required.

While we have shown a few examples that you can calculate manually, more complex ones are not so easy to demonstrate. So, in brief, all Monte Carlo achieves is to throw a series of random numbers at a series of probabilities, often shown as distributions, to come up with a single answer.

Reliability: Obsolescence

23.1   INTRODUCTION

Another business problem that will be encountered in practice is the decision of whether to repair or replace a specific piece of equipment. For example, computers only have a limited life during which they function reliably. After that time the computer will either become unreliable, or obsolete, and will need to be replaced. So the decision is whether to carry on using a computer until it fails, or to replace it after a fixed period of time.

You see this type of replacement strategy commonly applied in the case of company car schemes. The strategy adopted in practice will depend on the probability of failure and the cost of repair and replacement. It will also be important to consider how essential the asset is to your operation. For example, the decision about when to replace the battery in a smoke detector clearly has much greater impact on the risk profile of an institution than would be the case when replacing coffee supplies in a coffee vending machine.

To explain and illustrate the types of models that may be used to solve this type of issue, we consider the operation and replacement decisions related to personal computers.

23.2   REPLACEMENT AT A FIXED AGE

A company knows that the cost of replacing a specific personal computer is £1,250. They also know that they need to consider the reliability of the equipment and any losses that will accrue if the equipment were to fail during the business day.

If the computer breaks down during the business day, management estimate that on average there will be a reduction in staff performance, which will cost the business around £1,750 per failure. The key variable in this case is the length of time that the company takes to replace the equipment, so this is where we will introduce the mathematical symbol n. In this case it is used to represent the amount of time until the computer is replaced. The company always replaced personal computers overnight so that in the morning there will be a complete setup and staff performance will therefore not be affected further.

Again we need to introduce some further mathematical notation. In this case we designate that the probability of a computer breaking down during its kth year is p_k. Of course the company will have had personal computers that will have failed before and is able to use this information to calculate a series of failure probabilities. These probabilities are summarised in Table 23.1.

The average life of a personal computer when purchased is therefore:

$$(1 \times 0.05 + 2 \times 0.10 + 3 \times 0.15 + 4 \times 0.20 + 5 \times 0.25 + 6 \times 0.25) = 4.25 \text{ years}$$

The question the company needs to face is what is the optimal time (n) to replace the computers in order to minimise the expected cost on a year by year basis.

Again we need to introduce further mathematical notation at this stage. Let C_B be the cost of installing a new computer, which is £1,250 in this example. Then let C_F be the cost

Table 23.1 Failure probabilities
for replacement at a fixed age

Year		Probability
1	p_1	0.05
2	p_2	0.10
3	p_3	0.15
4	p_4	0.20
5	p_5	0.25
6	p_6	0.25

incurred by a complete failure, being the cost of the replacement together with the loss of performance caused by a failure during the working day. In the example this is given by £1,250 + £1,750 = £3,000.

Finally let

$$\bar{P}_k = 1 - P_k = \sum_{i=k+1}^{\infty} p_i$$

which is just saying that the probability that a particular computer will last k years, is the total of all of the probabilities for the computer lasting any amount of time up to k years.

If a scheduled replacement takes place after n years then the expected cost is given by the probability that the computer will have failed, together with the probability that it is still functioning. There are always two opportunities: the computer could fail prior to the replacement date and be repaired, or there is the chance that the computer will remain reliable right up to n years. In mathematical notation this is shown as:

C_B Prob(computer is unbroken)

$+C_F$ Prob(computer fails prior to the $(n + 1)$th year) $= C_B \bar{P}_n + C_F P_n$

The expected number of years between replacement of the personal computer, if it is replaced every n years, is then given by:

$$\sum_{i=1}^{n} i p_i + n \bar{P}_n = \sum_{i=0}^{n-1} \bar{P}_i$$

The first sum allows for the computer breaking down and then being repaired, prior to the normal replacement time. The second term represents the period of unbroken service. The expected cost per year is now given by the following mathematical equation:

$$C_n = \frac{C_B \bar{P}_n + C_F (1 - \bar{P}_n)}{\bar{P}_0 + \bar{P}_1 + \cdots + \bar{P}_{n-1}}$$

For the example considered above, all these costs are summarised in Table 23.2.

By looking at the column for expected cost per year it can be seen that the minimum total costs corresponds to replacing the computer after four years, where a value of £607.14 is shown. As expected, the cost for replacing before this time is larger since reliable computers will on balance be discarded. The cost increases after this stage as the computers become more unreliable and are more prone to failure.

Table 23.2   Cost per year for replacement at a fixed age

i	p_i	$\bar{P}_i$	$\sum_{j=0}^{i} \bar{P}_j$	C_i
0	0.00	1.00	1.00	
1	0.05	0.95	1.95	£1,337.50
2	0.10	0.85	2.80	£775.64
3	0.15	0.70	3.50	£633.93
4	0.20	0.50	4.00	£607.14
5	0.25	0.25	4.25	£640.63
6	0.25	0.00	4.25	£705.88

23.3   REPLACEMENT AT FIXED TIMES

This type of technique may be extended to deal with additional constraints that the company may wish to impose. Let us assume that the company imposes a rigid rule that every computer must be replaced after every nth year regardless of any intermediate replacements.

Let f_i denote the probability that there is a failure i years since the last replacement. The f_i are related to the probability of a computer breaking down during its ith year, p_i. This relationship is summarised in Table 23.3, where, for example, to calculate f_3 you must consider the option of failing after either year 1, year 2 or year 3.

Table 23.3   Failure probability for replacement at fixed times

Failure probability

$$f_1 = p_1$$
$$f_2 = p_2 + p_1 f_1$$
$$f_3 = p_3 + p_2 f_1 + p_1 f_2$$
$$\vdots$$
$$f_n = p_n + \sum_{i=1}^{n-1} p_{n-i} f_i$$

The variable F_n is used to denote the number of failures that occur if we replace the computer after n years. This variable has an average value of $\bar{F}_n$. This consists of the probability that there will be a failure at year 1, together with that for year 2, including and up to a failure occurring in year n. This can be mathematically shown as:

$$\bar{F}_n = f_1 + f_2 + \ldots + f_n.$$

The expected cost per year is therefore the probability that the computer is unbroken added to the sum of the probabilities of breakage, or:

$$C_n = \frac{C_B + C_F \bar{F}_n}{n}.$$

In this case the costs are summarised in Table 23.4.

Table 23.4   Cost per year for replacement at fixed times

n	p_n	$\bar{f}_n$	$\bar{F}_n$	C_n
1	0.05	0.0500	0.0500	£1,400.00
2	0.10	0.1025	0.1525	£853.75
3	0.15	0.1601	0.3126	£729.29
4	0.20	0.2258	0.5384	£716.29
5	0.25	0.3027	0.8411	£754.63
6	0.25	0.3447	1.1858	£801.23
7	0.00	0.1515	1.3373	£751.70
8	0.00	0.1983	1.5356	£732.08
9	0.00	0.2338	1.7693	£728.67
10	0.00	0.2553	2.0246	£732.39

There is still a minimum at four years of £716.29. However, the minimum cost now oscillates with the next lowest point being £728.69 which appears at nine years. For a large number of years, it would be expected that, in the limit case:

$$C_n = \frac{C_F \bar{F}_n}{n}$$

Since we know that $\bar{F}_n/n$ is simply the failure rate of the computer, we can now calculate the actual costs. We calculated that the average life of the personal computer on purchase, from Table 23.1 was 4.25; therefore since $1/4.25 = 0.2353$, the cost is then given by the following calculation:

$$(£1{,}250 + £1{,}750) \times 0.2353 = £705.88.$$

This is less than the two options calculated above and would therefore suggest that the optimum solution is to replace the computer only when it actually fails.

So we can see that using different modelling approaches does come up with different solutions. Again this highlights the fact that applying a sub-optimal modelling technique that fails to take into account all the potential variables could result in the company choosing a sub-optimal solution.

24

Project Evaluation

24.1 INTRODUCTION

Project evaluation techniques are widely used in business to decide whether a particular project should be undertaken. They are also used to enable a number of projects to be compared and, on considering explicit criteria, the company will select those that are to be approved.

In this chapter we consider net present value techniques, the internal rate of return of a project, the price earnings ratio and the payback period method of project appraisal. The payback period does have some advantages over the other methods, but, as with any other modelling technique, there are also disadvantages. However, when you are doing project evaluation the payback period is a method that does need to be considered, but is frequently forgotten.

In particular it is a technique where the lessons are easily learned and where management are likely to have a higher level of understanding of the message delivered than might be the case for some of the more complex methods.

We start by looking at net present value.

24.2 NET PRESENT VALUE

In this approach the borrowing costs that the firm incurs, or the cost of capital, is taken as the discount interest rate, which is then applied to cash flows arising from the project at a series of future dates. Some of these cash flows could be positive while others might be negative. The total net present value (NPV) of the project will be the total, or sum, of all these cash flows discounted by the cost of capital. The amount by which the NPV of these future cash flows is positive will be a measure of the extent to which the project has achieved its cost of capital and therefore is value enhancing to the institution.

24.2.1 An example of net present value

A bank proposes to purchase a new printing machine for £6,500. The machine has an expected life of three years and a scrap value of £1,000. The running costs of the machine are £3,500 per annum and the expected return is £6,000 per year, measured in terms of improved productivity and efficiency. The bank's required cost of capital is 10%. The question that the management will need to answer is whether the project (purchasing the printing machine) is likely to achieve the firm's required cost of capital and will therefore be sufficiently value enhancing.

In this case the bank has set the required rate at 10%, which is likely to be significantly above the bank's actual costs of capital. This will enable the bank to reject projects that are insufficiently value enhancing at an initial stage.

Again it is best to introduce some mathematical notation which assists in understanding the problem being addressed. If the interest rate is i and the project is expected to realise a single

Table 24.1   Net cash flow

Year	Net cash flow (y)	Discount factor	Present value (x)
2002	$-6,500$	$\dfrac{1}{(1+0.1)^0} = 1$	$-£6,500.00$
2003	$6,000 - 3,500 = 2,500$	$\dfrac{1}{(1+0.1)^1}$	$£2,272.73$
2004	$6,000 - 3,500 = 2,500$	$\dfrac{1}{(1+0.1)^2}$	$£2,066.12$
2005	$6,000 - 3,500 + 1,000 = 3,500$	$\dfrac{1}{(1+0.1)^3}$	$£2,629.60$
Net present value			**£468.44**

receipt of £x after n years from an initial investment of £y, then mathematically,

$$x = y \left(1 + \frac{i}{100}\right)^n$$

We can use this equation to provide a solution to the project of purchasing printing equipment to establish whether it meets the criteria required by the bank (see Table 24.1).

The discount factors take the discount rate agreed (the required capital return rate) for each of the years under consideration. On these terms the project would appear to be a success and is equivalent to investing £6,500 + £468.44 = £6,968.44 for the three-year expected life of the equipment.

Of course to do this evaluation we have ignored a range of other events, including inflation and taxation. We have also ignored any opportunity cost that arises because the bank is not able to do something else. All companies normally operate under conditions where capital is scarce and so undertaking one project normally means that some other project will be rejected.

In this case the return is a pure return based on the current cost of capital that has been set for the bank and therefore will only tell them that, on balance, the project does not detract value and achieves the required costs of funds.

In summary, the net present value (NPV) method compares a project's cash profile to the cost of investing the same funds invested in the project at the company's current corporate borrowing rate. If the NPV is zero, then the return from the project is exactly the same as the cost of capital that has been used for discounting the cash flows from the project.

24.3   INTERNAL RATE OF RETURN

The internal rate of return (IRR) method determines the interest rate at which the NPV is reduced to zero. It is therefore the expected earning rate of return for the project. Calculation of the IRR for returns over a number of years is a mathematical exercise; however, the basic functionality exists on many spreadsheets and will certainly be available within your company.

24.3.1   An example of the internal rate of return

A company has a project costing £1,500 in 2005 which is expected to earn £700 in 2006, £600 in 2007 and £500 in 2008. The company wishes to know the internal rate of return for the project.

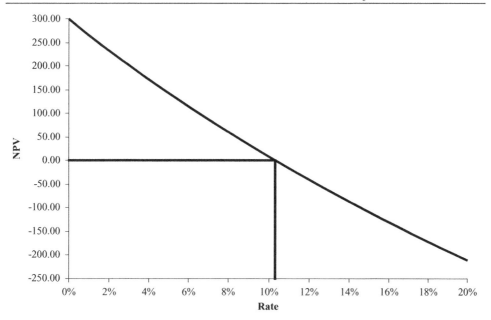

Figure 24.1 Internal rate of return.

The NPV values for a range of interest rates and the IRRs relating to them are set out in Figure 24.1. From the graph it can be seen that the NPV becomes zero at a rate of 10.3%. Therefore, if the cash flows were discounted at a rate of 10.3%, the NPV of the project would be zero.

If a package is not available then some form of interpolation could be employed which uses a series of starting guesses that shoot either side of the solution. For example, a rate of 10% returns an NPV of £7.89 while 11% gives a value of −£16.80. The calculations in respect of the 10% returns are set out in Table 24.2.

For 11% the divisor in the discount factor would become $1 + 0.11 = 1.11$ to the appropriate power. Joining these estimates by a straight line gives:

$$NPV = -2,468.90 \times IRR + 254.78$$

Table 24.2 Specimen calculation for 10%

Year	Net cash flow (y)	Discount factor	Present value (x)
2005	−1,500	$\dfrac{1}{(1+0.1)^0} = 1$	−£1,500.00
2006	700	$\dfrac{1}{(1+0.1)^1}$	£636.36
2007	600	$\dfrac{1}{(1+0.1)^2}$	£495.87
2008	500	$\dfrac{1}{(1+0.1)^3}$	£375.66
Net present value			**£7.89**

This then gives a value of 10.32% since, when the NPV is zero, the transept becomes:

$$\text{IRR} = \frac{254.78}{2,468.90} = 10.32\%$$

24.4   PRICE/EARNINGS RATIO

The price/earnings (P/E) ratio is a measure of the number of years profits in a company that is effectively bought when a share in that company is purchased. Therefore, using mathematical notation, if the share price is £x, N shares are issued and the annual profit is £P then the P/E ratio is given by Nx/P in years.

This is a widely used measure within the investment community. Of course alone it is not sufficient since it ignores such items as the underlying asset value of the company, which will act as a support to the share price. It also ignores any return that arises on the shares – for example, dividends. In many ways it is a measure of the perceived quality of the management in the company and an investor is likely to pay more for companies where there is expected growth or strong management. If a company has a high P/E ratio it could be expected to grow more quickly in terms of profitability than a company with a low P/E ratio. However, some sectors are able to command higher P/E ratios than other sectors purely due to their being in vogue. This can result in unsustainable P/E ratios being maintained for normally relatively short economic cycles, leading to significant potential future investor losses.

24.5   PAYBACK PERIOD

The payback period of project appraisal is a technique often neglected by modern business people, but still has significant importance to project appraisal in the modern world. It gives a measure of the time a project takes to 'pay back' its original investment. In so doing it takes little account of the size or profitability of the project.

What the payback period is able to do better than any other method is to show the assets that will be available for alternative uses, linking into the opportunity costs of not doing something. It is often the inability to account for these capital inflows properly that undermine some of the other methods. Of course, we would recommend that the payback period should be used in conjunction with the other methods, rather than as a replacement for them.

24.5.1   Mathematical background to the payback period

Again it is easier to manipulate a problem if we introduce mathematical notation. In this case, for a specific project, the expected cost is defined to be C. The cash inflow in year i is given by $S(i)$, and the project has an expected life of n years.

The basic definition of the payback period P is that it represents the first year in which cash inflows received to date exceed the original cost incurred, that is

$$C \leq S(1) + \ldots + S(P)$$

and P will be the first time that this occurs.

As the project progresses, better estimates of P may be obtained and further unplanned costs could also be incurred. We can define the outstanding costs at year i as being $C(i)$, then,

$$C(i) = S(1) + \ldots + S(i) - C$$

and the payback period P is now required such that $C(P) = 0$. The latest two sets of returns may be used to obtain an estimate of P by assuming a linear relation between i and $C(i)$. This calculation takes the form of a simple equation:

$$i = aC(i) + b$$

We can replace i with an actual value m in the above equation and obtain the following:

$$C(m) = S(1) + \ldots + S(m) - C = C(m-1) + S(m)$$

Then for $i = m - 1$ the linear equation becomes:

$$m - 1 = aC(m-1) + b = a[C(m) - S(m)] + b$$

and at $i = m$ the linear equation becomes:

$$m = aC(m) + b$$

You can solve these simultaneous equations, giving:

$$a = \frac{1}{S(m)} \quad \text{and} \quad b = m - aC(m).$$

If $C(P)$ becomes zero then an estimate of P is $m - [C(m)/S(m)]$. Clearly once the inflows exceed the project cost there is no need to extrapolate further. You are then able to construct tables that relate these key financial measures.

24.5.2 Mathematical background to producing the tables

For payback period P, internal rate of return IRR, project life n and uniform cash flow, the following relationship holds

$$\text{IRR} = Q - Q(1 + \text{IRR})^{-n}$$

where Q is the payback reciprocal, $Q = P^{-1}$. This is a fairly typical set of assumptions for this kind of work. In fact it is unlikely that there will be uniform cash flows, so the impact of this on the accuracy of your analysis will need to be considered.

This equation may be rearranged to make n the subject, as follows:

$$n = -\frac{\ln\left[(Q - \text{IRR})/Q\right]}{\ln(1 + \text{IRR})}$$

with the necessary constraint that Q is greater than the IRR, so that the log may be taken for a positive amount. Some values arising from the use of this equation are shown in Table 24.3.

Therefore if $P = 4(Q = 0.25)$ and IRR $= 0.20$, then n is 8.8. This means that if the project life is 8.8 years, and the project pays back in four years, then the IRR of the project is 20%.

Table 24.3 Project life in years: analysis of payback period and IRR

IRR	\	\	\	\	\	Payback period	\	\	\	\	\	\	\	\
	3.00	3.10	3.20	3.30	3.40	3.50	3.75	4.00	4.25	4.50	4.75	5.00	5.50	6.00
0.01	3.1	3.2	3.3	3.4	3.5	3.6	3.8	4.1	4.4	4.6	4.9	5.2	5.7	6.2
0.02	3.1	3.2	3.3	3.4	3.6	3.7	3.9	4.2	4.5	4.8	5.0	5.3	5.9	6.5
0.03	3.2	3.3	3.4	3.5	3.6	3.8	4.0	4.3	4.6	4.9	5.2	5.5	6.1	6.7
0.04	3.3	3.4	3.5	3.6	3.7	3.8	4.1	4.4	4.8	5.1	5.4	5.7	6.3	7.0
0.05	3.3	3.5	3.6	3.7	3.8	3.9	4.3	4.6	4.9	5.2	5.6	5.9	6.6	7.3
0.06	3.4	3.5	3.7	3.8	3.9	4.0	4.4	4.7	5.1	5.4	5.8	6.1	6.9	7.7
0.07	3.5	3.6	3.7	3.9	4.0	4.2	4.5	4.9	5.2	5.6	6.0	6.4	7.2	8.1
0.08	3.6	3.7	3.8	4.0	4.1	4.3	4.6	5.0	5.4	5.8	6.2	6.6	7.5	8.5
0.09	3.7	3.8	3.9	4.1	4.2	4.4	4.8	5.2	5.6	6.0	6.5	6.9	7.9	9.0
0.10	3.7	3.9	4.0	4.2	4.4	4.5	4.9	5.4	5.8	6.3	6.8	7.3	8.4	9.6
0.11	3.8	4.0	4.2	4.3	4.5	4.7	5.1	5.6	6.0	6.5	7.1	7.7	8.9	10.3
0.12	3.9	4.1	4.3	4.4	4.6	4.8	5.3	5.8	6.3	6.9	7.4	8.1	9.5	11.2
0.13	4.0	4.2	4.4	4.6	4.8	5.0	5.5	6.0	6.6	7.2	7.9	8.6	10.3	12.4
0.14	4.2	4.3	4.5	4.7	4.9	5.1	5.7	6.3	6.9	7.6	8.3	9.2	11.2	14.0
0.15	4.3	4.5	4.7	4.9	5.1	5.3	5.9	6.6	7.3	8.0	8.9	9.9	12.5	16.5
0.16	4.4	4.6	4.8	5.1	5.3	5.5	6.2	6.9	7.7	8.6	9.6	10.8	14.3	21.7
0.17	4.5	4.8	5.0	5.2	5.5	5.8	6.5	7.3	8.2	9.2	10.5	12.1	17.4	
0.18	4.7	4.9	5.2	5.4	5.7	6.0	6.8	7.7	8.7	10.0	11.7	13.9	27.8	
0.19	4.9	5.1	5.4	5.7	6.0	6.3	7.2	8.2	9.5	11.1	13.4	17.2		
0.20	5.0	5.3	5.6	5.9	6.2	6.6	7.6	8.8	10.4	12.6	16.4			
0.21	5.2	5.5	5.8	6.2	6.6	7.0	8.1	9.6	11.7	15.2	31.4			
0.22	5.4	5.8	6.1	6.5	6.9	7.4	8.8	10.7	13.7	23.2				
0.23	5.7	6.0	6.4	6.9	7.4	7.9	9.6	12.2	18.3					
0.24	5.9	6.3	6.8	7.3	7.9	8.5	10.7	15.0						
0.25	6.2	6.7	7.2	7.8	8.5	9.3	12.4							
0.26	6.6	7.1	7.7	8.4	9.3	10.4	16.0							
0.27	6.9	7.6	8.3	9.3	10.5	12.1								
0.28	7.4	8.2	9.2	10.4	12.3	15.8								
0.29	8.0	9.0	10.3	12.4	16.8									
0.30	8.8	10.1	12.3	17.6										
0.31	9.8	12.0	17.9											
0.32	11.6	17.4												
0.33	16.1														

It is difficult to formulate an easy equation for the IRR as it is difficult to make the IRR the subject of the equation. The problem can be rearranged to that of finding a root of

$$f(\text{IRR}) = Q - Q(1 + \text{IRR})^{-n} - \text{IRR}.$$

If $\text{IRR}(m)$ is the mth estimate of the IRR and the derivative is

$$f'[\text{IRR}(m)] = nQ[1 + \text{IRR}(m)]^{-n-1} - 1$$

then you have to use what is known as a Newton–Raphson iteration. This is beyond the scope of this text and is therefore not explained here. If you require further information on this we

Table 24.4   Internal rate of return

Life (n)	Payback period (P)												
	3.00	3.10	3.20	3.30	3.40	3.50	3.75	4.00	4.25	4.50	4.75	5.00	5.50	6.00
3.50	0.072	0.056	0.041	0.027	0.013									
4.00	0.126	0.110	0.096	0.082	0.068	0.056	0.026							
4.50	0.167	0.152	0.137	0.124	0.111	0.099	0.070	0.044	0.021					
5.00	0.199	0.184	0.170	0.157	0.144	0.132	0.104	0.079	0.057	0.036	0.017			
5.50	0.223	0.209	0.195	0.183	0.170	0.159	0.132	0.107	0.085	0.065	0.047	0.030		
6.00	0.243	0.229	0.216	0.203	0.191	0.180	0.153	0.130	0.108	0.089	0.071	0.055	0.025	
6.50	0.259	0.245	0.232	0.220	0.208	0.197	0.171	0.148	0.127	0.108	0.091	0.075	0.047	0.022
7.00	0.271	0.258	0.245	0.233	0.222	0.211	0.186	0.163	0.143	0.124	0.108	0.092	0.064	0.040
8.00	0.290	0.277	0.265	0.253	0.242	0.232	0.208	0.186	0.167	0.149	0.133	0.118	0.092	0.069
9.00	0.302	0.290	0.278	0.267	0.256	0.246	0.223	0.202	0.184	0.167	0.151	0.137	0.112	0.090
10.00	0.311	0.299	0.288	0.277	0.266	0.257	0.234	0.214	0.196	0.180	0.165	0.151	0.127	0.106
15.00	0.329	0.317	0.307	0.297	0.287	0.279	0.258	0.240	0.224	0.209	0.196	0.184	0.163	0.145
20.00	0.332	0.321	0.311	0.301	0.292	0.284	0.264	0.247	0.232	0.218	0.206	0.194	0.175	0.158

suggest that you refer to a specialist numerical analysis text. We then get the following result

$$\text{IRR}(m) = \text{IRR}(m-1) - \frac{f\,[\text{IRR}(m-1)]}{f'\,[\text{IRR}(m-1)]}$$

to obtain an estimate of the IRR. The initial value of the IRR is taken as Q [$\text{IRR}(1) = Q$]. Some values obtained from the use of this equation are shown in Table 24.4, in which it can be seen that if P, the payback period, is 4 and n is 5, then the IRR is 0.079, or 7.9%.

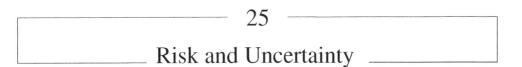

25

Risk and Uncertainty

25.1 INTRODUCTION

In this chapter we consider the degree of uncertainty associated with financial decisions. The business risk of taking investment decisions is considerable and the models used can significantly influence the actual outcome from the decision-making process. Generally there is a lack of understanding as to the weaknesses inherent in some of the models that are used. In other cases there may be programming or logic errors that potentially undermine the accuracy of the decision-making process.

25.2 RISK

Normally when you are undertaking project appraisal, the future outcome will not be known. However, a range of possible future outcomes may be predicted with some associated probabilities, although these are also uncertain. These probabilities are typically generated by management using a combination of personal knowledge and experience.

Some managers will normally be optimistic and will overestimate the income and underestimate the related costs. Others are normally pessimistic and will overestimate the cost and underestimate the profit. Also, office politics can be involved, with a manager choosing to underestimate the income flowing from a certain project when he or she would want that project to be rejected (and perhaps another personal project to be approved).

By taking a series of such estimates over a period of time, the risk management function will be able to assess whether some of the management are normally optimistic and others pessimistic. They will then start to make additional changes to their estimates to take account of this, as appropriate.

If you are able to estimate the outcome of the project with reasonable certainty then the approaches used in Chapter 24 can be used, although you must always make sure that management are aware of the level of uncertainty inherent in the analysis.

25.3 UNCERTAINTY

However, in other cases the future outcomes will not be capable of being predicted with any real degree of confidence. Past management knowledge may not provide sufficient guidance or the issue might be being faced for the first time. An example of this might be the decision by a company to test drill for oil in a new area. There might be oil, or there might not. It might be worth exploiting, or it might not. It might be feasible to exploit, or again it might not.

It is not enough that a project might be expected to earn a high return, if it is associated with a significant risk that could potentially lead to a lowering of the company's market value. It may also be more acceptable to make a lower profit than could otherwise be the case if this results in an acceptable level of potential loss being totally avoided. There are a number of ways in which problems of this type may be analysed.

25.4   ADJUSTING THE DISCOUNT RATE

In the adjusted discount rate approach, a factor is added to the discount rate purely to ensure that the company is compensated for the additional level of business risk it has accepted. The choice made by the company in respect of the increase in the discount rate is subjective, but, depending on the level of presumed risk, factors of 5% or 10% are typically added.

If this approach is to be adopted it is recommended that the company should set out clearly the type of risks that need to be considered and the impact on the discount rate of this analysis being applied. The way that this is achieved should be formally adopted as a policy. The use of standardised incremental increases in discount rate on a known and well-understood basis has the advantage of being transparent to all management. They will understand how a decision is arrived at and are therefore more likely to give it their support.

25.5   ADJUSTING THE CASH FLOWS OF A PROJECT

This adjusted cash flows approach evaluates the net present value of the project under certain options. These might be:

1. Increase the initial cost of investment by 10%.
2. Increase running costs by 15% or decrease savings/returns by 15%.
3. Increase costs by 10% and lower savings by 10%.

Management will be applying their judgement in deciding which levels to use. Again, as in section 25.4, we recommend that standard policies for this analysis should be formally adopted and implemented.

25.5.1   An example of expected cash flows

A project has the expected cash flows that are set out in Table 25.1. The company's cost of capital is known to be 7.5%. Management have decided that the cash flows should be reduced by uncertainty factors of 40%, 50%, and 60% for successive years of the project. This will recognise the increasing uncertainty of these cash flows as the project progresses. The net present value both with and without these factors, may be calculated using the equations taken from Chapter 24, If the interest rate is i and the project is expected to realise a single receipt of £x after n years from an initial investment of £y, then mathematically:

$$x = y \left(1 + \frac{i}{100} \right)^n$$

These calculations are shown in Table 25.2.

If i years have elapsed since the start of the project, the cash value in year i is C_i, the uncertainty with regard to that cash flow is u_i and the cost of capital is p, then the present

Table 25.1   Expected cash flows

Year	2002	2003	2004	2005
Cash	−£7,000	£5,000	£3,000	£2,500

Table 25.2   Corrected cash flows

Year	Cash	Present value	Uncertainty	Adjusted value
2002	−£7,000	−£7,000.00		−£7,000.00
2003	£5,000	£4,651.16	40%	£1,860.47
2004	£3,000	£2,596.00	50%	£1,298.00
2005	£2,500	£2,012.40	60%	£1,207.44
Net present value		**£2,259.56**		**−£2,634.10**

value is given by:

$$PV = \frac{C_i}{(1+p)^i}$$

and the adjusted value is given by:

$$\frac{u_i C_i}{(1+p)^i} = u_i PV$$

The figures in Table 25.2 have been calculated by using the above equations, taking the figures for 2005, where $i = 3$ (that is, $2005 - 2002$), $C_i = £2,500$, $u_i = 60\%$ and $p = 7.5\%$. For the present value this gives:

$$\frac{2,500}{(1+0.075)^3} = 2,012.4$$

For the adjusted value this gives:

$$\frac{2,500 \times 0.6}{(1+0.075)^3} = 1,207.44$$

If these uncertainty factors were considered by management to be appropriate then the project would be rejected as being too risky since, on balance, it will detract value from the company. This is shown by the adjusted value of −£2,634.10 in Table 25.2.

25.6   ASSESSING THE MARGIN OF ERROR

In this approach, an evaluation is made of the increase in costs or reduction in returns that would enable the project to break even. This gives some financial indications to management of the amount of slippage that could occur before the project falls into loss. They can then see how much cost overrun or loss of income would lead to the project failing to make an adequate return.

25.6.1   An example of break-even analysis

A company has a project under consideration with cash flows as presented in Table 25.3. If the company has a cost of capital of 7.5%, the question then is how sensitive is the project to changes in the levels of costs and the expected level of savings?

The figures in Table 25.3 show the cash flows discounted by the company's cost of capital using the equation for discounting set out in Chapter 24. The running cost and savings are

Table 25.3 Projected cash flows for break even analysis

Year	Purchase cost	Running cost	Savings	Net cash flow
2002	−£8,000			−£8,000
2003		−£1,500	£6,000	£4,500
2004		−£2,500	£7,000	£4,500
Net present value				**£1,000**

Table 25.4 Corrected cash flows

Year	Purchase cost	Running cost	Savings	Net cash flow
2002	−£8,000.00			−£8,000.00
2003		−£1,395.35	£5,581.40	£4,186.05
2004		−£2,163.33	£6,057.33	£3,894.00
Net present value				**£80.04**

adjusted using the present value equation:

$$PV = \frac{C_i}{(1 + p)^i}$$

After this analysis has been conducted and the adjusted net cash flows have been obtained, the project still has a small positive net present value and would still just about appear to be worth while. Management might wish to know what changes in the cash flows would have to have occurred for the project to just break even. This position corresponds to the net present value reducing to zero.

From the above calculation we know that the purchase costs would need to increase by a present value of £80.04, which corresponds to:

$$\frac{80.04}{8,000} \times 100 \quad \text{or} \quad 1\%$$

This means that a 1% increase in the original cost of the project would make the project only break even when discounted by the company's cost of capital. Similarly, running costs could also increase by a present value of £80.04, which corresponds to:

$$\frac{80.04}{1,395.35 + 2,163.33} \times 100 \quad \text{or} \quad 0.25\%$$

Therefore, a 0.25% increase in running costs would result in the project breaking even.

Finally, savings would need to fall by a present value of £80.04, which corresponds to:

$$\frac{80.04}{5,581.4 + 6,057.33} \times 100 \quad \text{or} \quad 0.69\%$$

We can now see that there are three levels of uncertainty, each of which individually is modest but would independently undermine the profitability of the project. When these are looked at in combination it may be difficult for the management to approve the project.

Combinations of any of the above situations should also be considered, since more than one eventuality could potentially undermine the project.

25.7   THE EXPECTED VALUE OF THE NET PRESENT VALUE

It might be possible to estimate a probability distribution for the expected cash flows, even though the actual cash flows are not known with certainty. This information may then be employed to:

- calculate the expected value of the net present value
- analyse the risks associated with this expected value.

The distributions adopted will be as discussed in Chapters 7 and 8 and will include the normal distribution, the Poisson distribution, the log normal distribution and potentially the binomial distribution. Other distributions may also be considered, with the final choice being based upon management's judgement.

25.7.1   An example of the use of the distribution approach to the evaluation of net present value

A company has a particular project under consideration where the initial outlay in 2005 is budgeted to be £8,000. The company's cost of capital is 7.5% and the expected cash flows are as presented in Table 25.5.

Table 25.5   Cash flows

Probability	2006	2007	2008
0.10	£2,500	£2,000	£1,500
0.25	£3,000	£2,500	£2,000
0.30	£3,500	£3,000	£2,500
0.25	£4,000	£3,500	£3,000
0.10	£4,500	£4,000	£3,500

The sum of the probabilities must equate to 1 so that it is expected that one of these results will occur. The expected cash flows may then be calculated in Table 25.6. The first figure for 2006 is obtained by multiplying the cash flow in Table 25.5 (£2,500) by the probability for that row, 0.10 (Table 25.5), to give £250 (Table 25.6).

Table 25.6   Expected cash flows

Probability	2006	2007	2008
0.10	£250	£200	£150
0.25	£750	£625	£500
0.30	£1,050	£900	£750
0.25	£1,000	£875	£750
0.10	£450	£400	£350
	£3,500	**£3,000**	**£2,500**

The total expected cash flows should then be discounted to present values using the company's cost of capital and the discounting equation from Chapter 24, providing the results shown in Table 25.7.

Table 25.7   Present values of expected cash flows

Year	Cash flow	Present value
2005	−£8,000	−£8,000.00
2006	£3,500	£3,255.81
2007	£3,000	£2,596.00
2008	£2,500	£2,012.40
Net present value		**−£135.79**

In this case the analysis has resulted in the project having a negative net present value, which suggests that the project should not be undertaken. Even this simple model actually has 125 possible outcomes, each with an associated probability and net present value of future cash flows. Calculations for some of these events are shown in Table 25.8.

Table 25.8   Detailed present values of expected cash flows

Probability				Cash Flows			Present value cash flows			
2006	2007	2008	Total	2006	2007	2008	2006	2007	2008	Total
0.10	0.10	0.10	0.0010	£2,500	£2,000	£1,500	£2,325.58	£1,730.67	£1,207.44	£2,736.31
0.10	0.10	0.25	0.0025	£2,500	£2,000	£2,000	£2,325.58	£1,730.67	£1,609.92	£2,333.83
0.10	0.10	0.30	0.0030	£2,500	£2,000	£2,500	£2,325.58	£1,730.67	£2,012.40	£1,931.35
0.10	0.10	0.25	0.0025	£2,500	£2,000	£3,000	£2,325.58	£1,730.67	£2,414.88	£1,528.87
0.10	0.10	0.10	0.0010	£2,500	£2,000	£3,500	£2,325.58	£1,730.67	£2,817.36	£1,126.39
0.10	0.10	0.10	0.0010	£4,500	£4,000	£1,500	£4,186.05	£3,461.33	£1,207.44	£854.82
0.10	0.10	0.25	0.0025	£4,500	£4,000	£2,000	£4,186.05	£3,461.33	£1,609.92	£1,257.30
0.10	0.10	0.30	0.0030	£4,500	£4,000	£2,500	£4,186.05	£3,461.33	£2,012.40	£1,659.78
0.10	0.10	0.25	0.0025	£4,500	£4,000	£3,000	£4,186.05	£3,461.33	£2,414.88	£2,062.26
0.10	0.10	0.10	0.0010	£4,500	£4,000	£3,500	£4,186.05	£3,461.33	£2,817.36	£2,464.74

The data is more easily summarised as a bar chart (see Chapter 2), as shown in Figure 25.1, and the company can now see that there is a wide range of possible outcomes, from the highly profitable to the highly unprofitable, when measured in terms of net present value. As these outcomes are widely spread, this would indicate that there is a high risk of an uncertain outcome being inherent in the project.

If a company has a series of repeated projects then they may be able to identify some average values that might be confidently employed. In this situation the required probabilities can then be reliably predicted and claims built upon them.

25.8 MEASURING RISK

In the problem considered above it was assumed that if the net cash flow in year 2006 was known, then the cash flow in the following two years was also known. If it is assumed that the probabilities of cash flows from year to year are unrelated, then again it will be necessary to adopt an alternative modelling approach. This requires calculation of the standard deviation (see Chapter 5).

Returning to the previous example, we can calculate the standard deviation of the cash flows in year 2006 by employing the figures in Table 25.7 and using the same mathematical notation

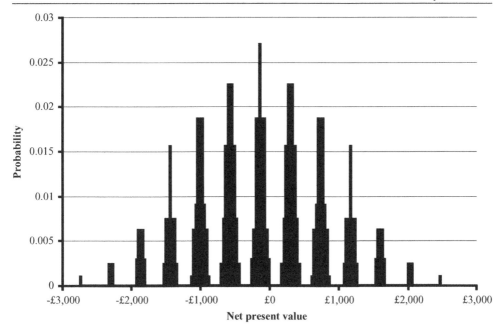

Figure 25.1   Bar chart of present values of expected cash flows.

from section 5.6. There, for a sample of n observations from a population, the variance, written as var(x) was defined to be

$$\text{var}(x) = \frac{\sum\limits_{i=1}^{n}(x_i - \bar{x})^2}{n-1}$$

and the standard deviation (see section 5.6), written as std(x), was defined to be:

$$\text{std}(x) = \sqrt{\text{var}(x)}$$

Here the variance is given by:

$$p_i C_i^2 - (p_i C_i)^2$$

which equates to:

$$12{,}575{,}000 - (3{,}500)^2 = 325{,}000$$

This gives a standard deviation $\sigma_1 = £570.09$ since 570.09 is the square root of 325,000.

Table 25.9   Calculation of the standard deviation

Prob p_i	Cash flow C_i	$p_i C_i$	$p_i C_i^2$
0.10	2,500	250	625,000
0.25	3,000	750	2,250,000
0.30	3,500	1,050	3,675,000
0.25	4,000	1,000	4,000,000
0.10	4,500	450	2,025,000
1.00		3,500	12,575,000

For the data in Table 25.7, the standard deviation is identical for all four years considered since only the mean is shifted through subtracting £500 from the cash flow in each year.

To convert to a present value, the company then needs to divide the cost by a factor $(1 + r)^j$ for the jth year of the project, with a required rate of return from the project of r. The divisor then becomes $(1 + r)^{2j}$ when introduced into the variance. Combining the values for the three years, a standard deviation for the net present value is arrived at which is,

$$\sigma = \sqrt{\frac{\sigma_1^2}{(1+r)^2} + \frac{\sigma_2^2}{(1+r)^4} + \frac{\sigma_3^2}{(1+r)^6}}$$

Given that $r = 7.5\%$ and $\sigma_1 = \sigma_2 = \sigma_3 = 570.09$, the corresponding expected net present value from Table 25.7 is $-£135.79$, with what we now know to be a standard deviation of £857.43.

25.8.1   An example of normal approximation

Another way that this problem may occur would be to solve the same issue and find the probability that a particular project will have a negative NPV given what is known in terms of costs, cost of capital and the expected distribution of returns. We will use the same information as shown in Table 25.7.

Here we need to refer to the notation and analysis set out in Chapter 8. We shall take z to be the standard normal variable $[z \sim \phi(0, 1)]$. In Chapter 8 we stated that the standard normal variable z has a mean of zero and a variance of 1, or using the mathematical notation from Chapter 8, $\phi(0,1)$. This standard normal variable has been tabulated in Chapter 8.

In this case the NPV denoted by x has a mean of μ and a variance of σ^2 which, again using the mathematical notation from Chapter 8, is written $\phi(\mu, \sigma^2)$. These terms are related by the equation:

$$z = \frac{x - \mu}{\sigma}$$

from section 8.2. In this instance $\mu = 135.79$ and $\sigma = 857.43$ and we are interested in NPV < 0, so we take $x = 0$. Therefore we are able to use this to calculate the final probability value.

$$\text{Prob(NPV} < 0) = \text{Prob}\left(\frac{\text{NPV} - (-135.79)}{857.43} \leq \frac{135.79}{857.43}\right)$$
$$= \text{Prob}(z \leq 0.1584) = 0.5629$$

So we now know that, in this case, given all of the assumptions that have been made, we estimate that there is a 56% chance of the project being a failure.

Two of the key assumptions that have been made are (1) that the probabilities related to the cash flows in different years are independent and (2) that the standard normal variable is appropriate (despite the appearance of Figure 25.1). In reality you will need to see if this is a suitable assumption for your specific case and, if not, then again use a different modelling approach. If you are in doubt as to what approach to adopt, then simulation should be considered, as set out in Chapter 22.

26

Time Series Analysis

26.1 INTRODUCTION

A time series is a sequence of values for some kind of variable where successive readings are recorded. Typical time series would include:

- the number of new depositors taken on, by month and by branch
- the monthly sales returns reported over the last two years
- the number of operational losses incurred over the last five years, by type.

Having obtained the data, the challenge is how best to portray the information. Consider the following table of commission earned at a branch on retail financial product sales, by year (Table 26.1). To enable the trend to be easily identified a graph would normally be produced, as shown in Figure 26.1.

Table 26.1 Annual sales

Year	1998	1999	2000	2001	2002	2003	2004
Sales (in £,000)	73	75	82	79	90	97	92

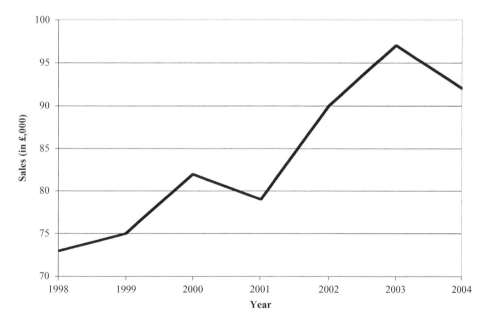

Figure 26.1 Annual sales.

Typically, the horizontal axis will be used for the independent variable, which in this case is time. The vertical axis is then used for the dependent variable, which is annualised sales.

The objective in designing a graph is to enable the underlying data to be more easily understood, to assist decision making by management. Typically the reader will be seeking to find any of the following:

- a trend that might be sustainable and may tell something about the future
- seasonality to identify changing resource requirements
- cyclical variations that may impact periodic financial reporting
- random variations (strikes, new products, etc.) which impact any trends that might be identified.

These differing sorts of variation will be discussed further in the following sections.

26.2   TREND ANALYSIS

This is the underlying movement in some observable dependent variable over time, which is the independent variable. Consider the following example.

A company is trying to better understand the processing costs underlying its products. At present, the budgets are set based on the number of staff, their total cost and the amount of processing conducted. This leads to a cost per unit as set out in Table 26.2.

Table 26.2   Annual performance figures

Year	Output per man-hour	Cost per unit	Number of employees
1998	45	2.35	70
1999	36	2.68	72
2000	39	3.21	68
2001	34	2.99	71
2002	32	3.12	72
2003	27	3.43	69

Even without producing the appropriate graphs, you can see that there is a downward trend in the output per man-hour and that this could be resulting in the increasing trend in the cost per unit. You can also see that the number of employees appears to be relatively static around the rounded mean value of 70, suggesting that this is not being increased or decreased in conjunction with business requirements. The ability to change a variable in accordance with demand requirements is referred to as *flexing*.

Clearly there will be trends in this data that the company will wish to consider further. This is even more clearly seen in Figure 26.2, which shows the annual output per man-hour, and Figure 26.3, which shows the annual cost per unit. The trends will now be even more evident to management.

26.3   SEASONAL VARIATIONS

These are fluctuations that may be explained by the time of year, the day of the week or the time of day. Typically there will be some change in at least one of the variables, and it may

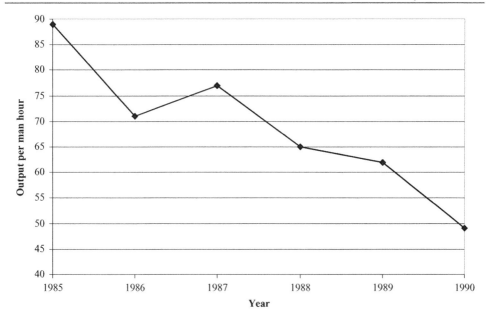

Figure 26.2   Output per man-hour.

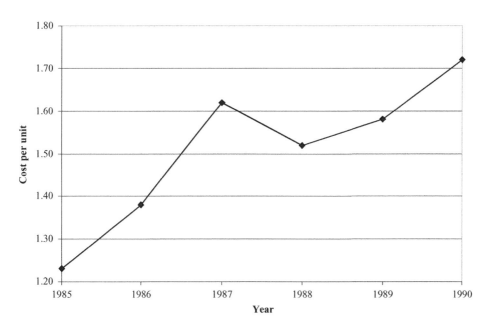

Figure 26.3   Cost per unit.

Table 26.3 Example of cyclical variation: Client visits per quarter

Year x_i	Quarter	Clients (000s) y_i	Trend (000s)
2000	1	48	43.21
	2	34	44.10
	3	60	44.99
	4	38	45.88
2001	1	47	46.77
	2	38	47.65
	3	65	48.54
	4	43	49.43
2002	1	51	50.32
	2	35	51.21
	3	69	52.10
	4	47	52.98
2003	1	56	53.87
	2	42	54.76
	3	73	55.65
	4	52	56.54

happen during any period, for example:

• The sale of football boots is higher in the winter, and cricket pads in the summer.
• Shops have higher receipts on Fridays than on Mondays.
• There are more phone calls during office hours than between 11 pm and 6 am.

The data presented in Table 26.3 represents the number of people visiting a major branch of a bank, with the information being presented by quarter. The information shown in the trend column is obtained by fitting a linear equation to the data. This approach is discussed in Chapter 13, with the resulting line being shown on the graph in Figure 26.4. The key parameter of the line is that the gradient is 3.55. This means that regardless of any cyclical trend, usage of the branch is increasing at a rate of 3.55% per annum. We can also identify that the intercept is −7,063.56 (see Chapter 13).

In section 13.2 we stated that the gradient is described by the following equation:

$$\hat{a} = \frac{\left(\sum\limits_{i=1}^{n} x_i y_i\right) - \frac{1}{n}\left(\sum\limits_{i=1}^{n} x_i\right)\left(\sum\limits_{i=1}^{n} y_i\right)}{\left(\sum\limits_{i=1}^{n} x_i^2\right) - \frac{1}{n}\left(\sum\limits_{i=1}^{n} x_i\right)^2}$$

The intercept was also defined in section 13.2 by the equation:

$$\hat{b} = \frac{1}{n}\sum_{i=1}^{n} y_i - \frac{\hat{a}}{n}\sum_{i=1}^{n} x_i$$

in which there are two variables, x and y, and a linear relationship has been constructed which is consistent with the n data points $(x_i, y_i : i = 1, \ldots, n)$; this has been described by the equation

$$y = ax + b$$

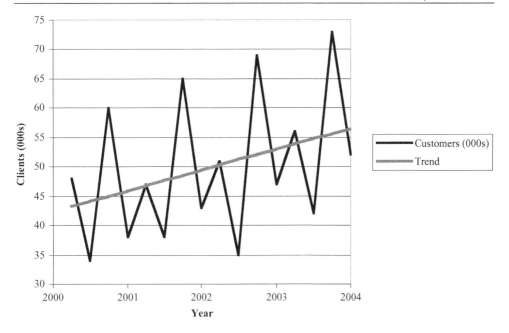

Figure 26.4 Quarterly numbers of clients.

where a is the gradient or slope of the line and b is the intercept with the vertical axis. If $x = 0$, then $y = b$, so the line starts initially with a value of b.

The trend information can now be extracted and shown in Table 26.4. However, in this case, from the graph you can see that there are large fluctuations around the line we have drawn to give the trend. These appear to be regular and therefore there is some evidence of a seasonal variation around an upward trend.

Table 26.4 Trend data compared to client numbers

Year	Quarter	Clients (000s)	Trend (000s)	Difference (000s)
2000	1	48	43.21	4.79
	2	34	44.10	−10.10
	3	60	44.99	15.01
	4	38	45.88	−7.88
2001	1	47	46.77	0.23
	2	38	47.65	−9.65
	3	65	48.54	16.46
	4	43	49.43	−6.43
2002	1	51	50.32	0.68
	2	35	51.21	−16.21
	3	69	52.10	16.90
	4	47	52.98	−5.98
2003	1	56	53.87	2.13
	2	42	54.76	−12.76
	3	73	55.65	17.35
	4	52	56.54	−4.54

26.4   CYCLICAL VARIATIONS

These are medium-term changes in results that are caused by factors that apply for a period and then gradually cease before returning later in a repetitive cycle. Such an effect is the economic cycle of changing interest rates, insurance premiums or commodity prices. These events may occur every few years and the trend that follows may exist for a period of years before a change in the trend takes place.

The data presented in Figure 26.5 represents the movement in UK base rates over the period August 1987 to October 2006. You can identify a number of separate trends – a general downward trend to January 1993, with an earlier spike, then a series of small trends leading to the secondary peak in July 1998.

During the period January 1993 to April 2001 there are three successive 'humps', each of which represents a separate cycle. A discussion of whether any of these have actually made any real difference, we will leave to economic texts.

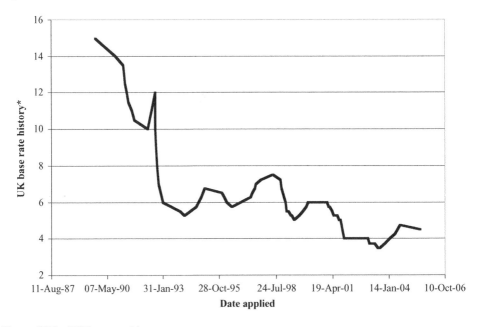

Figure 26.5   UK base rate history.

26.5   MATHEMATICAL ANALYSIS

Having recognised the various causes of variation introduced above it is necessary to ensure that you have identified the right trend when conducting data analysis. If a Board makes an incorrect analysis of future profitability on the basis of an identified trend, then in future periods they will find their results difficult to explain. This impacts the analysts' view of the quality of management and potentially the market value of the company. They will need to be able to identify whether a change is caused by any of the following causes:

- An upward trend.
- Cyclical variations due to changes in the interest rates.

- Seasonal variations, such as the end of the personal tax year.
- Random fluctuations, for example those that are due to changing legislation.

The most common problem, examined below, is the correct identification of a trend within seasonal variations.

26.6   IDENTIFICATION OF TREND

There are three basic approaches to this problem. In the first example shown in Figure 26.1, you could just estimate where to draw a trend line, which roughly bisects the recorded values. In the example set out in Figure 26.4, more detailed linear regression has been undertaken to enable a line to be drawn through data that has a greater degree of variability. The third approach is to make use of moving averages to smooth out seasonal effects.

26.7   MOVING AVERAGE

This is an average taken at the end of each time period and considers a fixed number of previous measurements terminating with the measurement that has just been taken. This measure is then related to the mid-point of the period represented by the values being employed. This sounds complicated but is easily demonstrated for sales data in Table 26.5 with moving averages in Table 26.6.

Table 26.5   Number of sales of financial service products made by a region of a bank

Year	1998	1999	2000	2001	2002	2003	2004
Sales (Units)	463	457	511	504	517	496	538

Table 26.6   Three- and five-point moving averages of the sales data

Year	Sales (units)	3 years moving average of sales	5 years moving average of sales
1998	463		
1999	457	477.00	
2000	511	490.67	490.40
2001	504	510.67	497.00
2002	517	505.67	513.20
2003	496	517.00	
2004	538		

On averaging the sales for 1998, 1999 and 2000 the mean is:

$$\frac{463 + 457 + 511}{3} = \frac{1{,}431}{3} = 477$$

This is the three-year moving average corresponding to 1999, which is the mid-point of the three-year period.

In Table 26.6, both three- and five-year moving averages have been calculated. The sales and averages are displayed in Figure 26.6.

While all the representations of the sales data exhibit an upward trend it is more apparent in the moving average figures, which have less negative increments. It is clearly important

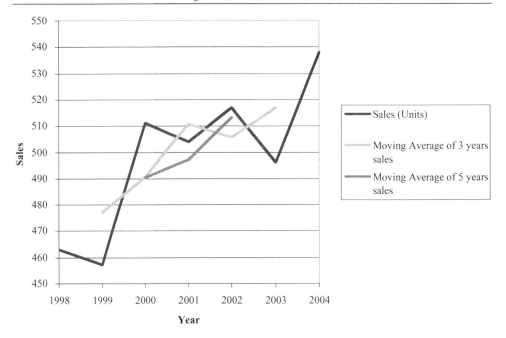

Figure 26.6   Three- and five-point moving averages of the sales data.

to adopt an appropriate interval for averaging. If there is a known cycle either in weeks or seasons, for example, then it is best to average over one full cycle.

26.8   TREND AND SEASONAL VARIATIONS

Consider Table 26.7, which shows daily confirmations issued. The basic trend appears to be slightly upwards, but is also subject to some level of fluctuation. In this instance a moving average would seem useful with five days being a suitable period. This is shown in Figure 26.7. The actual figures are presented in Table 26.8.

The seasonal variations were obtained by subtracting the five-day moving average from the actual confirmation statistics. These differences have been summarised in Table 26.9 so that the daily effect may be more easily assessed.

Table 26.7   Daily confirmations statistics

| | Week | | |
Day	1	2	3
Monday	195	198	200
Tuesday	226	233	241
Wednesday	213	217	221
Thursday	246	252	259
Friday	173	175	177

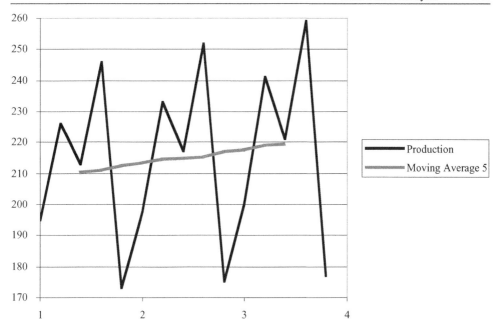

Figure 26.7   Five-day moving average for daily confirmation statistics.

Table 26.8   Five-day moving average for daily confirmation statistics

Week	Day	Production	Five-day moving average	Seasonal variation
	Monday	195		
	Tuesday	226		
1	Wednesday	213	210.60	2.40
	Thursday	246	211.20	34.80
	Friday	173	212.60	−39.60
	Monday	198	213.40	−15.40
	Tuesday	233	214.60	18.40
2	Wednesday	217	215.00	2.00
	Thursday	252	215.40	36.60
	Friday	175	217.00	−42.00
	Monday	200	217.80	−17.80
	Tuesday	241	219.20	21.80
3	Wednesday	221	219.60	1.40
	Thursday	259		
	Friday	177		

The average 'seasonal' variation for each day, over successive weeks, indicates that there are expected deviations from the general trend due to seasonality. Had a perfect description of the fluctuations in the data been obtained, these averages would all sum to zero. The apparent error (0.33/5) therefore has to be removed from each average. These daily estimates, plus the predicted trend line, may then be employed to predict future changes to volumes of confirmations.

Table 26.9   Variation for daily confirmation statistics

	Week			Average	Adjusted average
	1	2	3		
Monday		−15.40	−17.80	−16.60	−16.67
Tuesday		18.40	21.80	20.10	20.03
Wednesday	2.40	2.00	1.40	1.93	1.87
Thursday	34.80	36.60		35.70	35.63
Friday	−39.60	−42.00		−40.80	−40.87
Sum				**0.33**	**0.00**

26.9   MOVING AVERAGES OF EVEN NUMBERS OF OBSERVATIONS

So far we have simplified slightly by only calculating moving averages for odd numbers of observations, where there is always a middle point. Now the even case is considered.

There is clearly no difficulty in considering even numbers of observations. The difficulty comes in allocating the measure to the appropriate time point to evaluate seasonal variations. This is overcome by taking a further moving average: a moving average of the moving averages. This problem is illustrated in the seasonal data presented in Table 26.10.

Table 26.10   Moving averages of even numbers of observations

Year	Quarter	Sales	Moving average – for four quarters	Mid-Point. moving average	Seasonal variation	Fitted seasonal variation	Predicted fit	Error
2002	1	4,743						
	2	6,987						
			5,164.00					
	3	3,061		5,210.88	−2,149.88	−2,263.97	2,946.91	114.09
			5,257.75					
	4	5,865		5,281.13	583.88	558.03	5,839.16	25.84
			5,304.50					
2003	1	5,118		5,304.50	−186.50	−183.91	5,120.59	−2.59
			5,304.50					
	2	7,174		5,328.00	1,846.00	1,889.84	7,217.84	−43.84
			5,351.50					
	3	3,061		5,386.50	−2,325.50	−2,263.97	3,122.53	−61.53
			5,421.50					
	4	6,053		5,468.25	584.75	558.03	6,026.28	26.72
			5,515.00					
2004	1	5,398		5,526.75	−128.75	−183.91	5,342.84	55.16
			5,538.50					
	2	7,548		5,561.75	1,986.25	1,889.84	7,451.59	96.41
			5,585.00					
	3	3,155						
	4	6,239						

Table 26.11   Fitted seasonal variations for even numbers of observations

Quarter	Year 2002	Year 2003	Year 2004	Average	Adjusted seasonal value
1		−186.50	−128.75	−157.63	−183.91
2		1,846.00	1,986.25	1,916.13	1,889.84
3	−2,149.88	−2,325.50		−2,237.69	−2,263.97
4	583.88	584.75		584.31	558.03
Sum				**105.13**	**0.00**

For instance, in respect of the four quarters for 2002

$$\frac{4,743 + 6,987 + 3,061 + 5,865}{4} = 5,164$$

This gives a four-point moving average at quarter 2.5 (mid-way between quarter 2 and quarter 3). Similarly the figure 5,257.75 is calculated at quarter 3.5, and therefore:

$$\frac{5,164 + 5,257.75}{2} = 5,210.88$$

occurs at quarter 3. The difference between this and the true value is given by $3,061.00 - 5,210.88 = -2.149.88$, which gives the seasonal variation, which has been highlighted. The seasonal variation is simply the difference between the final moving average and the actual sales. This is then combined with the trend value to give a predicted value and its deviation (error) from the true value calculated. These are shown as the average value and the fitted value in Table 26.10, which shows the final, fitted seasonal value.

These provide the fitted seasonal variations employed in Table 26.11. Therefore for the third quarter in 2002 in Table 26.10, the actual sales were 3,061, the four-point moving average is 5,210.88, and the difference between these two values is −2,149.88. This is then taken forward to Table 26.11 as an estimated seasonal variation. In this case the fitted seasonal variation from Table 26.10 is −2,263.97. The predicted value is:

$$5,210.88 - 2,263.97 = 2,946.91$$

and the discrepancy is:

$$3,061 - 2,946.91 = 114.09.$$

The seasonal corrections are summarised in Table 26.11.

The seasonal variations (highlighted) have been carried forward from Table 26.10, and the average for each quarter is calculated. The sum of these averages should become zero. To ensure this is the case $1/4$ of 105.13 is subtracted from each quarterly average to give the fitted values.

Table 26.12   Raw sales data for a Z chart

Year	Month	Sales	Annual cumulative sales	12 month moving total
2003	1	450	450	
	2	324	774	
	3	481	1,255	
	4	418	1,673	
	5	387	2,060	
	6	324	2,384	
	7	324	2,708	
	8	450	3,158	
	9	481	3,639	
	10	544	4,183	
	11	450	4,633	
	12	324	4,957	
2004	1	481	481	4,988
	2	355	836	5,019
	3	576	1,412	5,114
	4	450	1,862	5,146
	5	450	2,312	5,209
	6	324	2,636	5,209
	7	324	2,960	5,209
	8	450	3,410	5,209
	9	481	3,891	5,209
	10	576	4,467	5,241
	11	450	4,917	5,241
	12	355	5,272	5,272

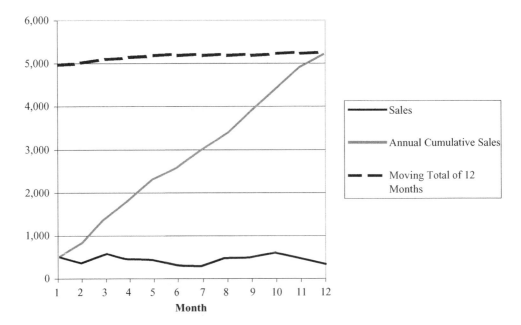

Figure 26.8   Graph of Z chart for sales data.

26.10   GRAPHICAL METHODS

Another approach that can be adopted is to use a Z chart. This can be used to simply present the cumulative returns over time, together with an appropriate moving total and the raw data.

Consider the following number of financial product sales for a bank (Table 26.12). Here we will take a 12-month moving total to ensue that any seasonal trends are properly covered. This means that starting with month 1, the first total will be calculated at month 12. When month 13 (year 2 month 1) arises, year 1 month 1 is dropped from the total and a new total is calculated. This information is shown graphically as Figure 26.8. In this case the moving total plays a similar role to the moving average. Here the upper line indicates any trend in the underlying data and the lower line shows the seasonal variations.

27
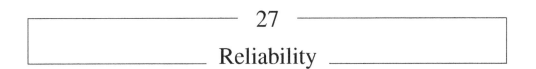
Reliability

27.1 INTRODUCTION

The reliability of a system or component is its ability to perform its designated task, for a particular period and in a specific environment. Clearly, reliability is linked to the probability of failure, effectively the unreliability of the system. In practice errors will occur in any process. This will not mean that the process itself is unreliable or should be changed; there may be an acceptable level of failures that can be accounted for within product costing.

Reliability is also is a time-dependent quantity, since failures will occur over time. Indeed the useful life of a piece of equipment will vary in some random manner between different installations. To examine and analyse this randomness and understand the nature of the replacement and repair decisions, statistical techniques must be employed. These will enable the company to predict the reliability of a system and analyse data on time to failure. This will then lead to the introduction of a sensible maintenance policy.

27.2 ILLUSTRATING RELIABILITY

For a sample of 100 new PCs, Table 27.1 shows the time taken before they have to be repaired for the first time. Here f_i is the number of PCs that required repairs during the ith month, F_i is the total cumulative number that had been repaired by the end of the month and R_i is the number that are still functioning. Thus,

$$F_i = \sum_{j=1}^{i} f_j \quad \text{and} \quad R_i = 100 - F_i$$

If you divide R_i by the total number of the sample (100 in this case), you will get the proportion of the sample that has not needed a repair before the end of the ith month. A similar scaling of the F_i column gives the probability of failure by the end of the ith month. Therefore the probability that a PC will require a repair before the end of the eighth month is 0.64, or 64%.

In the final column, the variable λ_i is referred to as the failure or hazard rate, and is obtained from the equation:

$$\lambda_i = \frac{f_i}{R_{i-1}}$$

with R_0 defined to be 100. These are all conditional probabilities since they are the probability of a repair being required in month i given that the PC had not been repaired at the start of the month. The failure or hazard rate (λ_i) is also a time-dependent quantity.

27.3 THE BATHTUB CURVE

Figure 27.1 shows a typical failure rate curve. Initially the failure rate is high, as faults overlooked at the final inspection appear almost immediately after the purchase. As these defects

Table 27.1 PC repair time

Month	f_i	F_i	R_i	λ_i
1	0	0	100	0.000
2	1	1	99	0.010
3	0	1	99	0.000
4	6	7	93	0.061
5	8	15	85	0.086
6	20	35	65	0.235
7	15	50	50	0.231
8	14	64	36	0.280
9	9	73	27	0.250
10	9	82	18	0.333
11	5	87	13	0.278
12	9	96	4	0.692
13	2	98	2	0.500
14	1	99	1	0.500
15	1	100	0	1.000

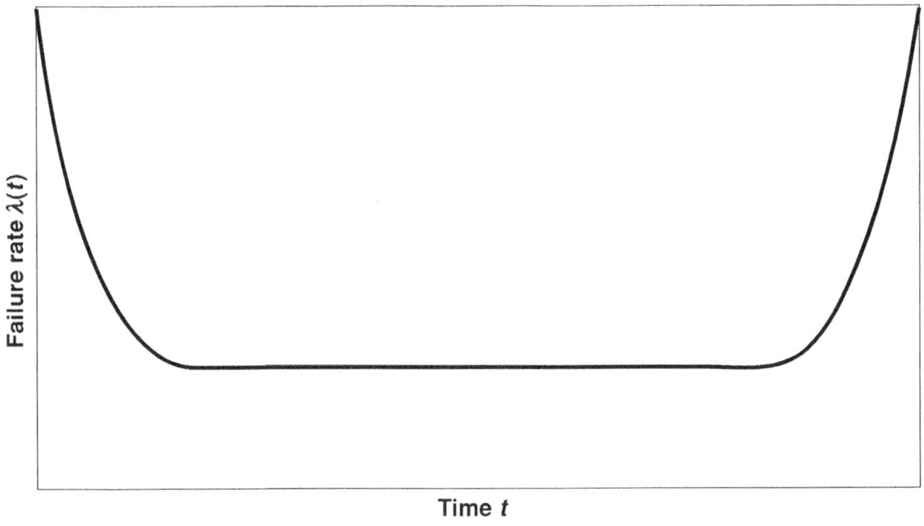

Figure 27.1 The bathtub curve.

are weeded out, this is normally followed by a period of failure-free use with an effectively constant failure rate. Finally, as the asset reaches the end of its expected life the failure rate rapidly increases until the asset fails.

A common example of this is the company car. Many faults are detected immediately the car is first delivered and during the following months. After this period, the car will tend to run fairly effectively until fair wear and tear take their effect.

It is often the case that an underlying distribution describes the rate at which individual discrete failures occur, with a frequency f_i, so that a model may then be employed to predict successive failures.

27.4   THE CONTINUOUS CASE

If the individual discrete failures are in fact reported at regular intervals, then this introduces what is called the *continuous case*. In the continuous case, written $f(t)$, failures are predicted at all times, t. The equation in this case is:

$$\text{Prob}(t \text{ lies between } a \text{ and } b) = \text{Prob}(a \leq t \leq b) = \int_a^b f(t)\,\mathrm{d}t$$

where the probability of a failure occurring at a time (t) between a and b is the area enclosed between the density function $[f(t)]$ and the limits a and b. (See Chapter 7 for related material.) Mathematically, the area under the curve is expressed as an integral, and is written as $\int_a^b f(t)\mathrm{d}t$. Integration is not discussed within this text, due to the level of mathematical knowledge required. In practice, the modeller that will be used within your business will normally undertake this type of calculation (integration) without actually using the term 'integration'. The number of cars that are still functioning is referred to as $R(t)$ and known as the *reliability*. It is calculated using the equation

$$R(t) = \int_t^{\infty} f(\tau)\mathrm{d}\tau \quad \text{or conversely} \quad f(t) = -\frac{\mathrm{d}R(t)}{\mathrm{d}t}$$

and the total number of failures is given by $F(t)$:

$$F(t) = 1 - R(t) = \int_0^t f(\tau)\mathrm{d}\tau \quad \text{or conversely} \quad f(t) = \frac{\mathrm{d}F(t)}{\mathrm{d}t} \tag{A}$$

Finally the failure rate $\lambda(t)$ is the ratio of the number of failures at a specific time to the number of items that are still functioning:

$$\lambda(t) = \frac{f(t)}{R(t)} \tag{B}$$

Combining equations (A) and (B) gives

$$f(t) = -\frac{\mathrm{d}R(t)}{\mathrm{d}t} = \lambda(t)R(t)$$

Solving the differential equation provides the following relationship, which we use later:

$$R(t) = \exp\left(-\int_0^t \lambda(\tau)\mathrm{d}\tau\right)$$

Again we are not explaining the working of differential equations in this text, so if you wish to know more about this you will need to refer to a more advanced work. However, in a few cases, algebraic forms of these functions are available. Failing this, appropriate modelling software will normally give you the ability to generate the function values. There are a number of other distributions, which may also be used to model the failure rate.

The simplest and most widely used distribution in this context is the exponential distribution, which is used to model the time between events in a Poisson distribution (see section 7.4). The Poisson distribution is typically used when you count the number of events across time or over an area. Areas of application would be

- the time until the next error
- the time until the next market crash
- the time until a new client calls
- the time to the next computer outage.

27.5   EXPONENTIAL DISTRIBUTION

This distribution was discussed in section 7.7 and is convenient to use since algebraic forms for probability of failure $f(t)$, probability function $R(t)$ and failure rate $\lambda(t)$ exist. The functions are:

$$f(t) = \lambda e^{-\lambda t}$$
$$R(t) = e^{-\lambda t}$$
$$\lambda(t) = \lambda$$

here there is a constant failure rate λ, which is the scale parameter. The mean time to failure is λ^{-1} and the standard deviation λ^{-1}. Examples of the exponential functions for $\lambda = 0.5$, 1 and 2 are shown in Figures 27.2, 27.3 and 27.4.

It is the failure rate curves that actually provide the input to the process and enable the identification of the appropriate distribution to take place. Having selected an appropriate distribution, it may then be used predictively as demonstrated by a number of examples later in this chapter. Examples of this distribution are presented below.

27.5.1   An example of exponential distribution

This example employs the equations of section 27.5, where $f(t)$ gives the failure rate at time t, $R(t)$ the reliability (the fraction that are still functioning) at time t and $\lambda(t)$ the failure rate at time t.

A company used five personal computers until they failed. The measured operating times prior to the failure of the each computer were 5,500 hours, 6,800 hours, 8,200 hours, 9,100 hours and 11,100 hours. The aim is to find the reliability at 1,000 hours – that is, the fraction of

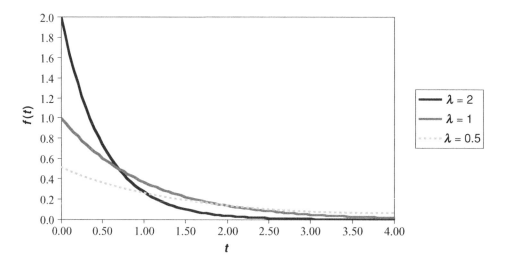

Figure 27.2   Exponential density function.

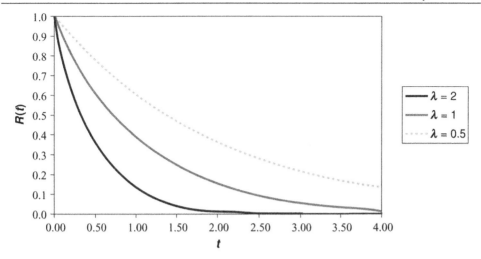

Figure 27.3 Exponential distribution reliability function.

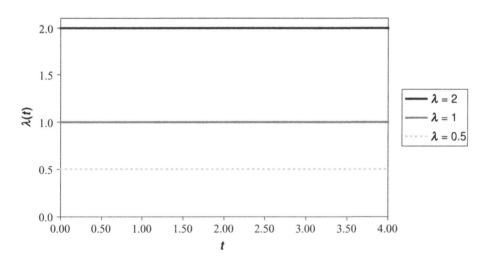

Figure 27.4 Exponential distribution failure rate.

personal computers still functioning and the time at which 15% of a large number of personal computers employed in similar environments might be expected to fail.

An exponential distribution (see section 7.7) is assumed to model the data, since failures are taken to be independent and occur at a fixed rate over time. Firstly, you need to evaluate the mean time to failure, which is given by:

$$\bar{t} = \frac{5{,}500 + 6{,}800 + 8{,}200 + 9{,}100 + 11{,}100}{5} = 8{,}140.$$

This provides an estimate of the number of failures per hour, λ, which is:

$$\lambda = \frac{1}{8,140} = 0.00012285$$

To work out the reliability at 1,000 hours, you use the definition of $R(t)$ from section 27.5, the reliability is $R(t) = e^{-\lambda t}$, so the reliability at 1,000 hours is:

$$R(1,000) = e^{-0.12285} = 0.8844$$

The time at which 15% of a large number of personal computers employed in similar environments might be expected to fail is found by solving $0.15 = F(t)$, which means that $0.85 = R(t)$ and finally $0.85 = e^{-\lambda t} = e^{-0.00012285t}$. This equation must be solved for t. Since the exponential function is the inverse of the natural logarithm (logarithm base e) then:

$$t = \frac{\ln(0.85)}{-0.0001228} = \frac{-0.1625}{-0.0001228} = 1322.90$$

Therefore, the time for 15% failure is 1,322.9 hours. Again in practice this type of calculation will be carried out within the software you are using, but at least in these cases it is possible to check the calculations manually.

27.5.2   An example of maximum of an exponential distribution

A company believes that, within a given portfolio of insurance policies, claims follow an exponential distribution with mean 10. The company has now observed 100 such claims with the largest loss being 50. The question is whether the company are still satisfied with the model they have adopted and would they change their view if the largest loss had actually been 100?

This example also employs the equations of section 27.5, where $f(t)$ gives the failure rate at time t, $R(t)$ the reliability (the fraction still functioning) at time t and $\lambda(t)$ the failure rate at time t. We know that policy claims follow an exponential distribution with mean 10, so $\lambda = 1/10$ (see section 7.7).

The assumption is that the 100 claims $\{x_1, x_2, \ldots, x_{100}\}$ are all independent and are identically distributed with probability density

$$\text{Prob}(X_1 \le x) = 1 - f(x) = 1 - e^{-x/10}, \quad x \ge 0$$

In this case we are interested in $M_n = \max(x_1, x_2, \ldots, x_n)$, since this would be the largest claim.

The probability that the maximum of 100 claims exceeds x [$\text{Prob}(M_{100} \ge x)$] is the complement that all claims are less than x. Since the events are independent, this is the product of the 100 individual probabilities, or, mathematically:

$$[\text{Prob}(X_1 \le x)]^{100}$$

These 100 probabilities will cover all possibilities:

$$\text{Prob}(M_{100} \geq x) + [\text{Prob}(X_1 \leq x)]^{100} = 1$$

On rearranging this, and using $\text{Prob}(X_1 \leq x) = 1 - e^{-x/10}$ from above, the required probability becomes:

$$\text{Prob}(M_{100} \geq x) = 1 - [\text{Prob}(X_1 \leq x)]^{100} = 1 - \left(1 - e^{-x/10}\right)^{100}$$

If we now consider a specific case, then for a maximum loss of 50 we replace x with 50 and obtain the following probability:

$$\text{Prob}(M_{100} \geq 50) = 1 - \left(1 - e^{-50/10}\right)^{100} = 0.4914$$

This means that the model calculates that there is a 49% chance that, in a sample of 100 claims, the largest would be 50. If the largest loss is then increased to 100, this gives a probability of:

$$\text{Prob}(M_{100} \geq 100) = 1 - \left(1 - e^{-100/10}\right)^{100} = 0.0045$$

So a loss of 50 is fairly likely, while a loss of 100 will only occur with a probability of 0.45% and is clearly therefore an extreme event.

27.6   WEIBULL DISTRIBUTION

The Weibull distribution is one of the most commonly used distributions in reliability because of the many shapes it attains for various parameter values (see Figure 27.5). It can therefore model a great variety of data. It is often used to model the time until a device fails, or the time to complete a task.

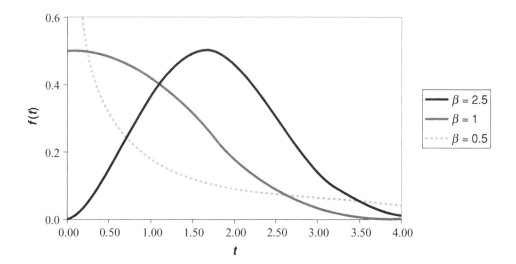

Figure 27.5   Weibull distribution density function.

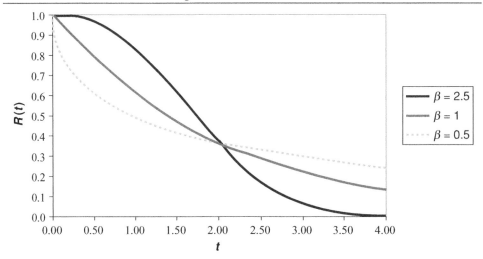

Figure 27.6   Weibull distribution reliability function.

Again closed forms exist for the functions of interest:

$$f(t; \beta, \alpha) = \frac{\beta}{\alpha} \left(\frac{t}{\alpha}\right)^{\beta-1} \exp\left[-\left(\frac{t}{\alpha}\right)^{\beta}\right]$$

$$R(t; \beta, \alpha) = \exp\left[-\left(\frac{t}{\alpha}\right)^{\beta}\right]$$

$$\lambda(t; \beta, \alpha) = \frac{\beta}{\alpha} \left(\frac{t}{\alpha}\right)^{\beta-1}$$

Here β is a parameter that is being taken to represent the shape of the curve, with α being the scale parameter that is used to scale time up or down. t is taken to represent time. These functions are shown in Figures 27.5, 27.6 and 27.7 for $\alpha = 2$ and $\beta = 0.5$, 1 and 2.5.

If the failure rate of the process decreases over time, you select $\beta < 1$, resulting in a decreasing density f. If the failure rate of the device is constant over time, you select $\beta = 1$, which produces the exponential distribution and again results in a decreasing function f. If the failure rate increases over time, you select $\beta > 1$ and obtain a density f which increases towards a maximum and then decreases. An example of the Weibull distribution is given below.

27.6.1   An example of a Weibull distribution

A company believes that the failure rate for a component is represented by a Weibull distribution with a characteristic life for the component of 250 hours and a shape parameter for the Weibull curve of 2.5. This example employs the equations and notation of section 27.6.

The reliability at 100 hours is

$$R(100) = \exp\left[-\left(\frac{100}{250}\right)^{2.5}\right] = 0.9038$$

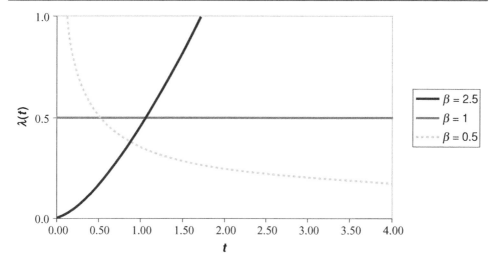

Figure 27.7   Weibull distribution failure rate.

since $\beta = 2.5$ and $\alpha = 250$. The first question to be answered is: At what time is the reliability 95%? The relevant equation becomes

$$R(t) = \exp\left[-\left(\frac{t}{250}\right)^{2.5}\right] = 0.95$$

and then taking logs gives:

$$\ln(0.95) = -\left(\frac{t}{250}\right)^{25}$$

We now need to make t the subject of the equation, so:

$$[\ln(0.95)]^{1/25} = -\frac{t}{250}$$

and multiplying by 250 gives:

$$t = 250[-\ln(0.95)]^{1/2.5} = 76.20$$

So at 76.2 hours we may expect 95% reliability.

27.7   LOG-NORMAL DISTRIBUTION

While the normal distribution has many useful properties (see Chapter 8), it does possess two tails. If used to model time, then negative times are allowed within the model. This is clearly nonsense and could undermine the quality of the modelling. To avoid this, a closely related distribution should be used, the log-normal distribution. If x is a random variable with a normal distribution, then e^x has a log-normal distribution.

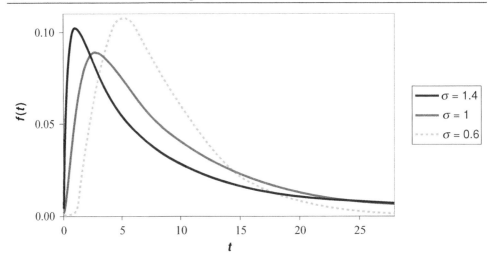

Figure 27.8 Log-normal distribution density function.

Here,

$$f(t; \mu, \sigma) = \frac{1}{t\sigma\sqrt{2\pi}} \exp\left[-\frac{1}{2}\left(\frac{\ln(t) - \mu}{\sigma}\right)^2\right]$$

where μ is the scale parameter and σ is the shape parameter, t represents time and $\ln(t)$ is the natural logarithm function (see section 3.3, which here has the base 'e').

The mean (see Chapters 5 and 8) is:

$$e^{\mu + \frac{1}{2}\sigma^2}$$

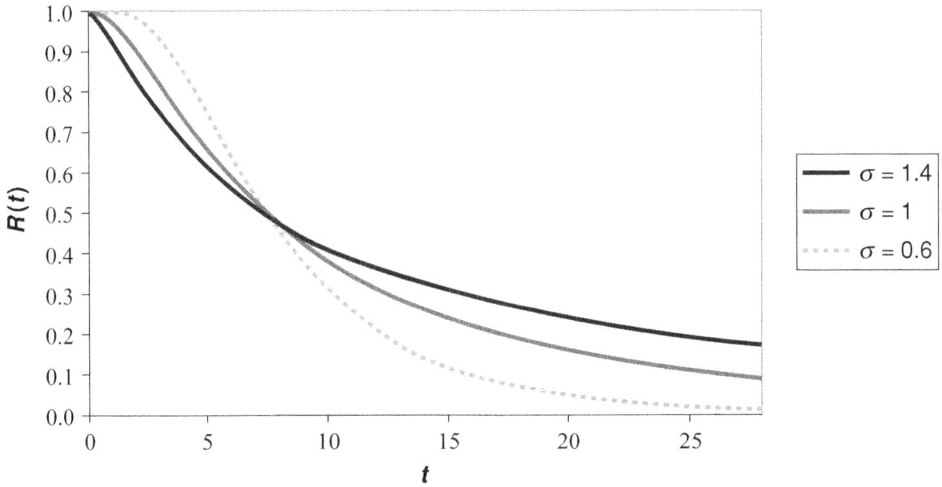

Figure 27.9 Log-normal distribution reliability function.

and the standard deviation (see Chapters 5 and 8):

$$\sqrt{e^{2\mu+\sigma^2}\left(e^{\sigma^2}-1\right)}.$$

The functions are shown pictorially in Figures 27.8, 27.9 and 27.10 for $\mu = 2$ and $\sigma = 0.6$, 1 and 1.4.

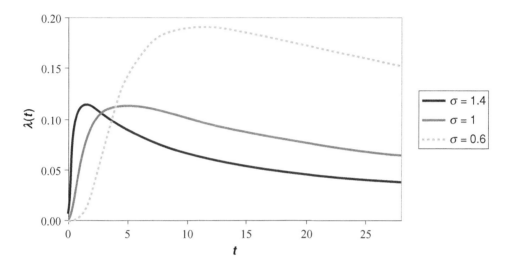

Figure 27.10   Log-normal distribution failure rate.

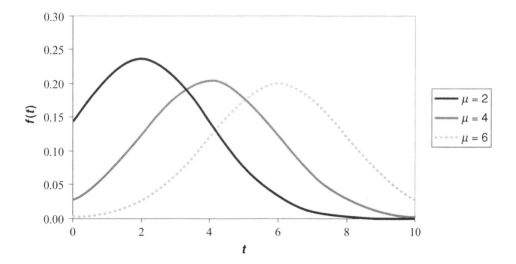

Figure 27.11   Truncated normal distribution density function.

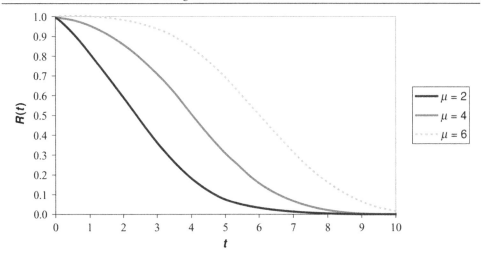

Figure 27.12   Truncated normal distribution reliability function.

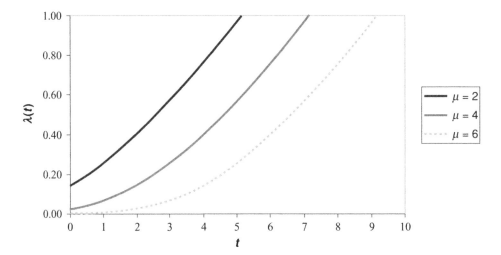

Figure 27.13   Truncated normal distribution failure rate.

27.8   TRUNCATED NORMAL DISTRIBUTION

An alternative to avoiding negative values in the normal distribution would be to use what is referred to as the truncated normal. This is a standard normal distribution, as discussed in Chapter 8, with the difference that no values are allowed to be negative.

Here, using the notation described in section 8.1:

$$f(t; \mu, \sigma) = \frac{1}{K_{\mu/\sigma}\sigma\sqrt{2\pi}} \exp\left[-\frac{1}{2}\left(\frac{t-\mu}{\sigma}\right)^2\right]$$

where $K_{\mu/\sigma}$ is the area under the standard normal curve between $-\infty$ and μ/σ (see Chapter 8). The functions are shown in Figures 27.11, 27.12 and 27.13 for $\sigma = 2$ and $\mu = 2, 4$ and 6.

28

Value at Risk

28.1 INTRODUCTION

Value at risk, or VaR is an attempt to estimate the greatest loss likely if a defined risk were to occur. For example, it could represent the loss in value of a portfolio of shares were a market slump to occur. Typically the way this works in practice is that the analyst calculates the greatest loss that would arise in 99% of all cases. That means that in 99% of cases the loss would actually exceed the amount of the calculated VaR, which is effectively a boundary value. This really is just a probabilistic statement. If a VaR is estimated to be £1 million with a 99% confidence, or a probability of 0.99, then a loss of more than £1 million might be expected on one day in every 100.

Generally there will be a range of factors that could influence the VaR calculation. In the case of portfolio analysis this would include market sentiment, the global economy and local factors such as interest rates and currency movements. What will also be available is historic knowledge and management's judgement to supplement any internally derived estimates. There are clearly uncertainties related to any prediction, or model building, which should be based on stable foundations.

A number of factors may affect the VaR. Many of these are effectively time effects which show movements in the key variables that impact the specific VaR. Consequently, showing the time trend inherent in the movement of the VaR tends to show additional information to management. When this is combined with movements in a key variable – for example, interest rates – then further information relating to correlation between these amounts can be identified.

VaR is probably the most important calculation undertaken within business and is required for trading portfolios, credit risk and also effectively operational risk within the banking industry. It provides a method to assess a risk and therefore an indication of the capital needed or management action required to address the risk. Although VaR was originally introduced to assess trading risks, the principle has now been extended to cover all elements of business from process risk to credit risk.

When viewed as a modelling process, VaR necessarily depends on the information available:

- What internal risks are likely and how can they best be quantified?
- What external risks are likely and how can they best be quantified?
- Are any of these variables correlated and, if so, is such correlation material?

Clearly if the risks are correlated then there is the potential for the VaR calculation to overestimate the level of risk if such correlations are ignored. In practice such correlations are frequently ignored since the VaR arising will be considered to be more conservative as a result.

There are always problems of data identification and quality. Remember the old acronym 'GIGO' meaning 'Garbage In, Garbage Out'. A model built on totally unreliable data is unlikely to produce meaningful results. While VaR is not always an ideal tool, since it can be difficult to use and interpret, it is currently the best tool available. When modelling unusual events a special family of distributions are employed.

28.2   EXTREME VALUE DISTRIBUTIONS

There is a requirement to model extreme operational risk events included within the Basel *Accord*. A major problem in this case is how to fit a distribution when there are relatively few extreme observations. Estimates based on these distributions are imprecise and become less reliable as the variable moves into the tail of the distribution. This is obviously a problem if the aim is to identify potential events beyond the range of previously observed data. Internal loss databases, for example, will only include data on events that have occurred to the bank.

It is therefore necessary to develop models to compensate for this lack of relevant data. This necessitates making a number of prior assumptions, which impact the quality of the ultimate results from the analysis. The objective is to come up with a distribution, of known properties, that can then be used to estimate what is happening at the extremes of the distribution. One possible solution is to apply normality, since the distribution is widely understood and estimation is straightforward. However, a normal curve is not a fat-tailed distribution and has both positive and negative tails. Indeed in the case of operational risk losses, where all the values are positive, a normal distribution is unsuitable. Likewise, a binomial distribution would have limited appeal since it does not have a long tail and is restricted to discrete observations. It is more sensible to initially adopt a distribution with a known fat-tailed characteristic whose parameters are estimated from the raw data.

Problems always arise since, by definition, most observations are centrally situated and the aim here is to fit extreme values. In the case of operational loss data, for example, most losses are small. Indeed when something goes wrong the usual result is that no loss occurs. Extreme events, like earthquakes and hurricanes, are relatively rare events.

Central to any theoretical approach is the extreme value theorem, which attempts to describe the limiting distribution of extreme values. Given observations from an unknown distribution function, the theorem states that the cumulative distribution of extreme observations converges asymptotically to

$$F(x : \mu, \sigma, \xi) = \begin{cases} \exp(-[1 + \xi(x - \mu)/\sigma]^{-1/\xi}) & \text{if } \xi \neq 0 \\ \exp(-e^{(x-\mu)/\sigma}) & \text{if } \xi = 0 \end{cases}$$

The parameters μ and σ correspond to the mean and standard deviation. The third parameter, ξ, is known as the tail index, giving an indication of the heaviness of the tail. The case of most interest in finance is $\xi > 0$ and the asymptotic distribution takes the form of a Fréchet distribution

$$F(x : \alpha) = \exp(-x^{-\alpha}), \quad x > 0, \quad \alpha > 0$$

This is a special case of the Weibull distribution $(\exp[-(t/\alpha)^{\beta}]$ with $\alpha = 0$ and β negative) (see section 27.6). This result allows estimation of the distribution without making any major assumptions about the underlying distribution of observations. If a distribution is available, it not only allows the estimation of actual results, but also provides the associated confidence limits.

28.2.1   A worked example of value at risk

The following describes the value at risk concept and provides a worked example. Consider the case of a portfolio worth $14 billion, where gold makes up 50% of the portfolio (i.e. $7 billion) and the remainder is split 40:40:20 into $, € and ¥ (i.e. $2.8 billion is held in dollars, $2.8 billion is held in euros and $1.4 billion is held in yen).

If the portfolio is managed in dollars, there are three currency-related risks:

1. The risk arising from movements in the dollar-denominated gold exchange rate.
2. The risk arising from movements in the dollar–euro exchange rate.
3. The risk arising from movements in the dollar–yen exchange rate.

The variance–covariance matrix (see section 5.6 for variance and section 13.3 covariance) for a 10-day holding period is:

$$
\Sigma = \begin{array}{c} \\ \text{Yen} \\ \text{Euro} \\ \text{Gold} \end{array} \begin{array}{ccc} \text{Yen} & \text{Euro} & \text{Gold} \\ \begin{pmatrix} 0.053\% & 0.004\% & 0.017\% \\ 0.004\% & 0.042\% & 0.012\% \\ 0.017\% & 0.012\% & 0.054\% \end{pmatrix} \end{array}
$$

So the variance of the yen exchange rate is 0.053%, while the covariance of the yen with the euro is 0.004%.

This type of data on variances and covariances are based on historical movements in asset prices and are published by a number of firms, for instance by JP Morgan as part of its RiskMetrics service.

The column vector of position (in $ million) is

$$
x = \begin{pmatrix} 1,400 \\ 2,800 \\ 7,000 \end{pmatrix}.
$$

Therefore we currently hold 1,400 yen, 2,800 euro and 7,000 gold all valued in $ million. For these purposes, we assume that we are interested in a 99% confidence level (which means that α is 2.33 in a normal distribution. VaR is calculated as:

$$
\text{VaR} = \alpha \sqrt{x^T \Sigma x}
$$

$$
= 2.33 \sqrt{ (1{,}400 \quad 2{,}800 \quad 7{,}000) \begin{pmatrix} 0.00053 & 0.00004 & 0.00017 \\ 0.00004 & 0.00042 & 0.00012 \\ 0.00017 & 0.00012 & 0.00054 \end{pmatrix} \begin{pmatrix} 1{,}400 \\ 2{,}800 \\ 7{,}000 \end{pmatrix} } = 461
$$

So this portfolio's value at risk is $461 million, i.e. this is the maximum amount we could expect to lose (with a 99% confidence interval) over the next 10 days. The VaR figure, in this example, reflects the maximum amount we could expect to lose over the next 10 days. However, there is a 1% chance that the actual loss will exceed this amount. Here the variance and covariance matrix is estimated from a long run of data (e.g. one to two years of data).

Consider now a $14 billion portfolio where gold makes up 20% of the portfolio (i.e. $2.8 billion) with the remainder split 40:40:20 into $, € and ¥ (i.e. $4.48 billion is held in dollars, $4.48 billion is held in euros and $2.24 billion is held in yen). The variance–covariance matrix is exactly as before. α, the new column vector of position is:

$$
x = \begin{pmatrix} 2,240 \\ 4,480 \\ 2,800 \end{pmatrix}.
$$

The value at risk is calculated as before:

$$\text{VaR} = \alpha \sqrt{x^{\mathrm{T}} \Sigma \, x}$$

$$= 2.33 \sqrt{\begin{pmatrix} 2,240 & 4,480 & 2,800 \end{pmatrix} \begin{pmatrix} 0.00053 & 0.00004 & 0.00017 \\ 0.00004 & 0.00042 & 0.00012 \\ 0.00017 & 0.00012 & 0.00054 \end{pmatrix} \begin{pmatrix} 2,240 \\ 4,480 \\ 2,800 \end{pmatrix}} = 340$$

The VaR of this portfolio is therefore \$340 million, some 26% below the VaR with a higher proportion of gold. This, as can be seen from the variance–covariance matrix, is because a portfolio containing more euros and less gold is less risky because the euro has a lower variance when compared to the dollar. It also has a lower covariance than gold and the yen. Using different values of α will alter the absolute figures, but does not affect the relative VaR of the two portfolios.

Clearly, when trying to do this type of calculation in practice, some form of commercially available modelling software will be employed. It is always worth remembering that the quality of the input data will impact the quality of the output. While we are giving an answer at a 99% confidence level, this does not mean that we are actually 99% confident in the analysis. When management improperly uses VaR figures, it is normally in the interpretation of the data arising that the business is let down. There are two percentages here – the 99% is based on the distribution and provides an element of analysis of the overall picture that has been estimated. The underlying data has an accuracy, which is certainly lower than 99% (i.e. there is only a 1% chance that the data will be unrepresentative or that the distribution selected will be inappropriate). Given the difficulties inherent with data fitting and the underlying data integrity problem, a much lower level of accuracy is actually achieved – perhaps only 80%.

28.3   CALCULATING VALUE AT RISK

Value at risk for a single position is calculated as:

$$\text{VaR} = \text{Sensitivity of position to change in market prices} \times \text{Estimated change in price}$$

or

$$\text{VaR} = \text{Amount of the position} \times \text{Volatility of the position} = x\sigma$$

where x is the position size and volatility, σ, is the proportion of the value of the position which may be lost over a given time horizon at the specified confidence level.

When looking at exposure to two or more risks – e.g. the risk in a portfolio of two assets, say gold and euros – the risk measures must take account of the likely joint movements (or 'correlations') in the asset prices as well as the risks in the individual instruments. This can be written as:

$$\text{VaR} = \sqrt{\text{VaR}_1^2 + \text{VaR}_2^2 + 2\rho_{12}\text{VaR}_1\,\text{VaR}_2}$$

where VaR_1 is the value at risk arising from the first risk factor, VaR_2 is the value at risk arising from the second risk factor, and ρ_{12} is the correlation between movements in the two risk factors. Given the definition of VaR above, this can be written as:

$$\text{VaR} = \sqrt{x_1^2\sigma_1^2 + x_2^2\sigma_2^2 + 2\rho_{12}x_1\sigma_1 x_2\sigma_2}$$

where σ_1 and σ_2 are the confidence level volatilities for the two risk factors (equivalently σ_1^2 and σ_2^2 are the confidence level variances) and ρ_{12} is the correlation between movements in the two risk factors.

Since the covariance of the two positions, $\sigma_{1,2}$ is given by

$$\sigma_{1,2} = \sigma_1 \sigma_2 \rho_{12}$$

and since the confidence level variance, σ_1^2, can be written as $(\alpha \sigma_1)^2 = \alpha^2 \sigma_1^2$, where α is the confidence level and σ_1^2 is the historical variance, the above can be rewritten as:

$$\text{VaR} = \alpha \sqrt{x_1^2 \sigma_1^2 + x_2^2 \sigma_2^2 + 2 x_1 x_2 \sigma_{1,2}}$$

This can be presented in matrix form:

$$\text{VaR} = \alpha \sqrt{(x_1 \quad x_2) \begin{pmatrix} \sigma_1^2 & \sigma_{1,2} \\ \sigma_{1,2} & \sigma_2^2 \end{pmatrix} \begin{pmatrix} x_1 \\ x_2 \end{pmatrix}}$$

In shorthand, this is:

$$\text{VaR} = \alpha \sqrt{x^T \sigma x}$$

where α is the confidence level, x represents the vector of position size, x^T is its transpose and σ is the matrix of historical variances and covariance's for the risk factors over the given holding period.

Generalising for more than two risk factors gives:

$$\text{VaR} = \alpha \sqrt{x^T \Sigma x}$$

where x is the matrix of positions (in \$), x^T is its transpose, α is the confidence level and Σ is the variance–covariance matrix of returns over the given holding period.

29

Sensitivity Analysis

29.1 INTRODUCTION

Sensitivity analysis is the impact on the business of a unitary increase in a key variable. Such a variable might be processing volumes, hours lost due to illness, number of working days in a month or a change to an interest rate.

Credit card losses (see Table 29.1) are one of the most stable forms of loss data that a bank is likely to have. Losses are both frequent and to be expected at a similar percentage. They therefore represent a good example of the use of sensitivity analysis. Given that a bank has this profile of losses on its credit card portfolio, what would be the expected loss for a 1% increase in business?

Table 29.1 Losses in a credit card portfolio

Year	Portfolio £'000	Losses £'000	Losses %
2000	1,500	27	1.8
2001	1,700	36	2.1
2002	1,900	41	2.2
2003	2,400	47	2.0
2004	2,300	49	2.1
2005	2,700	42	1.6
Total	**12,500**	**242**	**1.9**

If we just take year 2005, then the 1% increase in portfolio size would increase the size of the losses by 1% or £420. The question is then whether just taking the single year alone is going to be valid in terms of the impact of a 1% change in the population. If we consider the entire five-year population of £12,500k, then a 1% increase would result in an additional loss of £2.42k over a period of six years.

Perhaps the best way to look at this would be to take the average loss percentage rate of 1.9% and apply that to the 1% population increase for 2005 (£27k) giving the following calculation:

$$£27k \times 1.9\% = £513$$

which is £93 more than had previously been calculated

29.2 THE APPLICATION OF SENSITIVITY ANALYSIS TO OPERATIONAL RISK

In June 2004 the Bank for International Settlements published 'International Convergence of Capital Measurement and Capital Standards' (the *Accord*). This paper set out how capital requirements for operational risk should be calculated. As part of this there is also a requirement to understand the nature of operational risk better. If a business grows the company needs to

Table 29.2   Processing losses by month

Month	Transactions processed	# Errors	# Error %	Value of errors (£)	Average loss values (£)
January	23,516	27	0.11	1,674	62
February	19,872	14	0.07	28,315	2,023
March	21,634	16	0.07	265,093	16,568
April	19,965	19	0.10	7,802	411
May	27,432	21	0.08	19,335	921
June	28,911	28	0.10	2,113	75
July	27,345	17	0.06	7,301	429
August	21,862	5	0.02	6,184	1,237
September	32,449	14	0.04	10,118	723
October	28,016	21	0.07	19,904	948
November	29,714	19	0.06	14,336	755
December	30,331	31	0.10	27,819	897
Total	**311,047**	**232**	**0.07**	**409,994**	**1,767**

know that it is able to cope with the business volumes that will result. Failure to do so can impact reputation and also potentially lead to regulatory sanction. In the *Accord* there is a general assumption that operational losses are a proxy for operational risk, together with a requirement for modelling, which we shall consider further in Chapter 30 when scenario analysis is discussed.

The idea is therefore to understand what a 1% increase on processing volumes means for operational losses. Consider the example given in Table 29.2. This is a typical data analysis that a bank will create to meet the requirements of the *Accord*. This, for example, requires five years of operational loss data to be collated. A 1% increase in annual transaction numbers would be expected to increase the annual loss by 1% or £4,099. However, we can see that there have been a few events that appear to distort the analysis. The average loss per transaction is between £62 and £2,023, with the exception of March where the loss has become £16,568.

Sensitivity analysis is best at dealing with the routine and regular errors, what would be referred to within the *Accord* as 'Expected errors'. The less routine amounts, deemed unexpected errors, are better dealt with by using scenario analysis. You would expect routine losses to be budgeted for and included within product pricing. Unexpected operational losses are different and are better dealt with through the maintenance of adequate capital.

Let us assume that on further investigation one of the errors for March is £225,000, and this is taken as being an extreme event that is not expected to recur every year. It makes sense for this loss to be excluded from the data for the purpose of sensitivity analysis. This then reduces the loss total to £409,994 − £225,000 = £184,994 in respect of 231 losses from a population of 311,046. The average loss per event has now reduced to £801 and therefore the 1% increase in volumes would be expected to result in a loss of 1% × £184,994 = £1,849.94. This would represent 1% of 231 losses, or a further 2.31 errors.

Clearly we are not actually going to get 2.31 errors, but this is the measure that will be used by management.

In practice there is normally a total risk profile on which sensitivity is applied. The total risk profile shows all of the risks that the bank is subject to in some standardised form such that they can be combined. Within the *Accord* it is currently assumed that all of these risks are additive

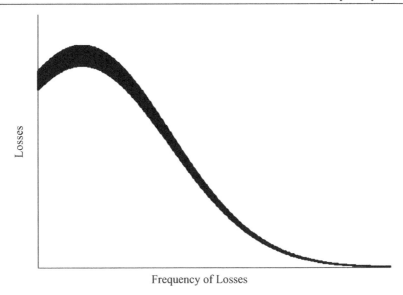

Figure 29.1   Graph showing impact of a sensitivity shift in a loss profile.

and, therefore, that no correlation exists between them. This will lead to a curve of loss, which accounts for the totality of the business that the bank undertakes. If business volumes increase by 1% it is likely that a relatively simple extrapolation of the data will be acceptable, and a new graph 1% above the earlier graph will be produced, with the area between the two graphs effectively being the sensitivity value, as shown in Figure 29.1.

However, if the impact of a larger level of movement is required, say a 50% increase in business levels, then there is no reason to suggest that losses will only increase by 50%. Indeed, it is likely that the business will then be operating under stress conditions causing increased loss incidence. Accordingly, sensitivity analysis can only really be employed for relatively small increases or decreases in business or processing levels where it is thought that a linear relationship (see Chapter 13) does in fact exist between the loss value and the frequency.

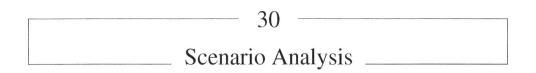

30

Scenario Analysis

30.1 INTRODUCTION TO SCENARIO ANALYSIS

Two papers from the Bank for International Settlements (BIS) have raised the importance of scenario analysis as a tool for risk management. The paper 'Sound Practices for the Management and Supervision of Operational Risk' published in February 2003 stated, 'some significant operational risks have low probabilities but potentially very large financial impact. Moreover, not all risk events can be controlled (e.g. natural disasters)'.

The problem with high-impact/low-probability events is that they will not have happened to your firm and therefore will not be reflected in your internal loss database. In another paper, 'International Convergence of Capital Measurement and Capital Standards' published in June 2004 and revised in November 2005, the BIS provided many of the details on how these events are to be considered.

It states (para. 665) that, for banks using the Advanced Measurement Approach (AMA), '. . . a bank's internal measurement system must reasonably estimate unexpected losses based on the combined use of internal and external loss data, scenario analysis and bank-specific business environment and internal control factors'. It further states (para 675): 'A bank must use scenario analysis of expert opinion in conjunction with external data to evaluate its exposure to high severity events. This approach draws on the knowledge of experienced business managers and risk management experts to derive reasoned assessments of plausible severe losses. For instance, these expert assessments could be expressed as parameters of an assumed statistical loss distribution.'

So the challenge is to use the information that is available to the bank to obtain a better understanding of the tail within a loss distribution. Within the BIS papers operational loss is taken as a proxy for operational risk, therefore the challenge is to understand what could be the potential loss arising from a potential event that might possibly happen at some time in the future, but has not actually happened to date.

Under these terms a scenario can be any event or series of events that you care to imagine. These could be as diverse as a three-day power outage, as experienced in New York in 2004, a flood or a severe operational breakdown that affects more than one business area. The suggestion within the papers is that we need to consider internal and external loss data.

30.2 USE OF EXTERNAL LOSS DATA

Most of the high-severity/low-likelihood events will not have occurred and therefore will not be included within a bank's internal loss database, which will necessarily focus on low-value/high-incidence events. These tell you a lot about the loss distribution at the expected end of the curve, but very little about the actual shape of the tail. To make the assumption that the expected part of the curve fits a standard distribution and therefore the tail of the curve will fit the tail of the same distribution, is at best brave.

The idea of using external loss data is that the event might have happened to somebody else and that a bank can use this information to work out what would be both the loss and likelihood of the event were it to occur to them. Clearly any such estimates are at best broad brush and cannot be seen to have any form of statistical rigour. Taking information from within loss databases, there are two types of loss database to consider. The first is the library style of loss database that includes analysis of a published actual event. This type of database is useful for scenario analysis since an event can be considered and the bank can then assess the impact the event would have on them, but there are three problems:

- Scaling
- Likelihood
- Relevance.

30.3   SCALING OF LOSS DATA

If we are to take an event that has happened to another bank then the event could be a different magnitude to the type of event that could occur to the bank we are considering. Let us consider the following example:

A bank has suffered a public fine of £24m for failing to adequately implement money-laundering deterrence procedures in respect of 'know your customer'.

Here is an external event that could happen to any bank and has certainly happened to one. If the market value of the bank that committed the event that resulted in the fine was £5,000m prior to the event, and the market value of the bank trying to use the data is £100m, then the scaled loss would be:

$$£24m\frac{100}{5,000} = £0.48m$$

So, the bank undertaking the analysis will take a £0.48m event into its loss database and loss-based probability distribution. However, at this stage it will not know what frequency to apply.

In other cases a loss will appear within a loss database that is not directly applicable to them. Consider the following example:

A bank has been fined £25m through an error in derivatives. Over a period of two years, the bank failed to price the instruments adequately and therefore entered into a series of transactions at non-market rates.

In this case, the bank undertaking the analysis does no business in derivatives. They could just say that this is not a relevant loss and ignore it as they do their analysis. Alternatively, and more correctly, they should analyse the event and consider what the message would be for their institution. The first question would be whether there are any instruments traded by the bank that are priced on the basis of some form of model. If there are, what is the amount that could be lost if that model were found to be defective? Secondly, what are the controls to prevent any transaction being undertaken at off market rates, and what would the loss be if these controls failed? If, in each case, the answer is favourable, then the same kind of scaling calculation is carried out.

30.4   CONSIDERATION OF LIKELIHOOD

Scaling will have at least suggested a calculation of a loss that can be used for the loss distribution, but what would be the likelihood that the event will happen? Clearly it is a lot less

Table 30.1 Assessment of likelihood

Description	Number of years for event	Percentage applied	Multiplier
Reasonably likely	3 years	33.3	0.33
Fairly likely	5 years	20.0	0.20
Possible	10 years	10.0	0.10
Unlikely	25 years	4.0	0.04
Extremely unlikely	100 years	1.0	0.01

than 1, since this is a high-severity/low-frequency event. In practice, all that can be done is to make some form of estimate of the consequences. A grid of possible solutions is normally the best way to introduce some degree of standardisation.

A typical structure is shown in Table 30.1, where management have concluded that a reasonably likely event will occur once in three years. Therefore, were an event to be evaluated as having a loss of £0.48m and be considered as possible by management, then the loss to be taken into the loss distribution would be £0.48m × 0.10 = £0.048m.

The way that this is actually done is to show a one-tenth event at £0.48m in the loss distribution. It will be the total of all of these scenarios that will make up the tail of the distribution, and therefore the unexpected loss for the bank.

This approach at least comes up with a loss to put into the tail of the distribution and scales it on a logical basis. However, it must be recognised that the level of accuracy of this type of information is low. There is unlikely to be a loss of £0.48m, that could happen at any time, or not at all. Instead of £0.48m, the actual loss figure used would be based on this analysis and on management's analysis of the issues involved. The approach does produce answers, but it cannot be expected to be anywhere as accurate as, for example, 99.9% confidence levels.

Over a period of years management will begin to understand the accuracy of their estimates. If an unlikely event frequently recurs, then it would be fair for management to reconsider their estimates and see if they are still happy. If a likely event does not occur, then the same reconsideration should be carried out. Consequently, over a period of time the analysis will improve.

30.5 ANONIMISED LOSS DATA

If the use of public loss data for scenario analysis is likely to produce a fairly inaccurate result, then the use of anonimised loss data must surely be even worse. The problem for many banks is that their loss databases will not include sufficient losses to come up with a meaningful distribution, even at the expected end of the curve. The idea is then to use anonimised loss data to complete the distribution.

The BIS papers require internal data to be held in a series of specific cells by business type (for example, corporate finance) or loss event type (for example, internal fraud). The bank that is conducting the analysis may have a corporate finance department but may have had no internal frauds. However their internal loss database does have losses of £27,000 in trading and sales, which is external fraud. The way that this works is for the £27,000 cell to be referred to as the anchor cell for the analysis. The bank then refers to the external loss database, which is made up of a series of losses provided to an external firm and stored in a database.

The bank finds that the figure in the database for trading and sales, external fraud, is actually £705m, whereas that for corporate finance, internal fraud, is £1,216m. The calculation that the bank then needs to do is to scale the losses shown in the anonimised database to populate their own loss database. This gives the following solution:

Loss for corporate finance, internal fraud = the anchor cell (£27,000) × new loss (£1,216m) ÷ the loss in the anonimised database for the anchor cell (£705m)

This gives a loss of £46,570 to be included within the actual loss database for the bank.

Well, that is the theory. In this case the bank potentially ends up with a larger loss in its database for an event that has not happened than would be the case for one that has happened. The chance of this type of calculation producing anything meaningful is at best remote. That regulators, for capital calculation, could use such calculations is also fraught with concerns. However, later amendments to regulatory rules will almost certainly deal with such matters.

An Introduction to Neural Networks

31.1 INTRODUCTION

In business you do occasionally encounter what are referred to as neural networks. These are typically used for pattern recognition and are based on a series of historic assumptions, assessments and/or observations.

Normally a set of observations is used as the input into the network, which is then trained to assign each of these observations to one class or more. The observations consist of a number of features and an associated class assignment, which may be continuous (so a full range of solutions are possible) or discrete (so only certain solutions are possible). Neural networks are often used for non-linear regression, where the task is to find a smooth approximation between multidimensional points. In all instances the input and output data are presented simultaneously to the network.

Expert systems are also sometimes referred to as being neural networks. Expert systems take the knowledge of the company, its advisers or experts, and put this into a form whereby it may be used for the general benefit of the company. These are not really neural in the way that we are setting out in this chapter, but rather are effectively intelligent scenario modellers.

A mathematical neural network is composed of basic neural units or neurons, normally referred to in business as *nodes*. These are designed to model the behaviour of biological neurons. Each node computes its output by weighting its inputs from other nodes, applying an optional bias, to break symmetry, to the weighted sum and applying an activation or transfer function to that sum. In business applications the neural modeller takes the attributes of the data entry and analyses it into its constituent parts. The information is then used to make assumptions regarding the population from which the data is drawn. As more data is sampled, then the model continues to improve in its accuracy.

31.2 NEURAL ALGORITHMS

In practice, many algorithms may be employed to model the neural networks. These include the following approaches:

- Back Propagation (used here)
- Adaptive Resonance Theory
- Bi-directional Associative Memory
- Kohonen Self-Organising Maps
- Hopfield
- Perceptron.

In this chapter we only explore back propagation. The other techniques are all a little different and are beyond the scope of this book. If you need to understand the specific details of these techniques you will need to refer to a specialist text. However, in general, the methods differ in their network topologies, how the individual neural units are connected, and in their learning strategies. This means that if your company is using a neural modeller you will need to understand which of the techniques is being used and any limitations that this introduces into the modelling process.

The topology is characterised by the number of layers, the number of neurons per layer, and the type of connections that exist between the layers. If there is a feed forward connection, this means that the information is used to influence the nodes that occur after that point. If there is a feedback connection, then the influence is on the preceding nodes. Finally if there is a lateral connection, then the influence is on the modes in that layer.

Activation or transfer functions scale their output between minimum and maximum values, for example to $[-1, 1]$ or $[0, 1]$. There are several activation functions that are used, with the sigmoid or S function being the most popular. Other popular functions are the hyperbolic tangent, the ramp or linear activation, and the step function. Again the explanation of these terms is beyond the scope of this work.

Learning strategies include supervised and unsupervised learning. In supervised learning, the net is given the output for a given input by the modeller, whereas unsupervised learning typically relies on clustering of like samples.

Supervised learning is applicable when there are known examples of the desired outcome. For example, the back propagation paradigm uses supervised learning. The goal is to develop a set of weights that will yield the best output for a given set of inputs. The steps of the back propagation process are as follows:

1. Calculate the output for given existing weights.
2. Determine the error between the desired output and the actual output.
3. Feed the error back through the system to adjust the weights.
4. Continue until the error is minimised across all training patterns.

Neural networks are used in combination with other techniques, such as fuzzy logic and genetic algorithms, to build predictive models. They can also create models that can rapidly analyse large amounts of data and make predictions in real time. The strengths of neural networks are as follows:

• They are applicable to a wide range of problems.
• They can be used for prediction, classification and clustering.
• They can produce good results in complicated domains.
• They are used for time series analysis and fraud detection.
• They can be used to process continuous and categorical variables.
• They are readily available in commercial off-the-shelf packages.

However, neural networks have the following weaknesses:

• They can sometimes yield inexplicable results where there is no logical explanation for the decision.
• The analysis may converge to what is actually an inferior or sub-optimal solution.

It is always necessary to undertake a reasonableness review of any output from a neural-modelling system. This will identify if the solution arrived at is obviously unreasonable. There are several other aspects that must be borne in mind when carrying out research into an application:

• The training data must have sufficient information to allow the possibility of making the kind of predictions desired.

- When performing one-step-ahead predictions one must really be certain that the model is predicting ahead.

In a time series application the network may be simply predicting that the level one-hour later will be the same as it is now, and new information may not be reflected until it is too late.

Above all, neural networks must be viewed as statistical tools. They are bound by the same restrictions on data information content, data quality and model generalisation as any statistical technique. No statistical technique can extract information when no information is available.

Appendix
Mathematical Symbols and Notation

INTRODUCTION TO NOTATION

Throughout this book common notation has been used to enable the mathematical terminology to be more readily understood. Every effort has also been made to replace the notation with words where this is possible and to provide some further explanation. This appendix provides a review of the key notation that has been used throughout the book. Some of this may appear rather obvious, but there are some interesting lessons to be learned even from the use of simple notation.

Addition (+)

The addition or *sum* of 2 and 3 is written $2 + 3$. Clearly $2 + 3$ is equal to $3 + 2$, so the order in which the numbers are written down has no effect when they are added. The fact that the order can be reversed means that the operation of addition is said to be *commutative*. When extending to more than two numbers, such as $2 + 3 + 4$, it makes no difference whether 2 and 3 are added first to get $5 + 4$, or whether 3 and 4 are first added to get $7 + 2$. Whichever way you carry out the calculation, you will obtain the same result of 9. This property of addition, where the order does not matter at all, is called *associativity*.

Subtraction (−)

The reduction or difference between 5 and 4 is written as $5 - 4$. Here the order in which the numbers are written down is important because, when subtracting, $5 - 4$ is not the same as $4 - 5$. Therefore subtraction is not commutative. Further, when two or more numbers are subtracted, the answer will demonstrate that subtraction does not have the property of associativity. In subtraction, the order in which the different terms are set out really matters.

Subtraction of a negative number is equivalent to adding a positive number. For example $5 - (-4) = 5 + 4 = 9$. So the operation of subtracting a number from a positive number is the same as adding two positive numbers.

The plus or minus sign (±)

This is a symbol used in cases where the answer may be plus or minus. For example 7 ± 3 represents the two numbers $7 + 3$ and $7 - 3$, that is 10 and 4 respectively. The usual context for this is to say that a number lies in the range 7 ± 3. This means that it can take any value from 4 to 10 inclusively.

Multiplication (×)

The operation of multiplying the numbers 6 and 7 is written as 6×7. This could also be stated as the product of 6 and 7, or six times seven being 42. The multiplication of two numbers is commutative, in other words 6×7 equals 7×6. It is also associative, when evaluating $5 \times 6 \times 7$, the result is unaffected if the product of 5 and 6 is evaluated first, or 6 and 7, the result is still 210. When multiplying positive and negative numbers the sign of the result is given by the rules in Table A.1.

Table A.1   Key issues when multiplying numbers

Operation	Result	Example
positive $\times$ positive	positive	$6 \times 7 = 42$
positive $\times$ negative	negative	$6 \times -7 = -42$
negative $\times$ negative	positive	$-6 \times -7 = 42$
negative $\times$ positive	negative	$-6 \times 7 = -42$

Division ($\div$)

The operation of dividing, or taking the quotient, of the two numbers 10 and 5 is written $10 \div 5$. It may also be written as 10/5 or $\frac{10}{5}$. Since 10/5 is not the same as 5/10, the order in which the numbers are presented matters. So the operation of division is not commutative. When dividing positive and negative numbers, the sign of the result is given by the rules in Table A.2.

Table A.2   Key issues when dividing numbers

Operation	Result	Example
$\frac{\text{positive}}{\text{positive}}$	positive	$\frac{10}{5} = 2$
$\frac{\text{positive}}{\text{negative}}$	negative	$\frac{10}{-5} = 2$
$\frac{\text{negative}}{\text{negative}}$	positive	$\frac{-10}{-5} = 2$
$\frac{\text{negative}}{\text{positive}}$	negative	$\frac{-10}{5} = -2$

The reciprocal of a number

The reciprocal of a number is found by dividing it into 1, that is 'turning it upside down.' This is also referred to as inverting it. The reciprocal of $\frac{4}{5}$ is $\frac{5}{4}$. Since an integer such as 3 can be written as $\frac{3}{1}$, its reciprocal of 3 is $\frac{1}{3}$.

Integer

An integer is any of the natural numbers, whether positive or negative, or zero. Integers are also referred to as whole numbers. They are numbers with no fractional parts, so if they were written in a decimal format with one decimal place, then the part after the decimal point would be zero.

Greater than ($>$), greater than or equal to ($\geq$)

A symbol meaning greater or more than, for example, $3 > 2$ is read as 3 is greater than 2. This may be extended to include equality, for example an account is not overdrawn if the balance $\geq$ £0, or, in words, the balance is greater than or equal to zero.

Less than (<), less than or equal to (≤)

A symbol meaning smaller or less than, for example, 3 < 4 is read as 3 is less than 4. This may be extended to include equality, for example an account has no funds or is overdrawn if the balance ≤ £0, or, in words, the balance is less than or equal to zero.

Not equal to (≠)

A symbol meaning not equal to, for example, 3 ≠ 4 is read as 3 is not equal to 4. It is used in mathematical notation to exclude a specific value. This occurs at any time when a known value cannot occur. For example, if the value of a security ≠ £10, then it can take any value other than £10.

Parentheses ( ), [ ], { }

Brackets or parentheses are used to enable the reader to know the order in which things need to be done – effectively which calculation is performed first and on what is the calculation conducted. Conventionally round brackets ( ) are used, however when a series of brackets are required both square [ ] and curly brackets { } may be employed. Effectively it makes little difference as long as people understand what you are trying to explain. For example, the result of $3 + 4 \times 5$ would be 23, since the multiplication is done before the addition. $(3 + 4) \times 5$ is 35, because in this case the parentheses override the normal precedence, causing the addition to be done first. Brackets or parentheses are also used to set apart the arguments in mathematical functions. For example, $f(x)$ is the function f applied to the variable x.

When evaluating complex expressions it is important to follow the rules in Table A.3.

Another important rule is that when you have several multiplication and divisions within expressions, always work left to right.

Table A.3   Order of operations rules

Priority	Operation
1	Calculations contained within parentheses are evaluated
2	Squaring (or raising to another exponent)
3	Multiplying or dividing
4	Adding or subtracting

Significant digits

Significant digits are the number of integers appearing in a figure after the decimal point. For example, 1.786 is to three significant digits, whereas 98.32 is only to two significant digits.

Rounding

The procedure of rounding has the effect of deleting the least significant digits of a number, then applying some rule of correction to the part retained. If you round a number to a certain number of significant digits and the first number rejected is less than 5 the last significant figure is rounded down. If the first number rejected is 5 or greater, then it is rounded up. What this means is that 12.7570 rounded to two significant places is 12.76, while 12.7540 rounded to two significant places is 12.75. As a general rule 5 is always rounded upwards, so 12.665 will be rounded to 12.67 whereas 12.664 would be rounded down to 12.66.

Exponent or power

If a number, referred to as the base, is multiplied by itself a number of times, then another form of notation is generally used. Referred to as the exponent or power, this records the number of times the base is multiplied by itself. The multiplier is shown as a superscript after the base number itself. A series of examples are presented in Table A.4.

Table A.4   Examples of exponent

Base	Exponent	Notation	Result
3	2	3^2	9
2	3	2^3	8
4	5	4^5	1,024

In words, 3^2 is referred to as three squared, whereas 2^3 is referred to as two cubed. Certain simple rules follow. Any base with an exponent 1 gives itself, that is to say the base number is not multiplied by anything. If the base is negative, the result will be positive for exponents that are even and negative for exponents that are odd. For example $(-1)^2 = 1$ on the same basis as before that the product of two negatives equals a positive.

Some basic rules for combining exponents are summarised below for any base x.

- Rule for multiplication: $x^n \times x^m = x^{m+n}$, for example $3^2 \times 3^3 = 3^5$
- Rule for division: $x^n \div x^m = x^{n-m}$, for example $3^2 \div 3^3 = 3^{-1}$
- Rule for raising a power to a power: $(x^n)^m = x^{n \times m}$ or $(3^2)^3 = 3^6$
- Negative exponents: A negative exponent indicates a reciprocal: $x^{-n} = 1/x^n$ or $3^{-2} = 1/3^2$
- Identity rule: Any non-zero number raised to the power of zero is equal to 1, $x^0 = 1$ (x not zero), so $9^0 = 1$ and $5,000^0 = 1$.

Square root ($\sqrt{\ }$)

The square root of a value, denoted $\sqrt{\ }$, is the number that when multiplied by itself gives the original value. Thus $\sqrt{9} = 3$, it corresponds to an exponent or power of $1/2$.

Absolute value ($|x|$)

The absolute value of a number is a measure of how far that number is from zero. It is a measure of distance and is always a positive quantity. Put simply, the absolute value of a number is its size regardless of its sign. The absolute value of a number x is denoted by $|x|$, with the number being referred to inside the bars. For example, the absolute value of the number negative three is $|-3|$. Since -3 is three units away from zero, the absolute value of -3 is 3, or using the symbols, $|-3| = 3$. Similarly, we know that the number 3 is also three units away from zero, so $|3| = 3$. Numerical opposites have the same absolute value, as they are the same distance away from zero.

Factorial symbol (!)

The factorial function is denoted by the exclamation mark '!'. The number 5!, is read as 'five factorial', or 'factorial five' and is a shorthand notation for the expression $5 \times 4 \times 3 \times 2 \times 1$. The factorial of 1, or $1! = 1$, and by convention 0! is defined as 1. However, factorials only apply to positive integers. In general, if n is a positive whole number then $n! = n \times (n-1) \times (n-2) \times \cdots \times 5 \times 4 \times 3 \times 2 \times 1$. In this expression the dots are taken to replace all the terms between $(n-2)$ and 5. Therefore $8! = 8 \times 7 \times \cdots \times 2 \times 1$ is the same as $8! = 8 \times 7 \times 6 \times 5 \times 4 \times 3 \times 2 \times 1$.

Greek alphabet

The Greek alphabet (Table A.5) is used throughout business mathematics to refer to different types of event. We saw a number of these characters throughout this text. Perhaps we use Greek (or collectively the Greeks) just to confuse the poor reader, or just to show how clever we all are. Nonetheless they are in common usage so will need to at least be recognised. If you mistake a gamma for a delta then you may find yourself taking the wrong action when buying or selling shares, for example.

Table A.5 Greek alphabet

alpha	A	α	iota	I	ι	rho	P	ρ
beta	B	β	kappa	K	κ	sigma	Σ	σ
gamma	Γ	γ	lambda	Λ	λ	tau	T	τ
delta	Δ	δ	mu	M	μ	upsilon	Υ	υ
epsilon	E	ε	nu	N	ν	phi	Φ	ϕ
zeta	Z	ζ	xi	Ξ	ξ	chi	X	χ
eta	H	η	omicron	O	o	psi	Ψ	ψ
theta	Θ	θ	pi	Π	π	omega	Ω	ω

Summary of operations

In this appendix we have covered the following general notation:

- Addition $(+)$
- Subtraction $(-)$
- The plus or minus sign $(\pm)$
- Multiplication $(\times)$
- Division $(\div)$
- The reciprocal of a number
- Integer
- Greater than $(>)$, greater than or equal to $(\geq)$
- Less than $(<)$, less than or equal to $(\leq)$
- Not equal to $(\neq)$
- Parentheses $((), [], \{\})$

- Rounding
- Exponents
- Square root ($\sqrt{}$)
- Absolute value ($|x|$)
- Factorial symbol (!)
- Greek alphabet.

This notation is used throughout the book and throughout business mathematics. A range of other notation is also required to fully understand business mathematics and is considered specifically within the relevant chapter to which it relates.

Index

Index compiled by Terry Halliday

Printed and bound by CPI Group (UK) Ltd, Croydon, CR0 4YY

23/04/2025

14660948-0002